WOOD HEATING HANDBOOK
2ND EDITION

BY CHARLES R. SELF

TAB BOOKS Inc.
BLUE RIDGE SUMMIT, PA. 17214

SECOND EDITION

FIRST PRINTING

Copyright © 1982 by TAB BOOKS Inc.

Printed in the United States of America

Reproduction or publication of the content in any manner, without express
permission of the publisher, is prohibited. No liability is assumed with respect to
the use of the information herein.

Library of Congress Cataloging in Publication Data

Self, Charles R.
    Wood heating handbook.

    Includes index.
    1. Fireplaces. 2. Stoves, Wood. 3. Fuelwood.
I. Title.
TH7425.S44   1982   697′.04   81-18298
ISBN 0-8306-0096-5   AACR2
ISBN 0-8306-1472-9 (pbk.)

This revised edition is lovingly dedicated to my wife Caroline, who is helping revise my life.

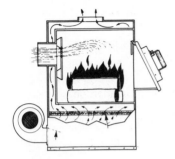

Preface

When I wrote the first edition of this book a few years ago, the wood-heating industry was barely in existence (after some decades of just about non-existence). The reasons for its resurgence are simple. The cost of all fuels has risen rapidly, since about 1973, to a point where it now costs nearly $300 more to fill a fuel oil tank than it did in 1972. That's an increase of something more than 600 percent; in 1972, it cost less than $45 for 275 gallons of fuel oil. The cost of electricity has reached astounding heights and natural gas has risen repeatedly and rapidly.

In 1976, there were probably no more than two dozen or so wood-stove manufacturers in the entire country. Today, the figure far beyond that, and local concerns have taken to producing their own versions of proven stove models. In the unassuming rural county where I keep house today, I could probably find several people who would be perfectly willing to weld me a metal-plate stove for a reasonable price. These people make several dozen stoves a year to supplement models shipped in from larger manufacturers. In a sense, a new cottage industry has formed. In addition, companies that had just started production of a single model five or six years ago often now have two, three or more models on hand. A prime example is the Vermont Castings Company. It started a few years ago with a single wood-burning stove of top-grade cast iron and fine design. It now produces two wood-stove models and one coal/wood stove. All of the stoves have the basic lines. They resemble the so-called Franklin stoves, but they are airtight and have an exceedingly long flame path to increase heat output.

Wood stoves have almost entirely replaced fireplaces as the heating unit of choice where no provision for wood heat is in place at the outset. In addition, there are a great many devices on the market for readily improving the efficiency of virtually any fireplace. Fireplaces such as Majestic's Warm Majic™ show signs of being nearly as efficient as a good wood stove.

The Warm Majic is a heat-circulating fireplace, but it is not designed like older heat-circulating fireplaces were. The firebox is vented to the outside so that it can be shut down at night, or so that it can draw outside air for really hot burning. In addition, the Warm Majic is delivered with glass doors. This combination allows one thing that fireplaces have always lacked; that is an ability to be shut down without drawing already warmed air up through an open

Fig. P-1. A modern wood stove (courtesy of Acme Woodstoves).

Fig. P-2. The Free Heat Machine (courtesy of Unique Functional Products Inc.).

damper. The exterior venting means that you need not allow warmed room air to be drawn up the chimney in order to get a good draft. All in all, these are significant improvements (Fig. P-1).

The line of adapters for fireplaces has become very wide. Extra heat can be gained with the use of various tubed grate devices (with or without optional fans). It is now easily possible to insert a unit in the fireplace and turn it very nearly into a wood stove. Unfortunately, these units, in general, are more costly than all but the largest and most expensive wood stoves. Wood stoves adapted at the factory for insertion into a fireplace are available, too, and tend to be a bit less costly. None are really inexpensive if they are any good at all (Fig. P-2).

Unfortunately, wood has become much more expensive to obtain, and some sources have almost dried up. It used to be easy to go to a landfill area and pick up trees and sections of trees dumped for disposal. I doubt now whether it would be even worthwhile to spend the time in search of such places.

The average cost of a cord of wood has risen rapidly. It seems only yesterday that in non-urban areas a cord of wood cost less than $50. It now approaches $100 for a cord of wood almost everywhere. Even in my locale, which is totally rural, a single full cord of green hardwood has risen to about $85.

Supply and demand factors are important reasons for the rise in price, but it also costs more than three times as much to fuel a chain saw as it did some five years ago. It costs more than three times as much to fuel the transportation of the wood. Chain saws certainly have not dropped in price (although they haven't risen as much as many other items).

There are compensations for the loss of landfill-destined firewood. More and more national forests and state forests have been opened to various types of wood cutting for fuel use. Permits must always be obtained for such cutting, but the red tape has usually been minimal. Local rangers or forest personnel can easily handle any requisite paperwork in a few minutes.

There are hazards. John McPhee recounts the tale of two people from Manhattan who, a few years ago, trotted into the upstate New York woods (if you can really call Carmel, New York, in Putnam County, upstate) to cut firewood. With the purchase of permits (nominal in cost), the cost of a chain saw, the cost of fuel, and the cost of renting a truck, they ended up laying out several hundred dollars for little more than a third of a full cord of wood.

Overall cost will drop as more wood is cut, and the chain saw is amortized, but rental of a vehicle is horrendously high these days. Chain saws can be rented, but that's not something I recommend for anyone who is serious about cutting firewood.

Wood Heating Handbook-2nd Edition begins with a thorough treatment of wood-burning appliances, from the masonry fireplace to the most modern stoves and appendages. How to plan for them and how to install them is explained. How to find wood, how to cut it, how to split it, how to season it and how to burn it is detailed. I also cover just about everything I've learned from years of burning wood, cutting wood and reading and talking about the subjects. Included are looks at the various tools related to the job. You'll learn how a masonry fireplace can cut 10 percent from your yearly heating bill, and how more efficient fireplaces can reduce your bills by as much as 75 percent. You will also find out how wood stoves can cut heating costs by nearly 100 percent, and how multi-fuel furnaces can add convenience to economy.

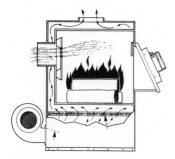

Contents

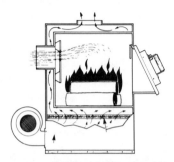

Introduction

Fireplace evolution probably began about as soon as early man discovered that an open fire in a ring of rocks in the center of a cave created almost as many problems as it could solve. The ring of rocks was essential to keep the fire from spreading to bedding. A cave with a hole in the roof had to be found to allow smoke to escape so eyes would not stream with tears.

From the hole in the roof, the move to the modern fireplace was a slow one. Designs are continuing to show improvement due, in part, to the new financial inducements for the use of wood heat. Thousands of years have been needed to move well away from the design of the original smoky campfires that required great gobs of wood to produce heat that sizzled you on one side while your other side formed icicles. The older style campfires and fireplaces probably did a better job of keeping bugs at bay than providing heat.

Modern wood stoves and fireplaces got great boosts from the work of Benjamin Franklin. Benjamin Thompson, known as Count Rumford, (1753 to 1814) receives credit for the discovery of convection currents (circa 1798) after he spent a great deal of time working on cures for smoky fireplaces in London. Benjamin Franklin and Rumford can be said to be the fathers of modern wood heat. Count Rumford is viewed as the father of the modern fireplace; his journals are still available in many larger libraries.

MODERN DESIGN

Unfortunately, many modern fireplace designs are still far from efficient heating systems. On an average, a masonry fireplace or a

1

metal-lined fireplace built according to today's accepted principles and using no accessories to increase heat output is likely to be, at the very best, about 10 percent efficient. Some are used so improperly, in addition to the low original efficiency, that an overall heat loss will often result. *Heating efficiency* is expressed as the percentage of heat a heating device can extract from the total heat available in a particular fuel. When a net heat loss occurs when using a fireplace, you'll be stuck with higher heating bills along with the cost and work of supplying the wood for the fireplace.

Still, more and more people buy fireplaces (Fig. I-1) and install them. Part of the satisfaction of the fireplace has always been the open fire mystique of relaxation. It is used as a focal point for a party, conversation, or romance. The look, feel, and aroma of burning wood adds great pleasure to the end of a hard day. It seems to matter little, if at all, that your backside is thoroughly chilled when your front is warm and your eyes are entranced.

Modern fireplace systems—carefully installed, fed, and maintained—can provide more than a fair amount of supplementary heat. Properly installed wood stoves can virtually take over the entire job of heating any house. Because of the much greater efficiency (from as little as 30 percent to 60 percent and a bit more), wood stoves have become the main heat source for a very large number of today's homes.

As an example, my cousin and her husband (a few miles from where I live) provide the total heat for their entire large farmhouse with a single kitchen wood stove. During the winter, Jim and Sandy shut down three of the upstairs bedrooms. The rest of the house is kept quite comfortable—though the kitchen does tend to be too hot most of the time—with the single large stove.

The stove is in the center of the room. About 15 feet of well-supported stovepipe goes back to the flue in one corner of the room. They use an auxiliary blower on the stovepipe to add to heat circulation on really cold days. There really aren't all that many cold days where we live in Virginia. I don't remember it being below zero in the past four winters. The stove was installed three winters ago. To date, the total purchase of fuel oil necessary has been 10 gallons to top the tank (most likely from evaporation and testing the furnace once every fall to make sure it still works).

The total outlay, including two chain saws, was something on the order of $800; over $400 of that was for the stove. Considering a minimal use of 1000 gallons of fuel oil per winter, the savings the first winter nearly paid for the stove and the saws. The cost for the

Fig. I-1. A modern fireplace (courtesy of Majestic).

second winter was about $100. The cost for the third winter was about $25 in fuel for the saws. The fourth winter will probably cost only $25 to $35 for fuel for the saws.

In four years, Jim and Sandra—for an outlay of $800 or so—will have saved at least $2800. Not everyone can do as well. The cost of fuel oil, or other heat sources, varies and so does the cost of firewood and the distance it must be transported. They are lucky to own a 54-acre farm with more than a little left in woods.

FIREWOOD

In the first edition of this book, I indicated that, in general, $5 worth of wood would produce more heat than $5 worth of oil, gas or electricity. I also stated that in some areas wood costs over $100 a cord around major urban areas and that the price of wood heat in areas such as New York City made it almost impractical.

Although wood has increased in price, that $5 worth of wood today will produce far more heat than will $5 worth of oil, gas or electricity. Since 1976, wood has about doubled in price in most areas. Fuel oil and its companions have more than tripled in virtually every case. Even in Virginia, where electricity is far cheaper than it is in many other areas of the country, the average daily rate has come up to almost a nickel per kilowatt hour. Just a few short years ago, that was the maximum figure you could find on charts for determining the cost of various electrical appliances. If you can buy a cord of wood for $100, you're sure to save money if your fireplace or wood stove has a heating efficiency rate of even as little as 30 percent (Fig. I-2).

Fig. I-2. A potbelly stove (courtesy of Portland Stove Foundry).

ECOLOGICAL CONSIDERATIONS

Burning wood as a fuel has not been demonstrated to cause ecological disasters when the waste products are released in the atmosphere. The waste products from rapid combustion are the same waste products released during slow oxidation of the wood. One of the most potentially harmful ingredients of all fuels is sulfur. Most woods contain less sulfur than do other fuels. More research is being done. In the near future, there will be more details on particulate matter and other emissions. In any case, you should avoid long-term and intensive inhalation of woodsmoke. It can be dangerous; this is especially true if the products of combustion replace oxygen in indoor air.

Cutting trees for firewood need not pose any real problem for ecologists if the cutting is done in a responsible manner. Trees, after all, are a renewable resource. Proper cutting can, in most instances, increase tree growth and wood yields of most forests. It is true that woodlands can be ruined by improper cutting methods—such as clear cutting and overharvesting—but these are rather easily avoided in most instances. Wood can, and should, remain a readily available renewable resource.

In the recent past, wood heat for prime or supplementary residential heating use was often associated with poverty. Today, wood heat is a very reasonable alternative heat source for an ever-growing number of people. With the current cost of even a moderately small home, poverty doesn't enter the picture when a cheaper heat source is desired, installed, and used.

There is a lot of wood still readily available. The price has increased (mixed slabwood—oak, poplar, and pine—from sawmills in Virginia in truckloads of about 2½ cords, cut to 16 inch lengths, increased in price from $20 in 1977 to about $55 in 1981) and there is sometimes a problem in making good use of the wood. Some forests in the Northeast and Southeast are in particularly rough shape. They are in virtually desperate need of thinning after years of no care or improper care. Large numbers of the trees in these forests are of no use as lumber or pulpwood. The potential for future tree crops can be increased simply by thinning out the less desirable growth and using it for firewood. One problem, and a relatively new one, might be that timber that is otherwise excellent for use as lumber for building might now be used as firewood. The increased profit derived from much higher cordwood prices can sometimes mean a tree is worth more as firewood than it is at the sawmill for lumber.

Getting wood to burn can be a problem when you install a wood stove or fireplace, but it can also provide a great amount of pleasure. The wood must be located, cut down, cut (or bucked) to burning length, seasoned, and stored. For those of you with little time to spare and sufficient money, buying cordwood is the simplest and easiest way to proceed. For the rest of us, with little enough time but even less money, a woodlot would be a big help. In such cases, a moderate-sized chain saw and an axe can easily provide enough wood to last all winter.

Woodcutting means fresh air and exercise, *lots* of exercise, so it's a good idea to have your doctor do a check-up if you have any reason at all to suspect physical problems. A heavy regimen of woodcutting is a reasonable amount of work, but it will almost

Fig. I-3. A wood stove designed for a mobile home must have low clearance (courtesy of Suburban Manufacturing Co.).

Fig. I-4. A wood stove installed in a mobile home (courtesy of Suburban Manufacturing Co.).

surely be more than desk-bound people are used to or are able to handle readily. There is certainly a great deal more work involved in using wood for heat than just turning a thermostat up or down. These days, a savings of a large percentage of any household heating bill can easily reach $1000 annually. That should certainly be worth a few hours' work!

SAFETY

Saving money by using wood for fuel is only acceptable if the method of heating is as safe as possible. Some insurance companies demand special methods of protection. If you have any doubts at all, check with your fire-insurance company and your local building inspector. They should be able to supply any additional information about insurance coverage and certificates of occupancy in your locality.

■ Always use manufacturer's suggested clearances for wood-heating appliances. If the manufacturer says the clearance to the back of a wood stove must be no less than 18 inches, don't try to get away with a foot (unless you take special precautions, such as installing a heat shield. (Figs. I-3 and I-4).

■ Keep a fire extinguisher on hand at all times. It should be close to the wood heating appliance, but far enough away and on a clear path that a small fire cannot keep you from reaching it. It is best to use dry-chemical fire extinguishers with wood stoves because water and CO_2 might make the metal of the stove warp when used. In the case of overheated cast iron, water could actually make the metal just about explode.

■ Make sure that everyone understands that wood-stove surfaces are not to be touched. For children and invalids, provide protection around the wood stove.

■ Make sure the chimney flue is cleaned at least twice during each heating system (and more often if green or resinous wood is burned).

■ Always place ashes in a metal container. Place the container outdoors on a fireproof surface. It is best if the container is also covered.

■ When joining stovepipe, use at least three sheet-metal screws at each junction.

■ Try never to use more than 10 feet of stovepipe.

■ When more than 10 feet of stovepipe must be used, always secure it to framing members—maintaining the correct distance from combustible surfaces—with heavy wire or plumber's strapping.

■ Check the chimney for leaks or obstructions or other problems before the start of each heating season.

■ Never use a volatile substance, such as kerosene or charcoal starter fluid, to start or "pep" up a wood fire in a fireplace or stove.

■ Never use charcoal in a wood stove or fireplace.

■ Use coal only in heating appliances designed for that fuel.

■ Size the heating appliance to the area to be heated, and then size the flue to the heating appliance (whenever possible). If the flue is in place, you're not going to be able to move up to 8 inches if it is masonry and 6 inches.

■ Keep a check on stovepipe all through the heating season. A twice monthly check is needed and you should concentrate on areas such as the flue entrance where it is most likely to pull loose.

■ Use only 22-gauge or 24-gauge stovepipe. Anything lighter is not truly safe.

■ Do not decrease the diameter of the stovepipe between the stove and the flue entrance.

■ Slope the pipe upward toward the chimney. Make sure it enters the chimney at a point higher than its exit from the stove.

■ Do not let the stovepipe project beyond the chimney flue liner into the chimney.

■ Do not pass standard stovepipe through floors, walls, or concealed space.

■ If you don't use a properly constructed masonry chimney, make sure the metal chimney you use is of the insulated type and UL listed.

■ Operate a hot fire at least 30 minutes each day so that creosote buildup is burned off a little at a time.

■ Don't use flammable liquids in the room with the wood stove or fireplace.

■ When cutting firewood, follow all the rules of chain saw safety (from proper starting procedure to proper felling bucking procedures).

■ Keep firewood stacks under 6 feet tall, even when they lean against a wall, and under 4 feet tall when they are self-supported.

Chapter 1

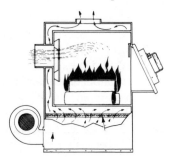

Fireplace Selection

The job of fireplace selection doesn't sound particularly difficult, and it doesn't sound at all confusing. After all, when everything's taken into consideration, all that is really needed is a fireplace of the proper size to provide enough heat to make a room, or several rooms, comfortable while not drawing so much air that it will smoke and cause other problems. The job really is simple except that modern manufacturers have provided such a wide variety of fireplaces that it is sometimes difficult to decide on any particular model.

Consider the typical fireplace. It is simply a hole in the wall where you burn wood to save on your fuel bill or to make the room cozy. In the days of masonry fireplaces, that was it. The alternative was the Franklin stove used as a fireplace, a cooking stove, or a wood stove. Today, though, you're faced with a seemingly endless variety of fireplaces.

THE MASONRY FIREPLACE

As a start, let's consider the traditional masonry-only fireplace. In most cases, consideration is just about all that should be given to a masonry unit. They are sinfully expensive to have built (and quite difficult to build yourself unless you're a very experienced mason). They are, in general, a great deal less efficient than most factory-built units. New damper systems can increase the efficiency of masonry fireplaces (as can many of the new heat transfer units and other modern devices). Usually you can get the same or better results with a factory-built unit for a great deal less money and work. I've mentioned the masonry fireplace and included a chapter on building them for the simple reason that there are still a large number of traditionalists among fireplace lovers. Their preferences are as valid as anyone else's, but harder to realize because of the higher cost in either cash or physical effort.

If you choose an all-masonry fireplace, particularly one to be built in a house already standing, you are limited as to where it can be installed. On existing houses, the expense of installing an all-masonry unit in the center of the house, say forming a wall between the dining room and living room, would be prohibitive. This is particularly true if the house has a basement or crawl space underneath. First, a solid foundation is essential to prevent settling problems because of the masonry's weight (which is considerable for even a small fireplace and chimney). The foundation of the fireplace must be carried down to the basement floor and below. Footings must be poured in a large enough size to completely support all the weight—probably several tons of brick and mortar. That means money! If the house is on a slab, that slab must be broken up and new footings of the proper size will have to be poured to support the new addition.

An all-masonry fireplace in an outside wall also needs footings, but the footings can be butted to the existing foundation with no need to rip out already poured and set concrete work. This can mean a very large savings right at the outset. Footings are simply poured alongside the original foundation (past the frost level). In most areas of the country; that should save several feet of excavation and masonry work.

For more practical applications, the factory-built fireplace is likely to be the choice in most of today's homes. They are made of steel, and many of them are guaranteed smokeless if manufacturer's installation instructions are carefully followed (Fig. 1-1). These fireplaces come in anything from the bare firebox/damper unit to those listed by the Underwriters Laboratory as zero-clearance types. (*Clearance* refers to the distance between the fireplace and the wall. *Zero-clearance* fireplaces are those placed either on the wall or in the wall.) Always look for the UL listing when you are getting ready to purchase a zero-clearance or low-clearance wood-burning appliance. Then follow any clearance directions, supplied by the manufacturer, right to the letter. The zero-clearance fireplace units can be installed almost anywhere in any house. The

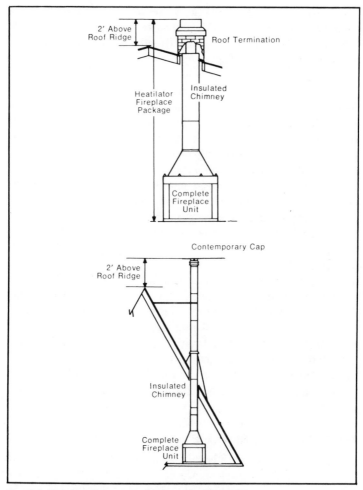

Fig. 1-1. Two Heatilator zero-clearance fireplaces.

chimneys are made up of locking sections (insulated or with air spaces between the inner and outer pipes). They require little skill and not much time to put together.

If you want a fireplace for heating a single room, or for appearance only, the basic factory-built unit is fine. I recommend that you get a zero-clearance unit to simplify installation. Although the unit will cost a little more at the outset, the time saved, the materials used to install the unit, and the extreme ease of situating the package just about anywhere, make the total investment a lot smaller.

In the true fireplace category are heat-circulating fireplaces made by companies such as Vega Industries (Heatilator), Majestic (Majestic Circulator), and Superior (Heatform). These units are far more adaptable to heating several rooms than all-masonry fireplaces. The heat-circulating vents in several of the models can be moved about to heat a single room more thoroughly. The vents can be moved through the walls to heat a second room (and sometimes even a third, although the heat in this case will be only a supplement to normal room heating because the fireplace probably won't produce enough heat to *completely* heat all three rooms.) These units have cold air vents at the bottom and warm air vents near the top of the firebox unit. Shafts or metal ducts lead to the areas to be heated (Fig. 1-2). The warm air movement can be increased by small electric fans at the proper spots in the shafts.

Probably the newest and most efficient of all fireplace systems is Majestic's Warm Majic. The new features, such as outdoor venting and the glass doors that cut down on heat loss at night when the fire is burned down, add a great deal to efficiency. In addition, an optional fan can be used to provide greater spread of the warmth in the firebox. This is a feature the Warm Majic has in common with many other earlier heat-circulating fireplaces. Installation is simple and straightforward; it should take about one weekend or two at the most. If the fan is installed, the work is a bit more complex. In most cases, it will make sense for you to hire a licensed electrician to carry out that portion of the job. Installation of this unit is described in a later chapter.

THE FREESTANDING FIREPLACE

The freestanding unit is a bit simpler to install, but it presents a few problems the zero-clearance unit does not. Foremost among the problems is the necessity of placing most units from 18 to 36 inches from any combustible surfaces. Any fireplace, regardless of design, must have at least 4 feet of clearance in front of the firebox. These distances can easily be reduced by covering nearby walls with one of the many brick imitations now on the market. Make sure the imitation is listed as non-combustible. Ceramic tile at least three-eights of an inch thick may also be used in addition to a variety of other materials capable of converting a combustible surface to a non-combustible one. Freestanding fireplaces generally must also stand on a hearth area which extends several inches to each side and over a foot in front of the fireplace. A fireplace that is 36 inches in diameter can end up using as much as 90 square feet of room space.

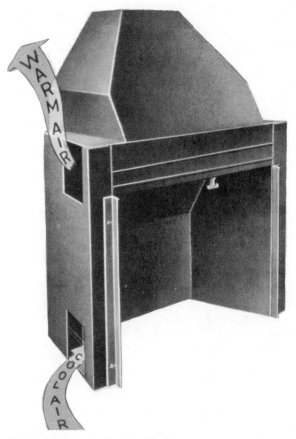

Fig. 1-2. A Majestic heat-circulator fireplace.

Clearances needed to the sides are generally about half those to the rear. There are some partially insulated freestanding fireplaces that need very little clearance in any direction. An argument strongly in favor of freestanding fireplaces is that many of the simpler units can be installed for not much more than $250—assuming the homeowner does the installation work (Fig. 1-3).

One other type of "fireplace" is available today: the old reliable, so-called Franklin stove (Fig. 1-4). This cast-iron unit, though not the stove invented by Benjamin Franklin and lacking almost all the features he designed into his unit, radiates a lot of heat from its sides, back, and from the open front door. Most Franklins can be used to burn coal (with the proper grate) as well as wood. Closing the doors turns it into a much more efficient space heater. The

Fig. 1-3. A freestanding fireplace.

Franklin stove suffers from the same troubles as freestanding fireplaces, but you can also use the same remedies. With its doors closed, a Franklin stove can put out more heat than many fireplaces several times its size. Particularly well built Franklins can be as much as 40 to 45 percent efficient. While that's not nearly as efficient as some of the more modern airtight designs, it is certainly respectable for an old compromise design.

With doors closed and the fire damped down, a Franklin stove will hold a fire much longer than any fireplace not equipped with a curfew. The heat loss up the chimney is a lot less when the fire does go out. These units fit well in a colonial decor and they make a very cozy evening fire. They really come into their own when you slide between the sheets with the knowledge that a banked fire will await you in the morning.

A standard in-the-wall fireplace of some type is certainly the safest unit for families with small children. Not too many people consider that the Franklin stove and most freestanding fireplaces have exposed-to-the-room exterior skins that get extremely hot. A child falling against this exterior can be severely burned. A properly screened fireplace, on the other hand, seldom has much hot surface exposed to the room

EASE OF INSTALLATION

Ease of installation is certainly a prime consideration for do-it-yourselfers, but it could prove a sensible consideration for just about anyone. The quicker a fireplace goes in, the lower the labor costs will be: Easy-to-install units can be serious moneysavers even when someone else does the job. In this respect, the freestanding units (including the Franklin stove) are best. Simply make some sort of hearth the proper size, place it in the appropriate spot, set the fireplace on it, and install the chimney sections. The most difficult jobs will be mixing and installing the refractory (a special heat resistant mix used in the hearth, or firebase, of the fireplace to keep the fire from burning through) and sealing the roof after the chimney has been brought through and capped. Because the chimney/roof sealing is needed for almost all fireplace and wood-burning stove installations, it's a job that really can't add points to installation difficulty.

Fig. 1-4. A Franklin stove with the doors open (courtesy of Portland Stove Foundry).

Zero-clearance, in-the-wall units are almost as easy to install as freestanding units. Two persons should be able to put a zero-clearance fireplace in most houses over a weekend and still have time for a leisurely Sunday dinner. Because these units are very light, needing no masonry foundation, they can be placed almost anywhere in a room. Such handyman's aids as lock-together insulated flue pipes and prebuilt chimney caps that just slip over the factory-built flue make installation a breeze. Masonry work is restricted to the hearth and any decorative trim you might care to add to the exterior of the unit.

Zero-clearance fireplaces with heat-circulating features are a little more difficult to install. The vents and venting stacks are the biggest problem. You'll have to open up more of your walls to insert these parts of the fireplace (particularly if you want to pipe heat to another room). Generally, simple carpentry skills will enable you to do the job. Adding electric motors to the heat-circulating vents will require running some wires. That is a good job to leave to your local electrician if you're not experienced in these matters.

Masonry-surrounded heat-circulating units are next up in order of difficulty of installation—and it's a large step. These units provide only the basic firebox and the heat-circulating venting. It's up to you to install any needed insulation (this is provided, but not attached), a masonry surround, and a standard fire clay flue and chimney. These fireplaces are much heavier when completed than zero-clearance units. The reason is simple. Although the zero-clearance fireplace requires almost no masonry, the heat circulators have to be surrounded with standard masonry (Fig. 1-5). The circulators themselves are quite heavy. Add a ton or more of masonry, including a fair amount of chimney, and you can understand why footings and a solid foundation are essential. The job is more difficult and more expense.

The most difficult unit to install is the all-masonry fireplace (though a bit of effort can now be saved with the damper kits sold by many manufacturers). This is the heaviest of all units; it is not much heavier than the standard heat-circulating types. Because of the complex masonry work needed on the firebox, smoke shelf, and throat, it is by far the most difficult to build. It is the fireplace that the homeowner must wait the longest to use at full blast after installation is completed. And it is the fireplace which can, over the years, cause more problems than all the others combined. It is a fireplace for traditionalists, and especially those traditionalists with more than a fair amount of extra cash or spare time.

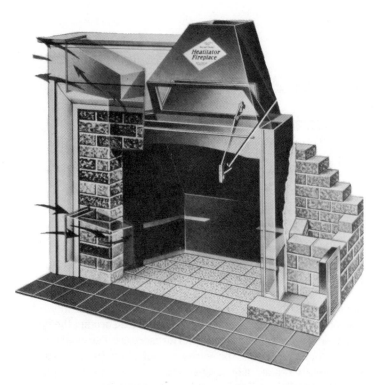

Fig. 1-5. A heat-circulating unit surrounded by masonry (courtesy of Vega Industries).

The prices for fireplace units installed by the homeowner can range from about $250 up to $750. Masonry fireplaces, whether of the heat-circulating or all-masonry type, will usually start at twice that price and go screaming upward to about three grand!

Chapter 2

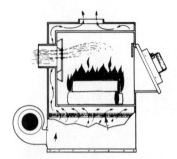

Wood Stoves

The most sensible and efficient source of wood heat for most of us will come from one or more wood stoves placed around the house. Today, wood furnaces and multi-fuel furnaces are also available, but the cost for those tends to be somewhat out of line (unless you need to completely replace a heating system for starters). A fireplace is generally inefficient if it is not furnished with one of the newer insert devices. Masonry fireplaces are impractical from a cost standpoint these days, even a relatively small brick fireplace costs as much as $3,000 to install (Fig. 2-1).

In cases where wood stoves are installed, some care is needed in the selection, and some grains of salt should be taken with any manufacturer's claim for an efficiency rating in excess of about 55 percent. Some manufacturers do claim over 60 percent efficiency, but I've seen no real evidence that wood stoves can be as efficient as, for example, an oil furnace that can usually be honestly rated at 65 percent efficiency in extracting heat from the fuel oil. This assumes the oil furnace is kept in good condition, and is cleaned and adjusted annually or more often.

Stove efficiency is usually related to the degree of airtightness possible in the stove. Controlling the amount of air entering the stove makes it easier to control the rate of burning; any excess air entering makes such control less efficient. Therefore, the old cast-iron models with many openings—that tend to leak a lot of air—are far less efficient than more designs such as Vermont Castings'

Fig. 2-1. An extremely fancy Franklin stove built without doors (courtesy of Portland Stove Foundry).

Vigilant and Defiant models. These models are cast-iron stoves, of absolutely top quality materials, designed to be airtight, or as nearly so as possible, and to provide a long flame path that extracts a great deal of heat that might otherwise simply go up the flue (Fig. 2-2).

There are also many stoves patterned along the line of the Fisher models (now sold all over the country), and some new designs that might or might not be as efficient as we would want them to be (Fig. 2-3).

Some models, such as the Arrow 2400 and 1800, are designed with heat exchange chambers (supplied by a circulating fan) that increase the heat output. These two models are specially designed for mobile home installations (Fig. 2-4). These heat exchangers serve the same purpose as baffles and long flame paths. They help to keep heat from rising up the flue and being wasted. Others, such as the Woodmaster line from Suburban Manufacturing Co., offer heavy steel-plate design. They have fireboxes lined with firebrick (which helps to hold the heat and to reduce the chances of firebox burnout) and cast-iron doors and flue collars (Figs. 2-5 and 2-6).

Fig. 2-2. A Franklin stove with the doors closed and the dampers open (courtesy of Portland Stove Foundry).

Fig. 2-3. A Monitor box stove (courtesy of Portland Stove Foundry).

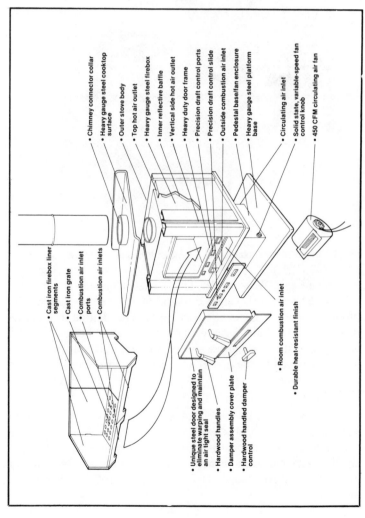

Fig. 2-4. An advanced-design Arrow wood stove.

- Cast iron firebox liner segments
- Cast iron grate
- Combustion air inlet ports
- Combustion air inlets

- Chimney connector collar
- Heavy gauge steel cooktop surface
- Outer stove body
- Top hot air outlet
- Heavy gauge steel firebox
- Inner reflective baffle
- Vertical side hot air outlet
- Heavy duty door frame
- Precision draft control ports
- Precision draft control slide
- Outside combustion air inlet
- Pedestal base/fan enclosure
- Heavy gauge steel platform base

- Circulating air inlet
- Solid state, variable-speed fan control knob
- 450 CFM circulating air fan

- Unique steel door designed to eliminate warping and maintain an air tight seal
- Hardwood handles
- Damper assembly cover plate
- Hardwood handled damper control

- Room combustion air inlet
- Durable heat-resistant finish

23

Fig. 2-5. A single-door, plate-steel Suburban Woodmaster stove.

Suburban's Woodmaster line includes mobile home wood stoves, and designs that allow the surrounding sheet metal top to be lifted to allow the use of two cooking eyes in addition to fireplace inserts, wood burning furnaces, and radiant wood heaters. Such a variety of heating appliances simply was not available anywhere a decade ago—not to mention from a single manufacturer (Fig. 2-7).

FEATURES

What you need in a wood stove will probably vary some from what I, or someone else, will need. Still, such variances come mostly in size and optional features such as blower fans to circulate air. The basics of stove construction quality need to be found in every wood stove bought and installed if problems are to be avoided.

There are three materials that provide the main construction of wood stoves. Least expensive are the sheet metal wood stoves. These are often made of metal as light as 24 gauge; more often, they are made of metal as heavy as 14 gauge and 18 gauge. This is usually rolled steel and the designs vary widely.

I heated for one winter with a sheet-metal stove of material little heavier than the 24-gauge stovepipe I used to attach the appliance to the flue. It had been used for a couple of previous heating seasons and needed some brazing to solidify things. It served exceptionally well. I probably saved several hundred dollars with an installation that cost me, including an oxy-acetylene for the torch to do the brazing, about $12.

Nevertheless, stoves such as these seldom last more than two heating seasons. They must receive great care to do even that well as far as durability goes. The stoves were then extremely inexpen-

Fig. 2-6. A larger Suburban Woodmaster plate-steel stove (courtesy of Suburban Manufacturing Company).

sive (in 1977, the model I had was selling for about $25), and I got mine for nothing. It provided enough heat to virtually run me outdoors in late January and early February when the temperatures were down near 10 degrees F.

SHEET-METAL STOVES

Any sheet-metal stove will require certain precautions at time of purchase and while in use. Check the internal supports of the stove (if any). These must be sturdy and well formed. Suburban Manufacturing lines their 14-gauge sheet-metal, radiant heater with 18-gauge metal in the firebox for long life and retarded chances of burnout. Many stoves don't have internal supports; the little oval job I had simply used metal crimping to provide external and internal support. Care must be used with any sheet-metal stove to prevent warping of the various parts. Getting the thing cherry red is almost certain to warp the stove and reduce efficiency (and it's not safe to get any wood stove that hot anyway).

Always make extra sure that any sheet-metal stove has a solid and safe covering under it. In other words, any wood or otherwise combustible floor must be especially well protected in case the bottom burns out of the stove.

If the stove comes without grates, as most sheet-metal stoves do, line the bottom with 2 inches of dry sand to help prevent burnout. If you buy carefully and tend carefully, you can extend a sheet-metal stove's life, even the least expensive stove, out to the third or even fourth year.

More and more stoves are now being made of mild steel plate (in thicknesses from three-sixteenths of an inch to five-sixteenths of an inch. In general, it makes no sense to buy a plate-steel stove that is constructed of material less than a quarter of an inch thick. The increased weight and cost of the heavier metal are well offset by the greatly increased durability. Most steel-plate wood stoves are of the type that have internal baffles for directing smoke and gasses around so that, presumably, better heating efficiency is obtained. I've worked with stoves with baffles and without baffles. My notes show mostly that those without baffles tend to smoke up a room more easily in heavy wind conditions than do those with baffles.

When looking over a plate-steel wood stove, check the way it can be loaded. Most stoves seem to have both front and top loading. This can be a handy feature. Top loading tends to let more smoke out into the room, but it also allows you to really cram the firebox

Fig. 2-7. This Woodmaster radiant heater offers two cooking "eyes" as well as supplementary wood heat (courtesy Suburban Manufacturing Co.).

with fuel when the day is exceptionally cold, or when you need a fuel firebox for overnight heating.

Next, check the thickness of the plate used. Often, the basic stove box will be of quarter-inch steel (with the top going to five-sixteenths inch plate). This is good because the top, if it opens, is one part that is very susceptable to warping.

Check the firebox. It is lined or unlined? Some are unlined, but most will be lined with firebrick. Lined is best because this cuts down on warping and burnout, and firebrick is easy to replace. Just get the correct size new brick, slip out the old, and slip in the new.

Plate-steel wood stoves are not as subject to warping as are those of lighter metals, but the possibility is still there if the fire burns too hot for too long. The heavier the plate the less the chances of warping. This can sometimes be counterbalanced by the need for a lighter-weight stove for an upper story of a house where the joists are not strong enough to support too much extra weight (Fig. 2-8).

Check the welds on the stove. These should be smoothly done and without air bubbles or signs of problems in the beads. A good weld will have an even, wavy appearance and will completely fill the joint. Joints should be welded both inside and outside the stove for greatest durability. Top loading doors must fit tightly. There will be, most often, a cord of asbestos or spun ceramic material used on the front loading door and the top loading door in order to assure a good seal.

Some plate-steel wood stoves have grates, but most of the models I've seen do not. In the cases where a wood stove has a grate, you simply install the thing and get right down to the business of lighting fires for comfort. When no such grate is provided, you should use the same technique as you would with a sheet-metal stove. Spread about 2 inches of sand on the bottom of the stove to help prevent burnout.

CAST-IRON STOVES

Cast-iron stoves come in the widest of all varieties of stoves. They range from the basic, old Franklin style, the parlor stove, the pot belly stove, and the Vermont Castings' Defiant and Vigilant models right on to the most expensive stoves of all, the Scandinavian models.

The older, or old-style, wood stoves don't even pretend to be airtight models at all. Most are assembled in units, and there is no sealing between the cast units. A few bolts hold the entire works together and a flashlight left in such a stove in a dark room will show all the gaping air leaks. Such stoves are often considerably less expensive than more modern designs. Even with their inconveniences, they can well serve as supplementary heating units.

My mother uses a parlor stove—a modern imitation of an old design—upstairs and an old Warm Morning upright coal and wood stove in the basement. Certainly the parlor stove is nowhere near airtight, but it will hold a good fire for 6 to 8 hours and the embers will keep a large portion of the house warm for another 2 hours or so. The Warm Morning model is much closer to airtight, but it is not completely sealed. It will easily hold a fire for 8 hours if it is well filled with wood. The firebox is deep and narrow, and it requires some fairly small chunks to fill it.

Fig. 2-8. The Fireplace Institute testing manufactured fireplaces at Auburn University.

When selecting a wood stove made of cast iron, once you decide on the specific design you want to buy, you should look for the thickness of the metal and see if you can check on the metal's quality. Cast iron is often hard to check for quality. Many manufacturers start out by painting the stoves black and that makes the check even harder: It is best to work with a reputable dealer in case anything goes wrong. Thickness of the metal is important for several reasons, but the foremost reasons are durability and freedom from warping over years of use. Also, heavier stoves hold more heat and they hold it longer, They also take longer to heat up on those cold mornings when you really want a blast of warm air.

It is on the very chilly mornings that inexpensive sheet-metal stoves are at their very best. The light metal heats rapidly and it gives off heat very quickly. As you check over a cast-iron wood stove, look for thin spots in the castings, and check for cracks. Many inexpensive stoves have been imported. They have very thin castings that often taper off to just about nothing in spots. This type of stove can prove dangerous.

If the cast-iron wood stove you are examining has an air-tight design, make sure the sections that bolt together are really close fitting. This is most easily checked in a dark or nearly dark room. Place a powerful flashlight inside the stove and check for light. Move it around until it has shone on every area where there might conceivably be a crack. Look carefully!

29

No stove is truly airtight, but good air control is essential to long burning of wood. The fewer air leaks in a stove's firebox the better your chances of keeping a fire going for (the often advertised) 14 hours or so. I've seen very few wood stoves that will really hold a fire longer than 10 hours. After that point, you're gaining heat mostly from embers (no matter the stove you use).

Some cast-iron stoves, particularly those of American design, come with grates to hold the logs off the bottom and to allow ashes to fall free where they can be more easily removed. Most Scandinavian stoves do not have grates and they are not designed to have them installed later. Instead, the usual process of spreading 2 inches of sand on the bottom of the firebox is followed.

No matter what material the stove you buy is made from and no matter what the basic design is, check for quality consistent with the price. With wood stoves now selling for as much as $750, buy the best quality you can afford, and make sure you check carefully.

Once the material of the stove is decided on, you can think about checking out the style of stove. Radiant heating stoves are probably the most common type to be found. This category includes cast-iron stoves, sheet-metal stoves, and plate-steel stoves in many different designs. Fisher stoves are radiant heaters and so are virtually all of the Scandinavian, American, and Canadian designed cast-iron stoves. Included in this listing are the old Franklin design, parlor stoves, and pot-bellied stoves.

Essentially, radiant heating stoves provide you with heat that radiates off its surfaces. It has advantages and disadvantages over heat circulators. The primary disadvantage is where there are small children or people who are partially disabled. Heat-circulating stoves usually are surrounded with sheet metal that remains relatively cool. Radiant-heat stoves have surfaces that get downright *hot*. A child or disabled person touching a surface on a radiant-heat wood stove is almost certain to get a significant burn.

Scandinavian airtight stoves control burning in a somewhat different manner than do circulating stoves using bimetallic thermostats for on-stove draft control. These stoves are the closest to being completely airtight. Systems of interior baffles force smoke and flame into an S-shaped pattern—albeit a sideways S—so that the wood does a cigar burn from front to back.

Draft controls, usually on the door, are closely machined to give good air flow control there. The doors, if not fitted with spun ceramic or asbestors rope for a seal, will also be machined to give a good, tight fit. I would say the quality of these stoves has to be seen to be believed. Everything from the fit of parts to the finish is exceptional. Many stoves (Fig. 2-9) can be obtained in various shades of enamel, such as red, blue and green, as well as the more standard black (the black is almost always inexpensive and it is easier to re-color should the enamel get chipped or discolor from too hot a fire).

The Scandinavian models are all made in metric sizes. I don't know of any United States source for metric-size stovepipe. The imported stuff costs about double or a bit more than does standard,

Fig. 2-9. A typical Scandinavian airtight wood stove (courtesy of Norwegian Woodstoves).

hardware store American-size stovepipe. The stovepipe isn't the only part of the system that is costly. Scandinavian airtights cost from 20 percent to 40 percent more than equivalent-size stoves made in this country.

As with all circulating stoves, children and invalids should be protected from the hot surfaces. When a circulating stove seems you best bet, and there are young children in your house, it often pays to build a wire mesh barrier around the heating appliance to prevent accidents.

Many circulator-type stoves have a bimetallic thermostat that opens and closes the stove damper at preset heating temperatures. None of these thermostats are exceptionally accurate, in my experience, and it has been my practice when using this style of stove to disconnect the thermostats and manipulate the stove damper(s) manually.

Getting sufficient draft can be something of a problem in some airtight stoves. If your chimney is not high enough to provide a good draw, the relatively small openings of the stove damper can cause the fire to smolder when you would like it to burn with a hot flame. In the case of non-airtight stoves such as Franklin stoves and parlor stoves, there is seldom any real problem getting a good, hot fire burning—unless the chimney is far short of requirements (the taller the chimney, in general, the better the draft). Basically, any chimney should rise 14 or 15 feet from the base of the firebox, or the hearth, to provide a good draft.

Airtight stoves are probably the wood stoves of choice if you expect to be doing most or all of your heating with wood. Many good brand names are on the market; some manufacturers are the King Stove Company, U.S. Stove Company, Ashley, Shenandoah, Suburban Manufacturing Company, Arrow Woodstoves, Fisher Stoves, Garden Way, Atlanta Stove Works, HDI Importers, Hunter Enterprises, Vermont Casting, Kickapoo Stove Works, Kristia Associates (Jøtul), Locke Stove Co., Malm, Riteway (which also makes an outstanding line of multifuel furnaces), and Vermont Woodstove Co. (with their DownDrafter the only *true* downdraft stove on the marketplace today). There are many others. See Figs. 2-10, 2-11 and 2-12.

It is impossible to list anywhere near all of the wood-stove manufacturing companies in this country (not to mention Europe and Canada). A decade ago, the entire list would not have been as long as that in the preceding paragraph. At one time, all companies selling wood stoves were swamped with orders as people began to

Fig. 2-10. The Better'n Ben 801 wood stove and coal stove.

install their first units. A wait of months was often necessary when you ordered a specific brand and model. As more companies came into existence, the first enthusiasm of the rush died and now long waits are no longer the rule.

MULTIPLE STOVES

If you go for airtight wood stoves for the entire heating needs of your home, some careful consideration must be given to the number of stoves needed and the costs of the individual heating appliances. Scandinavian woodstoves are so much more expensive than others that the need to buy three such units, even if of relatively small size, would force you into a position where the investment just isn't worth it. Amortization, or repayment, would take too long. While a standard box stove will use twice as much wood, generally, to provide as much heat as, for example, a Jøtul airtight box stove, the investment is on the order of four times as much for the Scandinavian stove.

SUPPLEMENTARY HEAT

Supplementary wood heat for a central heating system can easily and readily be supplied with non-airtight wood stoves such as

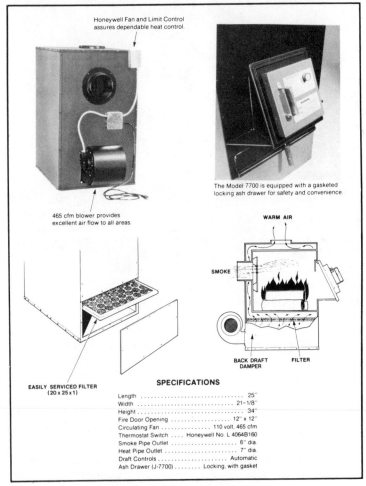

Fig. 2-11. Johnson Energy System's wood furnace.

Fig. 2-12. The wood burning Furnacemaster from the Suburban Manufacturing Co.

the Franklin, a pot belly or two, or parlor or box stoves such as the Monitor produced by the Portland Stove Foundry. Such stoves will almost always, if properly installed, hold a fire for at least 6 hours. They will provide good heat and burning for four or more of those hours, so that daytime needs are easily met. If filled right at bedtime, they will provide sufficient heat until the small hours of the morning. Then your heating plant can begin using fuel oil, natural gas, or whatever other fuel is feeding it. In other words, with about four or five loadings per day, non-airtight stoves can provide you with a situation where your central heating will be in use fewer than four hours a day. Your stove will often provide enough heat to keep the central heat off for the full 24 hours. The sharply lower cost of non-airtight stoves makes them attractive. If you decide to get one of the fancier parlor stove models with a lot of chromed geegaws, then the price, naturally, runs right up the scale. If you live, as I now do, in an area where the temperature seldom dips below about 15 to 20 degrees F., such a stove might be all that's needed in a moderate-size to small-size house.

Wood stoves should be selected with an eye towards the heating needs of a particular house, and not for size or appearance alone. Getting a stove that is too small is more of a problem than is getting one that is too large (but in either case you're wasting money). A wood stove that is too small tends to get burned out more rapidly because they will often need to be kept at full blast simply to keep the place at a moderate temperature. Wood stoves that are too large can run you out of the house with excess heat or they can cause excessive creosote build-up in the chimney. Constantly burning wood at a lower level will virtually always mean the flue temperature is low enough to allow creosote build-up.

STOVE LOCATION

Wood stove installation should be planned with an eye to the greatest possible heat dispersal throughout the house (or the series of rooms the stove is meant to heat). A central location is best, but it is not always practical. Many stoves are intended to heat only a single room and they would best do that job if placed in the dead center of the room. But not many of us want a wood stove as a central decoration in the middle of a living room.

If you have a chimney, the location of the wood stove is at least partially dictated by the location of flue openings on that chimney. It is quite possible to run long strings of stovepipe across a room, but this is not often very practical. Nevertheless, it can be made reasonably safe with the proper installation procedures. With a permanent installation, such long stovepipe runs are rather hideous looking. Come summer, do you really want to be staring at 20 feet or more of stovepipe running across a frequently used room?

At one time, we installed a circulator-style wood stove in a house in upstate New York. Because there was no available flue, I made an asbestos, metal, and wood frame to hold the pipe and I fit it in the upper half of a double-hung window. No problem. To get the heat to spread upstairs, we had to place the stove 10 feet or so off one wall in the dining room and 8 feet off another wall.

One stove provided heat for a three-bedroom house (the second story did get more than slightly cool on very cold mornings). It was an ugly arrangement, though temporary, and the cleaning of the stovepipe was a real problem because each junction was made with three sheet-metal screws. These had to be taken out in four different places to allow the cleaning. The shorter the stovepipe run, in most cases, the better. On the other hand, long runs do give back a lot of heat that might otherwise shoot on up out of the flue.

Wood stoves are installed in pretty much the same manner as are freestanding fireplaces. They have many of the same general requirements: proper clearances (according to the wood stove manufacturer's directions and local codes, if any) from combustible surfaces; a good layer of non-combustible material under the wood stove and off far enough to the front, back and sides to catch most sparks and falling embers; proper flue installation, etc.

Generally, a fireplace will be directly vented (flued right to the outdoors with the chimney directly over the firebox). This direct venting is one cause of the great heat loss with fireplaces (as much as 95 percent in some cases). A wood stove is more efficient, in part, because of a generally smaller flue size (in relation to firebox size) and it is not really directly vented.

Wood stoves use all three modes of heat transference—radiation, convection and conduction. *Conduction* is the transfer of heat by direct contact. *Convection* transfers heat by movement of air currents. *Radiation* transfers heat by rays. The fireplace, unfortunately, relies almost entirely on radiation for providing your home with heat.

WOOD-BURNING RANGES

Wood-burning kitchen ranges can serve as double money savers in some homes. The high cost of cooking gas or electricity does add a great deal to overall costs in running a home. To start, a stove or range the size of most of those used in kitchens will readily heat the kitchen for most of the day. Then, of course, you save the cost of the fuel used to cook your food. Still, most kitchen ranges have small fireboxes that will not hold enough fuel to provide a really long-term heating job for anything more than a single room. They should not be depended upon for more than supplementary heating of the kitchen.

Though it may seem quite odd, wood ranges really are not difficult to cook with. With a bit of experience, the results can be better than those with an electric range or a gas range. The type of fuel used is of great importance. For rapid heating, when you need to boil water for instance, is best done with small pieces of firewood from the softwood groups (and a lot of people use dried corncobs to get a hot, fast fire going). The slower burning hardwoods provide the best type of heat for slow cooking or baking.

You must keep an eye on anything being cooked in the oven and turn it from time to time so that any food being baked or roasted has the various sides presented, for about equal lengths of time, to the hottest side of the oven (invariably the side on which the firebox is located). A kitchen range with a water reservoir can be a good source of hot water and it can add a great deal to room humidity. A warming oven on top of such a range keeps bacon and biscuits warm, at no extra cost, while eggs are cooking.

WOOD-BURNING FURNACES

Wood-burning furnaces, and even multi-fuel furnaces, are now readily available. The primary manufacturers today include Riteway Stoves and Furnaces, Harrisonburg, Virginia; Bellway Manufacturing, Grafton, Vermont; Charmaster Products, Grand Rapids, Michigan; Combo Furnace Co., Grand Rapids, Michigan; Dual Fuel Products, Inc., Simcoe, Ontario, Canada; Duo-Matic Div., Manoir Int., Park Forest S., Illinois; Hunter Enterprises, Orillia, Ontario, Canada; Integrated Thermal Systems, Portsmouth, New Hampshire; Kickapoo Stove Works, LaFarge, Wisconsin; Longwood Furnace Corp., Gallatin, Missouri; Malleable Iron Range Co., Beaver Dam, Wisconsin; Marathon Heater Co., Marathon, New York; Suburban Manufacturing Co., Dayton, Tennessee; Wilson Industries, St. Paul, Minnesota; Johnson Energy Systems, Milwaukee, Wisconsin. There are other manufacturers and there probably will be more in the near future.

As a good example of a supplemental wood furnace for existing hot-air heating systems, the Johnson Energy Converter hooks into existing ductwork fairly easily (using 7-inch pipe into the present assembly). Johnson provides 14 models that vary in size and available features. The model J-7700 offers heavy-duty, cast-iron grates and a locking ash drawer. It has a fully filtered air intake system, a cast-iron door, a 465-cubic-feet-per-minute blower, and a limiter control (Fig. 2-11).

Suburban Manufacturing offers two basic models. One model (the FM-80U) is designed to provide supplemental heat, and the other model (the FM-80UC) is designed to provide a central furnace. At present, the FM-80U model sells for approximately $600; the FM-80UC model sells for approximately $900.

Many of the new wood-burning furnaces are thermostatically controlled and require only one or two feedings a day to keep an eight-room house very comfortable. Many also offer humidifiers, and some come with hot water boilers to cut another portion of your home fuel bill into little pieces.

USED STOVES

Five years ago, used wood stoves were fairly hard to come by without fairly hard searches (though they could be found). Prices were often reasonable, but stoves more than 75 years old are considered antiques in many places and the prices rise accordingly. Unless you have a desire to collect antique stoves, I would say it isn't really worth the bother.

Used parlor stoves, Franklin stoves and some airtights are now fairly often found on the market. A large number of people start to use wood heat and then find it is simply too much effort. Too many people start out figuring it will be as easy as turning up a thermostat. It isn't, by far, so more and more used wood stoves come on the market.

In general, no used wood stove should cost more than 60 percent or so of what a new one of the same model would cost. After that, make sure the stove was designed for wood, not coal, or for coal and wood use. It is easily possible to use coal in a wood stove (but not coal in a wood stove). Older coal stoves are almost always lined with firebrick or asbestos that will almost always be in pretty poor condition. Replacement of the lining is not hard, but it is another cost to be considered. Coal stoves almost always have fireboxes much smaller than wood stove fireboxes. They also have smaller loading doors. Getting enough wood in to fuel them for a full night of heating is often impossible.

THINGS TO CHECK

Check the stove for cracks; use the flashlight test in a dim room as described previously in this chapter. Cracks can be a real problem in cast-iron stoves. A crack in the wrong place will virtually guarantee you a smokey room a great deal of the time. Cracks also reduce efficient and uniform heating of the wood stove. Small cracks can be readily repaired using furnace cement, but larger cracks will require braze welding in cast iron. Most of the time, braze welding gives a better union in cast iron than does fusion welding (and is easier to do). Firebox welding must be done immediately. Welding of cracks in range tops and other non-critical areas can be delayed if needed.

Rust on interior parts of the stove will be more of a problem than will rust on exterior parts. Unless, in either case, the rust situation is really extreme, neither place will give you too much difficulty. Chemicals such as *naval jelly* do a reasonably good job of removing most rust. Using the naval jelly with a wire brush or steel wool will really cut through deposits. Advertisements claim one application will remove almost all rust. If the build up is moderately heavy, several applications will certainly be needed (even with the wire brush). Fortunately, naval jelly is not overwhelmingly expensive, it is easy to use, and it needs only be kept off the hands and painted surfaces to be safe. Just brush it on, let it stand about 20 minutes, and rinse away thoroughly with a garden hose. Dry the surface. Coat the surface with stove black or stove paint immediately after drying. Nothing will re-rust more rapidly than bare surfaced cast iron.

When you are looking over a wood stove, check the grates. If they are in place and unbroken, you might be ready to buy the used stove. If they're missing, you should avoid that particular stove unless you are sure you can easily find grates for it, and that the cost of the grates is not too high. Cracked grates can be braze-welded quite easily.

Once the stove is obtained, it becomes a matter of installation to proper clearances so that fire danger is reduced as far as possible, and so that heat circulation is best utilized. Keep the stove as central as possible. Keep the clearances right and the chimney cleaned.

Chapter 3

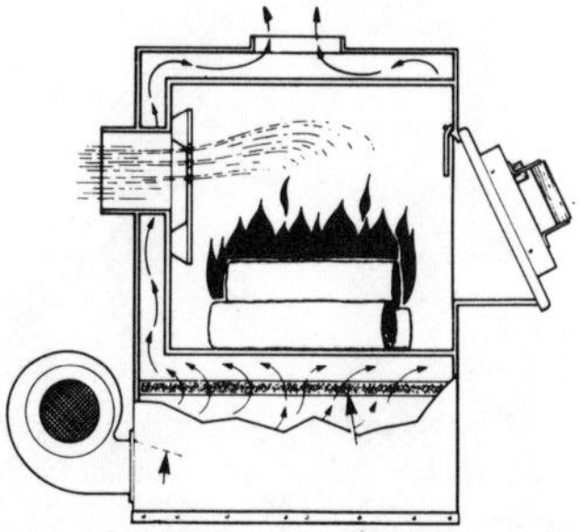

Fireplace Planning

The properly planned fireplace is a joy to see and use. The stuck-in or stuck-on fireplace, one that is just crammed into any available space, will probably not add much to the appearance of your home. Planning for a fireplace heightens the anticipation for the unit.

HOUSE TRAFFIC

Studying home traffic patterns is a large part of fireplace planning. You don't have to position the fireplace so it doesn't disrupt planned or established traffic patterns, but you must make sure the fireplace is easy to tend and easy to feed—without a disruptive flow of traffic near the hearth.

FIREPLACE SIZE

Fireplaces in walls must be proportional to the wall size. Fireplaces on long walls can be large and still appear to be proportional to the wall (as well as provide more access to the hearth for a larger number of people; see Fig. 3-1). Long walls also provide more space for indoor storage of wood. There should be enough room to store at least a one-day supply of wood for any fireplace or wood stove.

The size of the fireplace is extremely important to the *overall* appearance of the room. Even those of us who love large fires in large fireplaces must admit we don't care to stare at a black gaping hole in the wall during all those months when there are no flames to

Fig. 3-1. A fireplace that is proportional to the wall it has been built into (courtesy of Majestic).

warm or entertain us. A too-small fireplace can look just as decidedly odd as one that is too large.

Good design, with room scale kept in mind, means a fireplace opening should have a width that just about equals, in inches, the number of feet in the width and length of the room. For example, if a room is 26 feet long and 17 feet wide, the fireplace, if placed on the short wall (17 feet), should have an opening no wider than 43 inches. However, if the fireplace is put on the long wall, its opening can be a little wider (perhaps as much as 60 inches. The height of the opening should be from two-thirds to three-quarters the width. You'll probably have little choice with this measurement if you purchase a factory-built fireplace.

Table 3-1 shows suggested room and fireplace sizes. Sizes close to those mentioned are available in many fireplace styles, including freestanding (Fig. 3-2). Franklin stoves are available in a wide variety of sizes and should be about two-thirds the size of any fireplace appropriate for a given room.

Fireplace size brings about another consideration: heat. If the fireplace is too large, the raging fire set in its depths will probably drive everyone well back from the hearth—maybe out of the room. If

Table 3-1. Suggested Room and Fireplace Sizes.

Room Size in Feet	Opening, in Inches (short wall)	Opening, in Inches (long wall)
10 × 15	24-25	24-32
12 × 16	28-32	32-36
14 × 20	32-36	34-40
16 × 24	32-40	40-48
16 × 28	40-44	44-60

the fireplace is too small, the fire won't provide much heat or entertainment.

Wood stoves need not be selected for size as fireplaces are. Stoves can be much smaller because they are many times more efficient. If a stove is 50 percent efficient and a fireplace is only 10 percent efficient, the stove need only be about one-fifth to one-quarter the size of the fireplace to throw out the same amount of heat. The stove's wood storage space also needs to be only about one-third that of the fireplace. Scale is less important with stoves because few people really care to have a wood stove as the dominating factor in a room.

Fig. 3-2. A freestanding fireplace that is proportional to the room size (courtesy of Majestic).

You'll need considerable room in front of the fireplace for comfortable seats because the fireplace will almost certainly, at least during the fall and winter months, become the focal point of the room—possibly the entire house. Selection of an interior or exterior wall might depend in large part on the type of fireplace you plan to install. A masonry or heat-circulating fireplace will require foundations and footings. Interior walls are nearly always a problem for these types. For a house built on a slab or over a crawl space, a masonry or heat-circulating fireplace built in an exterior wall is more practical. Interior-wall fireplaces can take up lots of space. It's possible to lose well over 15 square feet of living room area to a zero-clearance unit placed in an interior wall.

In general, for already existing houses, a fireplace on an exterior wall will be a little less expensive to install (Fig. 3-3). An exception is the zero-clearance fireplace. This type might actually cost more on an exterior wall where some sort of decorative covering might be needed for the chimney.

FIREPLACE VARIETY

There are so many different kinds of fireplaces that selection ultimately becomes a matter of taste. There are many double-

Fig. 3-3. A fireplace joined to an exterior wall (courtesy of Majestic).

Fig. 3-4. A Majestic corner fireplace.

opening fireplaces (facing two rooms) in either metal-lined or zero-clearance styles. There are units for corner installation (Fig. 3-4). There are units that can be opened on three sides (serving as a room heater, room divider and dramatic decorative device). There are even units that open on all sides (Fig. 3-5).

Metal hoods of various styles can provide dramatic accents or can be used to actually overshadow the fireplace itself. Another benefit of hoods is that, as a hood warms up, it holds heat. This slowly releases warmth to the room, and increases the heat production of the fireplace by a modest, though appreciable, percentage.

WOOD STORAGE

Too often wood storage is considered *after* the fireplace is constructed. A one or two day supply of wood is an extremely handy thing to have inside the house (assuming the wood is seasoned and free of bugs). Estimating your needs for one or two days of wood-burning can be difficult if you've had no experience at using a fireplace or wood stove. The amount of wood you use depends on how often the fireplace or stove is used and how high the flames are kept. Just as much depends on the types of wood used, how it's seasoned, and how it has been cut and split. For supplementary wood

45

heating when using a fireplace, try storing some wood indoors in an area at least 4 feet wide and 2 feet high (assuming the logs are 2 feet long). This should leave space for kindling, small starter logs, and a decent supply of dried, split logs for main burning chores. Storage areas can be right next to the fireplace, underneath the hearth (with a raised hearth), or against the wall in which the fireplace is installed. Arrangements can be made for a storage area with a door in the living room. A weathertight storage area outside the house can hold enough wood for days.

All kinds of things—baskets, boxes, racks, and contraptions of all kinds, some attractive, some not so attractive, and some down-

Fig. 3-5. A suspended fireplace that is open on all sides (courtesy of Majestic).

right ugly—can be used for wood storage. I've always found that a reed basket or wicker basket makes a fine-looking holder for small kindling and newspapers for starting the fires. Not entirely new, but much more popular now than in the past, are the large metal hoops that can hold as much as a quarter of a cord of dry wood for your fire.

The advantage of indoor storage of wood is that you will always have a supply of dry wood on hand (even if your main supply outside gets drenched with rain). The indoor supply allows you to move some damp wood indoors as the already dry wood is fed to the fire. By the time you start running out of dry wood from indoors, the wet stuff will be dry enough to provide good heat.

FURNITURE PLACEMENT

Furniture placement around a fireplace depends in large part on your family's preferences. Generally, a furniture grouping allowing comfortable seating facing the fire is preferred. There should be plenty of room for tending the fire but not quite so much room that traffic constantly flows directly in front of the fireplace.

Basically, the furniture placement should make *you* comfortable. Regardless of what so-called experts say about furniture placement, it's still your home and the place where you most need to be at ease. If the experts are nervous because you like to put the soles of your shoes almost in the flames, let them worry—but keep a bucket of water close just in case!

In general, the distance of furniture from the fireplace should depend upon the size of the fireplace and the size of the furniture.

Fig. 3-6. Typical furniture placement around a relatively small fireplace (courtesy of Majestic).

Small furniture, small fireplace: shorter distance. Large furniture, large fireplace: greater distance (Fig. 3-6). Not only does this look more pleasing to most people, it also tends to be more comfortable.

HEARTHS

The hearth is a very important part of fireplace planning. The hearth's foremost function is preventing sparks from flying onto an unprotected floor. After that, the hearth becomes a decorative item that is something to look at and enjoy or sit on and enjoy.

The basic hearth is usually a rectangle of masonry or ceramic or stone laid in front of the fireplace. There can be many variations. Instead of the standard rectangle extending 6 inches to each side of the firebox and at least 2 feet in front of it, you extend the hearth several feet into the room. It can be of decorative brick, stone, or tile.

You can even drop the hearth below floor level. There are many ways to do this, including dropping the entire area around the fireplace to form a sort of conversation "pit" with a stone or tile floor.

The hearth can be raised and used as seating directly in front and to the sides of the fireplace. A raised hearth can also be used as a handy wood storage area. Hearth variations seem almost innumerable. Your choice of a hearth will depend, for the most part, on your tastes and your bank account.

WALL COVERINGS

Wall coverings for around the fireplace offer a great many intriguing variations and possibilities. With zero-clearance fireplaces, there's little need to make entire walls from heavy masonry—unless you want to. Newer, lighter forms of masonry can be used to save weight and bypass the need for major foundation work or reconstruction of your present foundation. Paneling or roughhewn beams can be used to continue the accent provided by the fireplace. The majority of panelings on the market today have a rustic look, but they can be more luxurious.

Zero-clearance units require no wall coverings. There is no need to rim the unit with fancy tiles or expensive masonry unless you prefer it and can afford it. A bit of work with a chain saw will provide rough-sawn paneling at a cost of one tree, or less, and still leave a fair amount of burnable wood trimmings.

Chapter 4

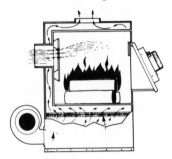

Installation of
Factory-built Fireplaces and Stoves

Factory-built fireplaces and wood stoves are shortcuts. There is no need, as there is for a masonry fireplace, to build the appliances from the foundation level to the chimney cap. However, strict adherence to proper methods of installation, for efficiency and safety, is required. Fortunately, the work involved in installation is a great deal easier than masonry work. (Figs. 4-1, 4-2, 4-3, and 4-4).

PRELIMINARIES

If you have no chimney installed, the number of packages dropped off by your local freight transporter is going to be fairly large. Your first job is to make certain no damage was done to the appliances and accessories during the transportation. Examine and then open the cartons. Remove each and every piece and examine them carefully. Any signs of damage should be checked before you sign the bill of lading for the materials. If all is well, you are now in a position to decide just where the particular unit will go. With a chimney already in place, your selection is somewhat limited. Underwriter's Laboratories recommends that you use no more than 10 feet of stovepipe to reach the flue with wood stoves (Fig. 4-5).

Once the exact location is selected, you'll know much more about what needs to be done. For in-the wall installation of prefabricated fireplaces, you must make your position selection with an eye

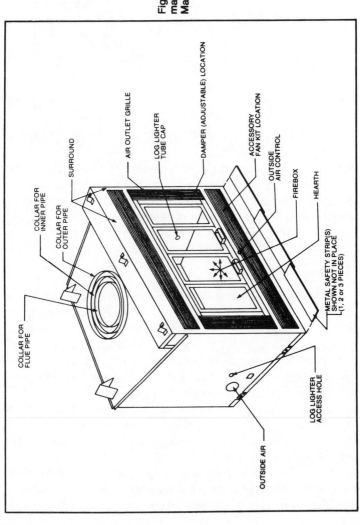

Fig. 4-1. Parts of the Warm Majic manufactured fireplace (courtesy of Majestic Co.).

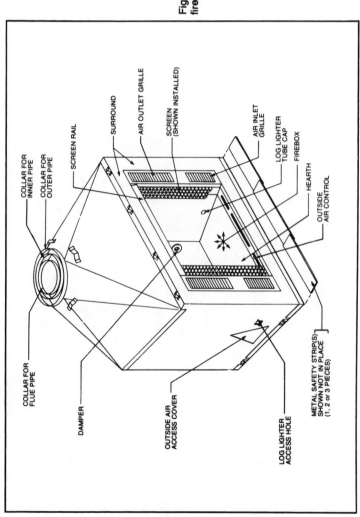

COLLAR FOR INNER PIPE

COLLAR FOR OUTER PIPE

COLLAR FOR FLUE PIPE

DAMPER

OUTSIDE AIR ACCESS COVER

LOG LIGHTER ACCESS HOLE

METAL SAFETY STRIP(S) SHOWN NOT IN PLACE (1, 2 or 3 PIECES)

SCREEN RAIL

SURROUND

AIR OUTLET GRILLE

SCREEN (SHOWN INSTALLED)

AIR INLET GRILLE

LOG LIGHTER TUBE CAP

FIREBOX

HEARTH

OUTSIDE AIR CONTROL

Fig. 4-2. The Majestic MHC series fireplace.

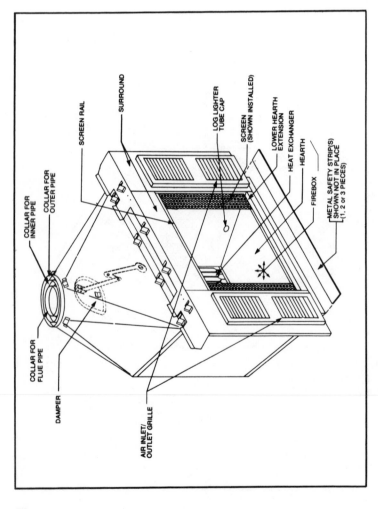

Fig. 4-3. Majestic's Energy Saving™ fireplace.

COLLAR FOR INNER PIPE

COLLAR FOR OUTER PIPE

SCREEN RAIL

SURROUND

COLLAR FOR FLUE PIPE

DAMPER

AIR INLET/ OUTLET GRILLE

LOG LIGHTER TUBE CAP

SCREEN (SHOWN INSTALLED)

LOWER HEARTH EXTENSION

HEAT EXCHANGER

HEARTH

FIREBOX

METAL SAFETY STRIP(S) SHOWN NOT IN PLACE (1, 2 or 3 PIECES)

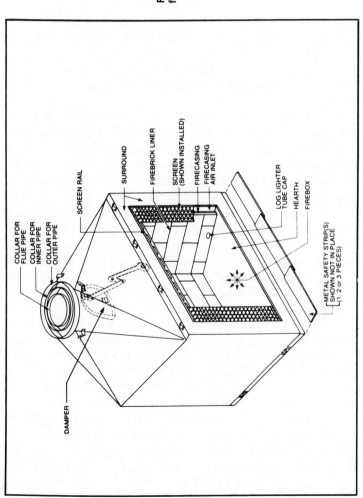

Fig. 4-4. Majestic's M/MD series fireplace.

COLLAR FOR FLUE PIPE
COLLAR FOR INNER PIPE
COLLAR FOR OUTER PIPE

SCREEN RAIL

SURROUND

FIREBRICK LINER

SCREEN (SHOWN INSTALLED)

FIRECASING

FIRECASING AIR INLET

LOG LIGHTER TUBE CAP

HEARTH

FIREBOX

METAL SAFETY STRIP(S) SHOWN NOT IN PLACE (1, 2 or 3 PIECES)

DAMPER

53

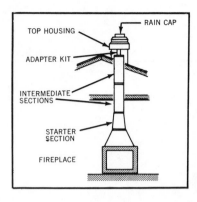

Fig. 4-5. Parts of a prefabricated fireplace (courtesy of Majestic).

for what might be inside the wall you're going to have to open up (the same idea goes for ceilings and roofs). Because most modern electrical codes demand an outlet at intervals no greater than a dozen feet along interior walls, you'll almost certainly end up having to move, or remove, at least one receptacle in any house built in the last 15 or so years.

In such cases, *make totally and absolutely certain* the power to the circuit you're working on has been cut off before tinkering with any electrical installation. Usually, the simplest method of doing such a job will be to simply reroute the cable and install the receptacle to one side or the other of the projected fireplace installation. Such a job is simple, but *must* be done in accordance with local codes.

Receptacles are always encased in metal or plastic boxes. Cut the power. Detach the wires from the receptacle. Pull the wires out of the box (after loosening the box clamp). Relocate the outlet box. Run the cable to the box. Allow it to enter just as it did in the original installation. Place the wires back, on their respective terminals, with the open end of the loop around the terminal facing the direction the screw will turn to tighten. Tighten.

Before closing up the wall, if you have any doubts at all or if your local codes require it, give your local building inspector a call and ask him to come out and check things over. I'm assuming that you've already checked with the building inspector to see if a building permit is needed to install either a wood stove or a fireplace. In the case of a fireplace, you will almost always be need a permit.

Much depends on the area where you live. In some areas, you will not even be allowed to change a simple wiring device from one place to another. A licensed electrician must do the work. In other areas, virtually anything you do that doesn't actually increase the value of the house is legal without permits. Whether permits are

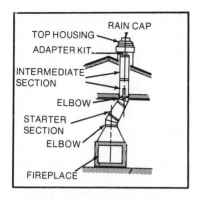

TOP HOUSING
ADAPTER KIT
INTERMEDIATE SECTION
ELBOW
STARTER SECTION
ELBOW
FIREPLACE
RAIN CAP

Fig. 4-6. Elbow installation of a fireplace using 15-degree and 30-degree offsets.

needed or not, proper installation of any relocated wiring is essential and so is proper installation of a wood stove or fireplace if you're to have a troublefree job (Figs. 4-6 and 4-7).

When checking for in-the-wall installation, make sure you don't consider breaking into a wall that has plumbing runs to either the kitchen, bathroom, or laundry room. Such runs are a great deal of trouble to relocate. If such a wall is where you plan to build, build *out* from it instead of tearing into it. This saves time, trouble, and expense.

Once the basic checks are done, consider your feelings and energy levels. This is one of the things you can do to help eliminate problems during the installation of a wood stove or manufactured fireplace. In most cases, when installing a manufactured fireplace, you will be doing the work in the evenings and over the weekends.

Fig. 4-7. Air flow through a Majestic heat-circulating fireplace.

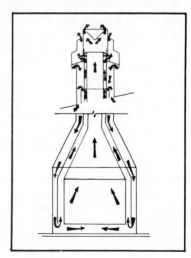

Make sure what you are using really is spare time. Working when you are too tired, irritated, tense, or otherwise upset is one of the fastest and surest ways to a botched job and personal injury. In such cases, you're far better off to put the job off for a few days until you've had the needed rest or handled any other problems that crop up.

Carefully follow directions. Clearance differences, unit size differences, and some basic installation procedures can easily change from time to time. Follow the manufacturer's instructions.

When installing prefabricated fireplaces, you don't have to be overwhelmingly handy, and you don't need many tools. Still, it will pay to have at least a bit of skill with basic tool use even though most manufactured fireplaces require little more than a screwdriver and a hammer to put together. You will need other tools to install bridging, bracing and to cut open ceilings and roofs.

To install zero-clearance factory prefabricated fireplaces you'll need a 2-foot level, (or a top quality shorter spirit level), a good claw hammer (a good hammer really *does* make nail driving an easier job), a keyhole or compass saw, a drill and bits, a miter box, and a backsaw (the last item is not always essential).

In addition, I would recommend a reciprocating saw for cutting through ceiling and roofing materials. For finish work, the miter box and backsaw again would be handy (a wooden miter box can be bought cheaply and used with a 10-tooth crosscut handsaw if you prefer). For masonry fireplace hearth materials, you will need some mason's tools such as a trowel, a brickerlayer's hammer, and a brick chisel.

Before opening up any wall, make a second check for obstructions to the venting that will be needed. You could find yourself facing bathroom or kitchen plumbing, extensive wiring, complex wall structures that you don't want to disturb, or vent pipes for any of a number of appliances. Determine the approximate route the venting (chimney) is to take through the ceiling (and the floor above if your house has more than one story) and the roof.

To do this with a prefabricated fireplace, first position the fireplace with the starter chimney section on top. Measure from two different room walls to the top of the starter section. Use these two measurements to mark the exact spots directly above the starter section where the chimney will rise through the house.

Don't forget that even zero-clearance chimneys require 2 to 3 inches of clearance (depending on the manufacturer's recommendations). This procedure will give you an indication of your roof exit position and must be checked again on the exterior of the roof to make sure the chimney will not be obstructed by trees, high vent pipes, power lines, or other items that might cause hazards or downdraft problems in the flue.

If the roof of your house is peaked, try to make sure you do not break through at the peak. A breakthrough in such a place complicates the framing needed to handle the firestop and chimney termination (Fig. 4-8).

When making your check for placement of the termination, make sure the sections your chimney will use are of sufficient length that the chimney will project at least 2 feet above all obstructions within 10 feet of the chimney if you have a house with a peaked roof.

Fig. 4-8. A Majestic heat-circulating fireplace showing hot and cold air vents.

If the roof is flat, the chimney must extend at least 3 feet above the roof surface (as well as being 2 feet above obstructions within 10 feet). If this quite basic rule of chimney design is not followed, your fireplace or wood stove will smoke and have a very poor draft.

You can readily route your flue around obstacles in the house by using chimney sections with offsets of 15 degrees and 30 degrees where needed. For freestanding fireplaces and wood stoves, you can avoid obstacles that would require an offset flue by simply relocating the unit and running stovepipe along at least 18 inches below any combustible surface. Try to keep the total stovepipe run to no more than 10 feet.

If you can't run the stovepipe as far down as 18 inches without running into difficulties, Country Stove and Shelter, Ltd. (265 Prestige Park Rd., East Hartford, CT 06108) offers an air insulated, double-wall stovepipe that cuts required clearances down as low as 9 inches. The pipe, called Canadian Connection or E-Vent, has been tested by Underwriters Laboratories of Canada. It comes in flue sizes of 4 inches, 5 inches, 6 inches and 7 inches. Available pipe lengths are 3 feet, 2 feet and 1 foot. There are 45 and 90 degree angles or elbows, and a tee and cap to make stovepipe cleaning easier.

A stainless steel liner is used. This stovepipe should definitely remain in place for a far, far longer period of time than will standard stovepipe. The price, however, is much higher. On a rough estimate, E-Vent is approximately 10 times the price of standard 24-gauge stovepipe (give or take a buck or two). In other words, current prices for a 36-inch section of 6-inch flue diameter E-Vent would be $32.40. That is very expensive. But only a couple of pieces are needed and you're virtually assured of not having to replace stovepipe for a good, long period of time. You will also be able to move pipe closer to combustible surfaces (walls or ceilings).

ZERO-CLEARANCE FIREPLACES

Many of today's zero-clearance fireplaces do not actually come under the heading of heat-circulating fireplaces (fireplaces with vents that directly circulate heated air to one or more rooms). They have raised firebox hearths that are designed to draw cool air from the floor level and thus increase the volume of warm air being passed to the room from the fireplace. Installation of such raised hearth fireplaces is very simple. In most one-story homes, it should require no more than a long holiday weekend of work.

Because the units are heavily insulated, you can sit them directly on a wood floor, or you can install the units on a prebuilt base of whatever height you prefer to use. This is the point where a raised hearth allowing for a seat in front of the fireplace, or a bit of storage for firewood becomes easy to envision and make. Build a frame (with 2 × 4s) larger than the fireplace unit, plus whatever hearth extension you prefer, cover the top with a good non-combustible material (brick or ceramic tile or slate), and leave the front open if you want to store wood underneath.

Heat production is increased to a fair degree with such a raised hearth fireplace. There is no need to run venting around the room or up the chimney as there is with heat-circulating models of various brands (Fig. 4-10). Such fireplaces can be positioned just about anywhere you might be able to imagine. They'll fit in the wall, out from a wall, on an interior wall, or in a corner. You can frame out around them with wood, surround them with ceramic tile trim, or use masonry.

Heat circulating zero-clearance fireplaces are not really a great deal more difficult to install than the raised-hearth models (Fig. 4-11). The primary difference is in the extra time needed for the

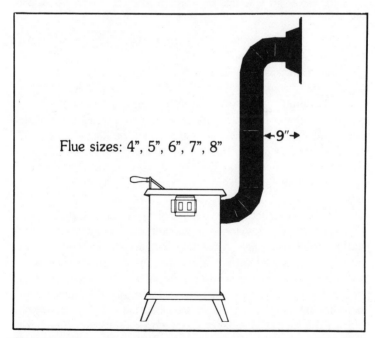

Fig. 4-9. Installation of an E-Vent stovepipe (courtesy of Country Stoves and Shelter Ltd.).

Fig. 4-10. Two styles of E-Vent stovepipe (courtesy of Country Stoves and Shelter Ltd.).

installation, on some heat circulating models, because you must install ducting and appropriate grills.

Heat from ducted heat-circulating fireplaces can be vented to other rooms through the ducting in order to benefit two or three rooms with supplementary heat. Cold air is drawn from vents placed low on the sides of the firebox (or under the firebox hearth). Hot air passes out of the upper vents alongside and is ducted to outlets placed where you prefer. Hot air ducts should always be placed a minimum of 6 inches below the ceiling and 6 inches above a floor (when the hot air is circulated to a second story). Grills are always installed with their louvers facing down.

If you've already lived in your house for a couple of winters, you will have located a few areas where there are cold spots or other heating problems. A heat circulating fireplace can be used to duct warm air to any such locations. Heat-circulating fireplaces are about the most energy efficient of all basic fireplaces. The amount of heat produced is probably about 50 percent more than the amount produced by any other kind of similar-sized basic fireplace. If you consider the ease of installation and the overall lower-cost of zero-clearance, heat-circulating fireplaces, as compared to masonry fireplaces, their higher efficiency seems an even bigger bargain.

Framing out a zero-clearance fireplace is a simple job whether the unit is installed in or on a wall. Start the job by forming a base, on the floor, of 2 × 4s of the correct size to fit the base of the model you are in the process of installing. Cut the wood to size and use at least two 12-penny nails to butt nail the base of 2 × 4s together (at each joint).

If the unit is going into a wall, you'll find that there is little else needed in the way of framing wood work. If the fireplace is to be installed on the wall, use standard wall-framing techniques around the base of the appliance.

After nailing up a doubled top plate of 2 × 4s, start by laying down a sole plate 2 × 4. Nail it to the floor, and nail in studs 16 inches on center. The studs are nailed to the top plate (before the second 2 × 4 is added), and this is set in place on the sole plate and the studs are toenailed at the correct intervals.

If you don't want to toenail the studs, get some of the simple framing anchors made by TECO and use these. If you don't have much carpentry experience, toenailing has a strong tendency to make the studs dance around more than a little. In most instances, 2 × 4s are the best choice of framing materials to provide a solid wall. But in many areas, you can use 2 × 3s because the wall serves no structural purpose. I doubt, though, you'll save more than $10 by using 2 × 3s. It may not even come close to that unless there's a lot of framing.

Fig. 4-11. Installing brick facing around a fireplace.

The final framing touch for both in-the-wall and on-the-wall installations requires a 2 × 4 header to be nailed across the front of the fireplace. You'll find a steel frame on the fireplace to help properly locate this header. The header is toenailed to the studs after being nailed to the fireplace. Check local codes before doing this portion of the work. A few areas require the use of a 2 × 6 header on top of the 2 × 4 header (which must also then be toenailed to the studs).

Front framing on in-the-wall installations is made both simpler and stronger if you use jack studs. Bring them inside the old studs, cut them off at the height of the header, and nail them directly to the old studding. The fireplace will have its front flush with the framing. You can apply decorative trim after the wallboard or paneling is installed.

If the ducting is to come out of the side of your fireplace, assuming the fireplace sides extend far enough into the room, just frame the side out to accept the ducts. If the ducting runs through walls and into other rooms, you'll certainly have to carve your way through some plasterboard or paneling in order to make the installation. Remove as little wallboard or paneling as is possible to do the job. The less cut away the easier you'll find the replacement.

In many cases, you'll find it simpler to remove an entire sheet of gypsum wallboard or paneling. Removing the entire panel, usually 4 × 8 feet, will generally make for a neater job (with fewer seams to be covered at the finish). If the ducting runs through a combustible wall close to the fireplace, you'll need to use a wall thimble. Thimbles can be adjusted to fit walls from 3 to 6 inches thick. This makes their installation quite simple.

Once the ducting has been run, you can install the grills (with the louver slats facing down). To produce a greater volume of heated air in the same room with the fireplace, or in another room, you can install small electric fans in the *cold* air vents to increase the volume of cool air reaching, being warmed, and passing on through the fireplace. Such fans must never be installed in hot air vents. In that spot, they would cool the already warmed air, interfere with the draft of the fire, and cause smoke problems.

Finishing touches on any of these zero-clearance fireplaces are entirely up to the person who installs them. The basic consideration is the weight your floor will support (Fig. 4-11).

Without proper foundations, an entire wall of unsupported masonry would take a bad tumble or cause the house to sag. Many of the new types of imitation masonry are extremely light and much easier to install than true masonry; little is added to the overall weight of the installation. Still, even a small manufactured fireplace and finishing touches can add several hundred pounds to your floor load. A Heatilator model 3138 heat-circulating, zero clearance fireplace weighs about 285 pounds and each chimney section adds 28 more pounds. Framing and a noncombustible hearth will readily add 150 or more pounds to this load. Slip in several hundred pounds of firewood stored near the fireplace and you can easily see how the extra weight can build up.

The final trim you use can be tile, stucco, barn paneling, rough-sawn wood, cedar shakes or almost anything in the way of attractive materials. Mantels are usually made of wood, but they can be made of slate or other materials such as brick or wood or other material covered with ceramic tile. Many, many Dutch-style homes in certain areas of New York State offer trim of ceramic tile in Delft patterns and they are exceptionally good looking.

A great many people feel a mantel is just something to collect dust and all sorts of odd trinkets while providing no real aesthetic addition to the fireplace itself. To a great many others, a mantel is an essential part of a fireplace; it is a type of completion. A mantel can be a graceful addition to period rooms and it can add a roughhewn look to more rustic rooms. Many types of stone such as slate, bluestone and granite, make exceptionally fine looking mantels. This is especially true when they are combined with worked wood panels to make a really elegant setting for the fireplace. This type of work tends to increase the cost of the installation. Few of us have the tools and skill to work materials such as bluestone or granite.

Raised hearths for zero-clearance fireplaces can be a continuation of the wall framing on which the fireplace stands. In such cases, the open-work studding in the hearth is sheathed with plywood and covered with masonry. Exterior grade plywood, one-half inch or heavier, is your best bet. Lighter grades of plywood will sooner or later be kicked in. That is why gypsum wallboard is not a good idea for such coverings.

There are many half-thickness brick styles available, and many even thinner bricks, as well as ceramic tile in a great many patterns. All of them can be very handy for finishing the front of a raised hearth. In any case, the hearth material should be at least three-eights of an inch thick and non-combustible. You might also want to leave part of the frame for the raised hearth open, finish off the sides of the opening with molding or masonry, and use the underside for wood storage.

However you do it, the top of the hearth is the most important spot. For the raised hearth, exterior plywood up to three-fourths of an inch thick should be used. Most of the time, the extra strength won't be essential. If someone accidentally drops a couple of heavy logs, as will happen sooner or later, you'll be grateful the strength is there.

Most floor-use ceramic tiles make a fine surface for any hearth. Although the finer handmade styles of ceramic tile are very expensive (as much as $10 a square foot), you'll seldom be using more than 6 to 10 square feet of the material. A hearth covered with such tiles can often become a pleasing focal point in any room.

In general, your hearth should be from half a foot to a foot wider than the fireplace opening (on each side). A hearth should extend out from the fireplace opening at 2 feet to keep flying sparks from charring floors or burning holes in rugs. If your fireplace unit is very large, say over 42 inches wide, you'll want a hearth that protrudes 3 feet or more from the firebox opening to make it seem proportionately acceptable to the fireplace.

WARM MAJIC

If I were to install a fireplace in my home today I would install one of Majestic's Warm Majic units. A description of its features rapidly shows why the unit is so much more efficient than even the best of other types of heat-circulating fireplaces. First, what Majestic calls the *fire-wrap* principle is used. In essence, this means that all sides of the firebox are wrapped with two constantly recirculating layers of air. When the heat is transferred, the air is sent into the room.

Efficiency nearly as good as a stove results if you use the optional fan kit at high speed, keep the flue damped to its lowest spot, and keep the glass enclosure doors closed. In addition, cool air is drawn in under the hearthplate, passed up the backwall and re-issued into the room after heating. In other words, heat transfer is maximized to about the greatest degree possible. Somewhat the same system is used in many wood stoves of the circulator type.

When you add in the glass doors that can be closed, and the exterior venting to the firebox that can be opened to provide combustion air, the efficiency is increased greatly. The appliance can be run just about full blast without room air being lost and it can be almost totally shut down without the loss of room air simply by shutting the glass doors and opening the outside air vent. The damper remains open as it does with any wood-burning appliance (the chimney or stovepipe damper), but room air is not used for combustion. Warm air is not lost up the chimney as would be the case with a standard fireplace.

The Warm-Majic, unlike most other manufactured fireplaces, comes in a single size. The firebox is 3 feet wide at the front and 22 inches deep. A good-sized fire can be kept burning. (Fig. 4-12). With the optional fan kit, the Warm-Majic should provide a more than fair amount of supplementary heat in many homes. The efficiency won't actually equal many wood stoves (though it will exceed some) because heat transfer from the back of the firebox, and its sides, must be again transferred to the front outlets to the room. But the design will provide about as effective heating efficiency as any we are likely to see in present-day fireplaces (Fig. 4-13).

You begin the Warm-Majic installation job by deciding where you want to locate the fireplace base unit. It can be mounted directly on a combustible surface that must be hard and flat and of sufficient size to support the entire base of the unit. You can use a raised,

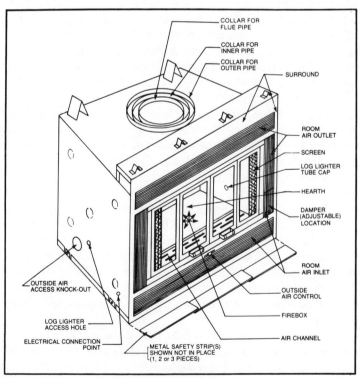

Fig. 4-12. Warm Majic (courtesy of Majestic).

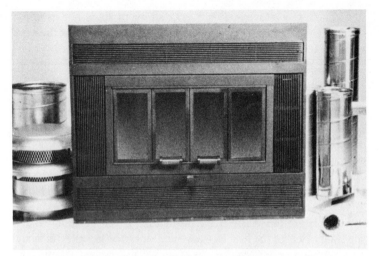

Fig. 4-13. Warm Majic Components (courtesy of Majestic).

wooden platform if you want a raised hearth, but the surface must be flat and uniform. The back of the fireplace can go directly up against a combustible wall, but adjacent sidewalls that are closer than 2 feet to the unit must be protected by wall shields of non-combustible material. If you install the unit in a corner, with the appliance's sides at 45 degree angles to combustible walls, no extra protection is needed.

For the simplest installation, you need only lay a hearth protector of three-eighth inch asbestos millboard or its equivalent (such as Babcock & Wilcox Insulating Products Division's Kaowool spun ceramic material). This can then be covered with a non-combustible decorative material to protect the millboard (from being crumbled as the stuff is easily crushed). Seal the gap between the fireplace hearth and the hearth extension with furnace cement.

Clean up the area on which the base unit is to sit. If needed, construct the raised box on which it is to sit. Move the base unit of the fireplace to its exact location and sit it in place. Lift the front of the base unit and slide the included metal safety strips in place so that they extend about 1½ inches back under the front of the base. The strips should overlap each other about half an inch. Turn down the four fastening tabs, two on each side, of the base unit and nail to the floor.

If your fireplace is located right against the wall in back of it, measure out 12½ inches and make a mark. Draw a line parallel to the back wall and you'll have the centerline of your chimney. Marks are made on the ceiling (Figs. 4-14, through 4-17). If the fireplace is

Fig. 4-14. Positioning the Warm Majic (courtesy of Majestic).

otherwise located, make an X mark on the flue opening on the base unit. Use a straightedge and chalk and make the distances between each point of the X's legs equidistant from any other adjacent to it. This will give you a centerpoint from which to work when you tape on two strips of cord that also form the X. Now, take a plumb bob and go to the ceiling. Position the point of the plumb bob so that it falls on the crossing point of the X. Mark the centerpoint on the ceiling (Figs. 4-18 and 4-19).

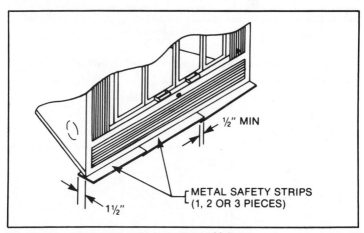

Fig. 4-15. Installing safety strips (courtesy of Majestic).

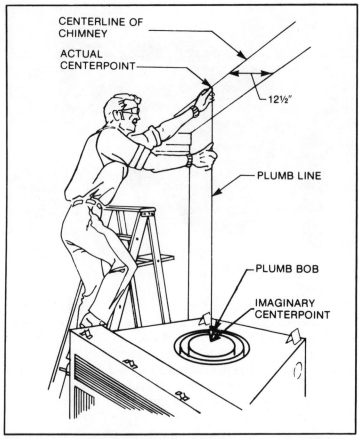

Fig. 4-16. Positioning for ceiling entry of the chimney (courtesy of Majestic).

Table 4-1. Installed Lengths of Chimney Sections.

| | DIMENSION IN INCHES | |
CHIMNEY MODEL NO.	TOTAL LENGTH (L$_T$)	INSTALLED LENGTH (L$_I$)
81	11½	10½
818	17½	16½
82	23½	22½
83	35½	34½
85	58	57

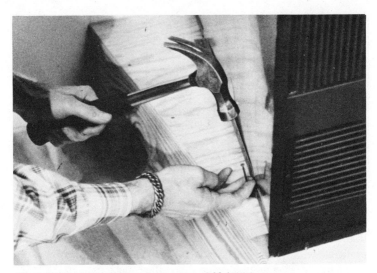

Fig. 4-17. Fastening the base (courtesy of Majestic).

If obstructions must be cleared, Majestic makes 15-degree and 30-degree offsets that can be used to move the chimney from its vertical rise. Table 4-2 gives dimensions of the offsets (815 is the

Fig. 4-18. Using a plumb bob to check the positioning (courtesy of Majestic).

Table 4-2. Height of Chimney Measured From Hearth to Chimney Exit.

15-degree and 830 is the 30-degree). Figure 4-20 shows the offsets attainable with those figures. No more than four elbows can be used per chimney. The chimney cannot be offset more than 30 degrees from vertical (each offset will require a pair of elbows). Whenever possible, straight on up is best.

Once you've got all this settled, move back to the centerpoint mark for the chimney and drive a nail through the ceiling. On the floor (or roof) above, check where the hole will be cut. Keep an eye out for possible obstructions such as wiring and plumbing runs. If there are too many obstructions, you might have to use offsets or reposition the fireplace.

Fig. 4-19. Marking the ceiling (courtesy of Majestic).

70

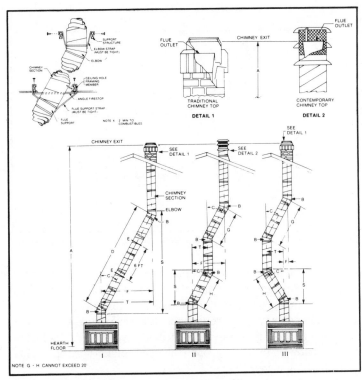

Fig. 4-20. The use of offsets (courtesy of Majestic).

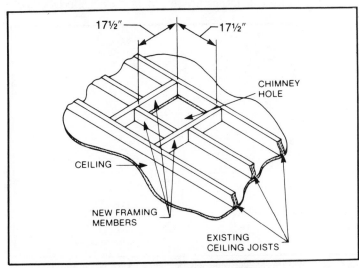

Fig. 4-21. Framing for the chimney (courtesy of Majestic).

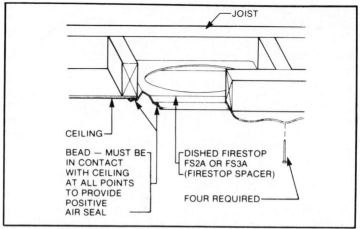

Fig. 4-22A. Setting the firestop when the room above is not an attic (courtesy of Majestic).

Cover the fireplace collar opening on the base unit and cut the hole for the chimney. Then frame the chimney hole as shown in Fig. 4-21. Use framing members the same size as those already in use. If the chimney comes into the ceiling vertical, inside dimensions of the frame will be 17½ inches by 17½ inches. If you need a 15-degree angle for entering the ceiling, open the inside dimensions up to 17⅞ inches by 22½ inches.

For a 30-degree ceiling entrance, you'll need inside dimensions of 17⅞ inches by 29⅝ inches. If the ceiling is over 8 inches thick,

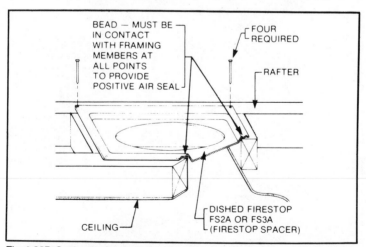

Fig. 4-22B. Setting the firestop when the room above is actually an attic (courtesy of Majestic).

other adjustments in the framing will need to be made (as indicated by the individual job).

If the chimney is not going into an attic, the firestop spacer (required for safety) is set in place with the flange on the ceiling side and the dished portion extending up into the hole. If the area above the ceiling is an attic, it is installed with the flange in the attic and the dished portion down. Nail each corner of the firestop spacer to the framing members of the chimney hole (Figs. 4-22A through 4-23).

Once the firestop is in place, you're ready to start attaching the chimney sections (Fig. 4-23). Start with the inner, or flue, pipe first; make sure the built-in snap fasteners lock as it is mounted. Now the inside pipe (this is a triple-walled pipe with air insulation) is added. Next, the outside pipe is added (Fig. 4-24).

Continue this process until all three pipes extend on through the ceiling. You probably will find it necessary to insert all three pipes inside each other for the last step. Then slip them all up through the ceiling hole (Fig. 4-25) and let them down one at a time to snap them in place. M⌐ke sure each section added snaps completely in place. Continue the chimney attaching job as needed until the roof is reached. Firestops must be added at each pass through of ceilings and floors, but none is needed when the roof opening is passed. If elbows are required, note that only the outer pipe has a snaplock. The inside and flue pipes telescope. Elbow straps must be nailed to a framing member unless the elbow is placed directly on the fireplace collar on the base unit.

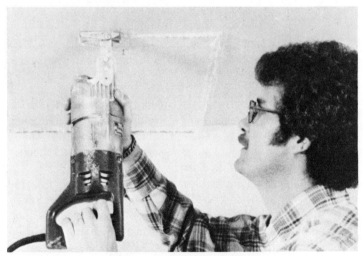

Fig. 4-23. Cutting through the ceiling (courtesy of Majestic).

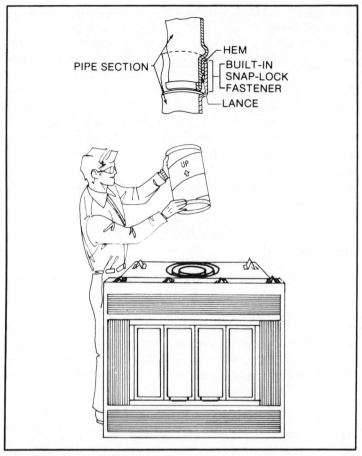

Fig. 4-24. Build-in snap-lock fasteners are used to attach chimney pipe sections (courtesy of Majestic).

Chimney supports are not needed for most residential installations. If the chimney height you require does exceed 45 feet, then chimney supports will be required. Elbow straps at intervals of under 30 feet can serve as chimney supports, but angled chimney runs must have supports as close as 6 feet.

If you must go through another ceiling, you can use the techniques previously described to find the centerline of the hole to be cut. (Fig. 4-26). When the time comes to penetrate the roof, driving a nail up through the roof at a marked centerpoint. (Fig. 4-27). The housing or termination you use will come with instructions for figuring the size of the hole needed. Once these are ob-

Fig. 4-25. Installing the first chimney section on the fireplace base (courtesy Majestic).

tained, you can mark the required hole size. Cover the top of the chimney and make the needed cuts, frame out as required, and secure the frame well. Use 16-penny nails in framing lumber the same size as that used in the original roof (Fig. 4-28).

Various termination or top styles will require various lengths of chimney to come up past the roof. Check the directions on the style

Fig. 4-26. Measuring from the roof to the chimney (courtesy of Majestic).

Fig. 4-27. Cutting through the roof (courtesy of Majestic).

you're using, carry the chimney up as far as it needs to go, and install the termination according to instructions (Figs. 4-29 through 4-32).

Once the termination is in place, you're ready to give some thought to installing the outside air system. You'll find two 16-inch sections of flexible duct included with Warm-Majic fireplaces (additional 4-inch duct is available). Duct length is limited to a total of 20

Fig. 4-28. Getting the chimney through the roof (courtesy of Majestic).

Fig. 4-29. Installing the termination (courtesy of Majestic).

feet. The vertical height *must* be at least 3 feet *less* than the chimney height. Ducting may run (as you see in Fig. 4-33) vertically through a wall or through the floor into a crawl space.

If the duct termination is an attic one, or in a crawl space, the area involved needs to have an absolute minimum of 100 square inches of ventilating area that is totally unrestricted. Install the duct

Fig. 4-30. Installing the cap (courtesy of Majestic).

Fig. 4-31. The job is complete (courtesy of Majestic).

termination so as to prevent blocking with insulation or dirt. Duct terminations installed on exterior walls should be placed so they are not blocked by shrubs or drifting snow. Terminations should never be run into garages or any area that might contain flammable liquids or fumes (Figs. 4-34 and 4-35). If the outside ducting system will not be used, there is a room air panel behind the bottom grill that must be removed (one on each end of the appliance).

Fig. 4-32. Other termination styles (courtesy of Majestic).

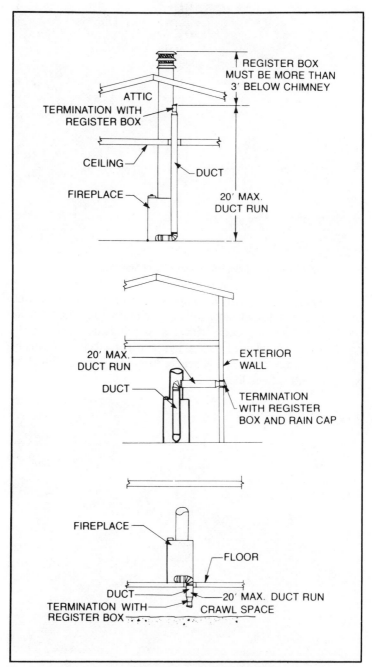

Fig. 4-33. Fresh air duct possibilities (courtesy of Majestic).

Fig. 4-34. Fresh air duct installation (courtesy of Majestic).

Framing is essentially the same as for any other manufactured fireplace except that all joints around the fireplace surround and the finish wall must be sealed with a non-combustible material. In addition, any mantel used must either be of non-combustible material or situated at least a foot above the fireplace opening (Figs. 4-36 through 4-38). Check local codes.

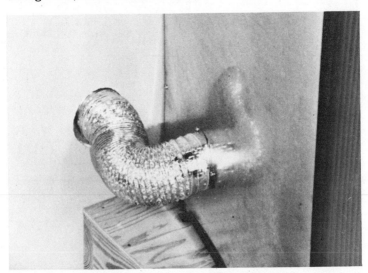

Fig. 4-35. Duct installation is complete (courtesy of Majestic).

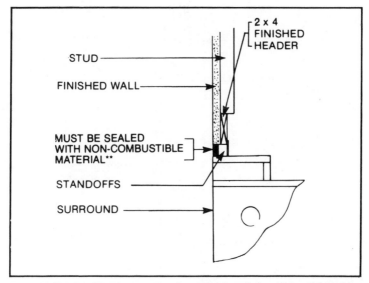

Fig. 4-36. Details of fireplace surrounds and finish walls (courtesy of Majestic).

Finishing up the hearth and the finish wall is pretty much your choice. The unit will be as attractive as any other fireplace, when done, it will be a great deal more efficient (Figs. 4-39, 4-40, and 4-41).

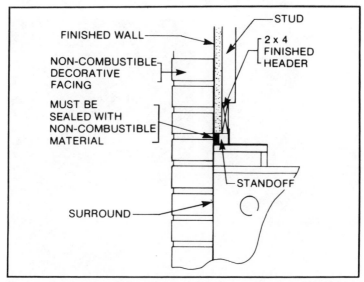

Fig. 4-37. Details of fireplace surrounds and finish walls (courtesy of Majestic).

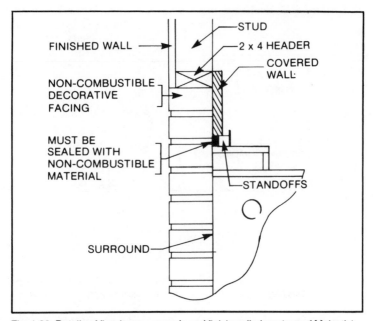

Fig. 4-38. Details of fireplace surrounds and finish walls (courtesy of Majestic).

FREESTANDING FIREPLACES

Freestanding fireplaces all come with manufacturer's recommended distances for clearance from combustible surfaces. You

Fig. 4-39. Finishing off the work (courtesy of Majestic).

Fig. 4-40. Finishing off the work (courtesy of Majestic).

must adhere to these instructions or make some kind of facing of non-combustible materials. If you decide to face a wall with non-combustible material, it is always a good idea to remember that such materials tend to pass heat on to the combustible materials behind them.

It is best to leave an air gap of 2 inches or a bit more to allow heat to escape (the escape is facilitated if the air gap is vented so that

Fig. 4-41. Finishing off the work (courtesy of Majestic).

heated air can pass out). In addition, freestanding fireplaces *cannot* stand on combustible surfaces without protection. In most instances, making a sheet-metal pan of appropriate size (it should extend at least 18 inches out in front of the firebox, and at least 10 inches out all around) and filling it with sand or decorative pebbles over a layer of sand is the simplest way of handling this.

You could use a sheet of asbestos millboard, but the stuff crumbles easily, and it is fairly expensive to start with anyway. I would simply make a sheet-metal box of 24-gauge galvanized steel, cutting the corners so that the box formed will be at least two inches deep. Use a plastic hammer to bend the sides up over a 2 × 4 used as a form, and then pop rivet the corners together. Next, fill with the non-combustible material of your choice and set the freestanding fireplace in place.

Any freestanding fireplace is best located so that its flue venting reaches the exterior as directly as possible. The more bends a fireplace flue has in it the higher the chimney must be to provide a decent draft for the fireplace. In addition, you'll need to keep a careful eye on traffic patterns around freestanding fireplaces (just as you do on wood stoves of other than the circulator style). These appliances present a great deal more heated surface to a room than any other type of fireplace. Children, especially, must be cautioned about playing too close to freestanding fireplaces and wood stoves. Also, you must make sure that there are no freeflowing combustibles around the fireplaces. In other words, make sure that a draft can't blow flammable materials too close to the fireplace.

When making the hearth box for a freestanding fireplace, don't try to work with sheet metal any thicker than about 18 gauge (someone with more tools might prefer 14 gauge). It gets very, very tough to handle because both cutting and bending are more difficult. For the neatest and safest hearth box, leave half an inch to an inch extra material on each side to be bent up. When the sides are in place, you'll be able to bend these tabs down to get a smooth edge that won't cause cuts. Fold the tab to the inside of the box for the smoothest looks and least likelihood of cuts.

If you plan to make a round hearth box, the same basic methods are used. Layout and cutting are a bit more difficult. Use a pencil and piece of string as an over-sized compass to mark out the diameter needed for the base, the sides, and the foldover tabs. Cut and fold as you would a square box, but make your cuts about 1 inch apart. Run them down within about half an inch or less of the part to be folded up as a sidewall.

When your hearth box is folded and riveted, you can clean it up, spray on a compatible primer, and then use whatever color of paint is best for your overall room decor to finish things off. When the paint is dry, cut a piece of one-fourth inch asbestos millboard to fit in the bottom or pour in a half inch of sand. Cover the board or sand with pebbles, brick or other material. If you use brick, you can lay out different patterns and then brush sand down in the joints for a finished look. That's it. Your hearth for a freestanding fireplace is ready.

There are many other ways to construct a hearth for a free-standing fireplace. Virtually any of these hearthbox and other hearth construction methods will serve equally well for woodstoves. Lay ceramic tile at least three-eighths of an inch thick in a bed of mortar. Brick, slate, or stone can be used on the floor.

Once your hearth box is in position, you can set the freestanding fireplace on it and pour the refractory hearth in the firebox hearth section. If you don't use the refractory hearth material, the fireplace will almost certainly burn out shortly before the end of a single season of heavy use. Refractory material is supplied with freestanding fireplaces and needs only to be mixed, poured, and spread to the manufacturer's recommended thickness.

If for some reason there isn't enough refractory compound to complete the job, do *not* use standard cement to replace any that's missing. Anything not specially compounded to withstand severe heat will crack quickly and be a waste of time and money. If there isn't enough of the compound, locate a masonry dealer who has firebrick mortar in stock and use that to make up the difference.

All freestanding fireplaces must be individually vented. Each must have a flue separate from any other appliance's flue. Trying to tie your fireplace (or a wood stove) into an old gas heater flue is especially dangerous. Most are not made to withstand the heat being sent up the chimney. If the gas furnace (or any furnace) is still hooked up and operating, there's just about no way on earth your fireplace can get a proper draft. There's no way the gas furnace will get a proper draft either. The money saved by not installing a separate chimney (Fig. 4-42) will eventually be wasted anyway.

For combustible walls to the rear of freestanding fireplaces, clearance can vary from 1 foot to 3 feet (depending on the unit's construction). A single manufacturer might easily make a half dozen different style units (each with a different recommended clearance). Some appliances are made to hang directly on a wall. Others can be readily placed in room corners with little or no clearance needed, but

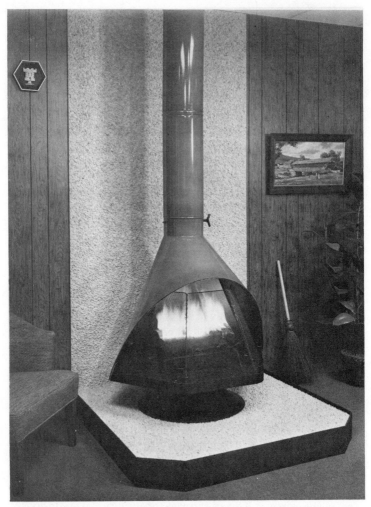

Fig. 4-42. A freestanding fireplace on a non-combustible base.

these are always specially insulated models. Wall-to-fireplace side clearance is usually from 30 to 36 inches. You will need at least 3 feet, and preferably 4 feet, in front of any freestanding fireplace that is free of combustible materials.

From this point in the installation, it is simply a matter of attaching the first section of stovepipe to the top of the fireplace, with the damper installed, and adding the other stovepipe sections until they approach the ceiling. Remember that any stovepipe passing along under a ceiling, parallel to the ceiling, must be at least

18 inches below any combustible surfaces unless the stovepipe is one of the air insulated types such as E-Vent.

At any point where the flue is to pass through a ceiling or wall, you must use a section of insulated chimney or an insulated wall thimble. Remember that even an insulated chimney will need at least 2 inches of clearance from combustible surfaces (this is usually provided by the firetop used to install the insulated chimney).

Firestop spacers must be used when you run an insulated chimney through a wall or ceiling. If your roof is flat, the chimney

Fig. 4-43. A flue provided with 2 inches of clearance from a non-combustible roof.

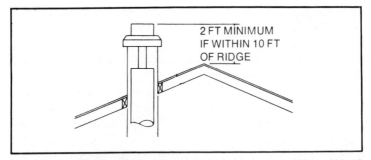

Fig. 4-44. The chimney top should extend 2 feet above any roof ridge within 10 feet of the chimney (courtesy of Heatilator).

must extend at least 3 feet above the roof surface. Peaked roofs need chimneys that extend at least 2 feet above any obstruction within 10 feet.

There are any number of chimney termination styles that can be used on an insulated chimney. Included are some designs you could make yourself, but in most cases terminations purchased from the

Fig. 4-45. Installing a chimney termination.

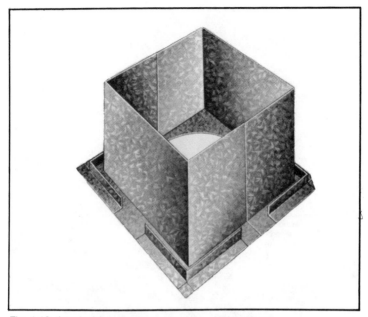

Fig. 4-46. A typical firestop spacer (courtesy of Heatilator).

manufacturer of the insulated chimney, is the easiest and simplest method (Figs. 4-43 through 4-46).

When you cut through the roof, do it from the outside. Lift shingles out of the way where you can in order to keep from destroying them. The fewer shingles destroyed or badly damaged, the easier it will be to install flashing around the termination. Make one or two marking cuts and drill a few marking holes. Then go to prying up the shingles, gently, with a broad-bladed pry bar. Move the bar in as close to each nail as you can. Once the shingles are removed, you can make the final cut for the chimney hole. While firestop spacers are not required at roofs, you might want to install one anyway (some terminations will not allow this). Insert the last section of insulated chimney, make sure it is locked in place, and slip on the termination cap (See Figs. 4-44 through 4-47).

To attach the flashing (sheet metal which is designed to prevent water seeping into the house), overlap the high side flashing over the low side flashing and drill one-eighth inch holes through the flashing and the termination panels (as shown in Fig. 4-48). Drill inward on all sides except the low side. Drill three holes per side; locate the holes 3 inches from the corners whenever roof pitch permits. Nail the flashing to the rafters and use roof cement to caulk around the

Fig. 4-47. Installing the final chimney section.

top, the sides, and panels at the roof line. *Do not* caulk around the low side; you want any water that manages to get in to flow back out on the low side.

Return the shingles to their positions and re-nail them. You can use some roofing cement on the shingles (around the nailheads) if it seems necessary. A dab of roofing cement under the flap of each shingle section will help keep the shingles from lifting in high winds (many shingles come with this dab already there, but removing them will almost certainly destroy the seal).

If you want, you can add insect (and bird) screening and a rain cap. Most contemporary terminations come with such items in place. Neither is essential, but both are nice and handy touches. If the chimney is newly installed and of the correct height, draft aids should not be necessary.

Now, go back and check over all your work. Make sure all firestop spacers are properly nailed, that all chimney supports, where needed, are firmly and securely nailed to house framing members (not siding or sheathing), that any refractory has been poured to the correct depth, and that the hearth is solidly in place. The hearth should be large enough and deep enough to serve its purpose (a minimum of three-eighth of an inch of non-combustible material is needed, and that is a bare minimum). A quick and orderly check of clearances from combustible surfaces is also in order. Though changes are difficult at this point in the job, corrections are easier to make now than later in the game when the wall or ceiling might begin to smolder from excessive heat.

You need to check your chimney installation for smoke leakage. This is a simple job. Place several layers of wet newspapers or a folded wet blanket (or some other material that will seal things) over the top of the chimney and then light a small smudge fire in the fireplace. If you have trouble getting a smudge fire started, simply tear up a few strips of builder's felt paper or tar paper and add that to the fire. Check all joints for smoke leaks. If there are any, check the locking action of the chimney sections and re-lock them. If there are no leaks, pull off the newspapers or blankets and go ahead and enjoy your fireplace.

WOOD STOVES

Installing wood stoves, like the installation of freestanding fire-places, is an operation that can vary a great deal. Much depends on the stove design itself. Almost as much depends on the presence or absence of a chimney, the type of building involved, and whether or not the installation is to be permanent or temporary. By permanent or temporary, I don't necessarily mean a one-winter phenomenon, but an installation that must be removed when the heating season is over.

At present, I am getting ready to install a wood stove in a mobile home, and this must be a temporary installation. The chimney units

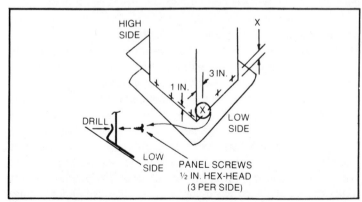

Fig. 4-48. Attaching flashing to the chimney termination (courtesy of Heatilator).

that go in through the roof will be permanently in place. The stove, because of limited wall space, will be removed—along with any interior stovepipe—late each April and will not go back in place before the middle of October.

Even if I really wanted the stove in place year 'round, there would be no possibility. The only available wall space in the 12 × 65 foot mobile home consists of three floor to ceiling windows. At present, the space is occupied by a desk that will have to be removed and stored for the winter. The stove will be placed on Kaowool millboard, and millboard will be placed behind it so that the framing around the center window doesn't flame up.

All of this will simply be set in place. The stove is fairly lightweight so removal and storage won't cause the problems they would with a cast-iron stove such as one of the small Vermont Castings' models (even their small model is quite heavy because of the weight and density of the top-quality cast iron they use to manufacture them).

The idea here is to cut the heating bill in the trailer without spending a great deal of money. The chimney will be Majestic's triple-wall, air-insulated material for a 6-inch flue, and E-Vent will be used to reach the ceiling. This keeps me from having to either extend the Kaowool insulation all the way up the window wall or move the wood stove 3 feet out (eating up already precious floor space).

A contemporary cap or termination will be used. I expect the savings to be on the order of 50 percent, possibly 60 percent, over last year (even though fuel oil has risen about 30 cents a gallon since then). Last year, fuel oil useage was on the order of 475 gallons during a mild winter. Expected use this winter is on the order of 175 gallons. Wood costs will be virtually nothing. The mobile home rests on 65 acres with a fair amount of wooded land, and quite a bit of blown-down timber. A chain saw is already in hand, as is a pick-up truck, so the basic costs will be those involved with fueling the two.

In any case, always remember that in virtually every instance a wood stove is going to have certain minimum space requirements. Very few are designed as zero-clearance units. You must make sure that there is sufficient space between the wood stove's heating surfaces and any combustible materials. Although the heat reaching a combustible wall might not *seem* any too great, most dried wood used to build houses will catch fire at about 250 degrees F. Any combustible wall near a wood-burning appliance *continues* to gather heat for as long as the stove or fireplace is producing heat.

Almost any wood stove must be placed no less than 2 feet from any combustible surface. Some stoves with insulated rears and sides can be brought in a lot closer. If you decide to shorten the distance, make certain that your wood stove is of the type with an insulated portion where it nears a combustible surface.

If after the stove is in use for about 6 to 8 hours, you cannot comfortably place your hand on any such surface and hold it there indefinitely, then the heating appliance is too clsoe. The stove must either be moved out, the wall must be protected with non-combustible material, or a heat-protecting shield must be built.

Replacing fireplaces with wood stoves has become common practice these days. A great many companies have designed special units to do the job. It is possible to convert a stove for use in a fireplace without an overwhelming degree of trouble. In most cases, you'll find it wisest to place the stove on the hearth in front of the fireplace. Box style stoves, whether airtights or not, are generally best for this. If the hearth isn't long enough, they can easily be turned sideways to fit.

Next, you need to seal the fireplace to cut down heat loss. Start by opening the fireplace damper as wide as it will go. Use two sheets of Kaowool millboard. The spun-ceramic fibers of the Babcock & Wilcox product are safer to use than asbestos.

Cut one sheet small enough to fit tightly inside the firebox opening, and the second large enough to have at least 1 inch of overlap at the top and both sides of the firebox. These two boards are then bolted together with washers used as interior spacers to give about a half-inch space between boards. Get some Kaowool rope and glue that around the edges of the board fitting the outside of the firebox with epoxy glue. This will provide quite a good seal.

Next, cut a round hole about two-thirds of the way up the millboard. The hole should be just large enough to take the particular size stovepipe you're going to use. The actual distance up the board will depend on the stove you're planning to use (as will the flue hole opening size). Check the stovepipe for fit in the hole. Run the stovepipe on through the hole and well into the fireplace. Now, make a check where the pipe falls in relation to the smoke shelf in the fireplace innards. If it isn't quite close, you'll be certain of a better draft if you place a 90-degree elbow on the pipe and run another section of the pipe part of the way up into the flue and past the fireplace damper. Place a stovepipe collar on the pipe and shove it tight against the Kaowool millboard to cut down on drafts through any innacurate cutting.

Sit the stove in place in front of the millboard and pipe and run a section of pipe to the stove (with a damper in place). You might, if you don't have a large enough hearth, want to make a hearth box to accept the wood stove. This process will give you a stove in place that can readily supply you with over a 200 percent increase in heat production compared to a basic fireplace (Fig. 4-49).

In addition, the Better'n Ben wood stove, available in many places around the country, is designed to slip right in place on most any fireplace. The model 801 is designed to use either coal or wood. The Better'n Ben 801 is built of one-quarter inch boiler plate, and it has a firebrick lining. In addition, it has shaker grates (essential when coal is used), and an airtight design.

It will accept logs up to 16 inches long or 40 pounds of coal. It produces about 40,000 Btu per hour. The stove is especially designed to fit directly into a fireplace and seal the opening (greatly simplifying your work). In addition, it is claimed that the stove will burn fuel for 24 hours on a full load of hard coal with very little attention needed. A basic problem is locating the anthracite to burn in the stove. Pennsylvania and Kentucky produce reasonable amounts of hard coal, but most areas of the country have bituminous coal—so-called soft coal—that does not burn as long or as clean as does anthracite.

Temporary wood stove installation is rather simply carried out in most instances. It can be an excellent idea if you happen to be renting a home. This is especially true for a home that has no chimney installed. It is possible to install temporarily a wood stove without installing a chimney. You will have to be exceptionally careful in how you carry out the process. Some sturdy supports will be needed. Check with your landlord before taking on the job.

Select a window that will allow prefabricated chimney sections to run unobstructed up the side of a house. Lower the top section of the window (if it's double hung in style). If the window is casement style, open one side and remove the screen. Cut a piece of plywood to fit the opening as tightly as possible. You'll find you need a generous amount of weatherstripping to keep errant breezes from defeating much of the purpose of your work. Use at least one-half inch thick exterior grade plywood for this job.

Cut a second piece of plywood to fit the interior portion of the window with an inch or two of overlap. Locate the centers of the two pieces of plywood and draw a circle large enough to fit your insulated chimney section at this point (or an insulated thimble into which you can insert stovepipe). Cut the holes.

Fig. 4-49. A Garden Way box stove installed in a fireplace.

Just inside the smaller piece of plywood, nail 2 × 4s (2 × 6s if the window is very deep) with 8-penny nails (that is, about 1 inch in from the edges of the exterior piece of plywood). Fill the resulting space with non-vapor, barrier-backed, mineral-wool insulation. Set the interior piece of plywood on the 2 × 4s and nail that in place. Place the unit in the window, and thoroughly weatherstrip it inside and out. Insert the insulated thimble or insulated chimney section.

From this point, run the insulated chimney up the side of the house. Use supports at 4-foot intervals. There is no fireplace underneath to support the weight of the chimney. Place your stove on a hearth box, as described earlier, and run stovepipe to the thimble connector at the window. The stove should be placed as close to the window as possible (so long as the distance is consistent with safe operation).

Permanent stove installations are little different from permanent installations of freestanding fireplaces. Make sure all clearances are correct. Hook the proper-size stovepipe onto the collar on the stove. Bring the stovepipe to the flue opening on the chimney. Use a material that is non-combustible under the stove. Make sure it extends out at least a foot, and preferably 18 inches, by any loading door—with a 10-inch extension at the sides and back.

To reduce the required distance to a combustible wall, you can use a heat shield that you can easily make yourself. Use at least one-fourth inch Kaowool millboard, placed in front of the combustible wall with a 2-inch to 3-inch airspace behind the board. Leave a 1-inch air gap at the bottom of this heat shield so that air flow of heated air is helped. The heated air will rise as cool air enters at the air gap and the heat shield will be even more effective).

Distance reductions can also be affected using 28-gauge sheet metal spaced at least 1 inch from the wall. According to the National Fire Protection Association guidelines, this is more effective than asbestos or Kaowool millboard.

Using millboard, when the recommended distance above the stove is 3 feet, you can bring the distance to 30 inches and reduce side and rear clearance to 18 inches. Using the 28-gauge sheet metal, you can bring the distance down to 18 inches above and a foot to the sides and rear. If the recommended distances to unprotected surfaces are 18 inches, the asbestos allows you to reduce clearance to 15 inches at the top and 9 inches at the sides and rear. The sheet-metal shield allows reduction to 9 and 6 inches respectively.

Wood stoves virtually always require a damper installation in the stovepipe (even though the stove itself might have one or more dampers). If none is required in the pipe, the stove manufacturer will usually say so in the installation instructions. In any case, it is usually a good idea to install a stovepipe damper even where none is called for. Such a damper can help in shutting off air if a chimney fire does occur. Chimney fires are absolutely nothing to fool with. A friend of mine had one take off in a fireplace flue a few years ago, and, fortunately, it did no damage beyond badly shattered nerves. Still, the fire was said to have sounded as if a freight train was running through the living room at top speed. Flames shot a dozen feet out of the top of the chimney, throwing sparks over a wide area, and filling the entire house with a thick layer of smoke. Snow had been heavy and the weather warm; the roof and surrounding woods were just about fireproof. That is not a condition you can count on happening very often during winter.

Installing a damper is a fairly simple process. Most stoves come with the damper plate and a spring loaded pin that fits through the holes in opposite sides of the plate (leaving the spring loaded handle outside the stovepipe). Presumably the pointed end of the damper pin can be used to punch the holes for its own insertion: don't try this. I did one time and I bent the pin and handle so badly I had to buy another damper. Drill the correct-size holes in a spot on the stovepipe where it will be in easy reach.

Stovepipe installation is the point where a lot of wood stove set ups soon become unsafe. Many people simply slip the stovepipe sections together and leave them, more or less, hanging there. This is totally unsafe. Any joint in stovepipe, even if you have only a single piece of pipe running into an elbow that runs into a flue, must be secured with three sheet-metal screws.

This sounds like a time-consuming job. It can be if you have several sections of pipe in 2-foot lengths. But it is also possible to buy sheet-metal screws with a nut head and it is possible to buy a nut driver for self-tapping screws that will fit in your electric drill. There the time reduction can be really considerable. When stovepipe is installed, it should have a slight upward slope to the flue opening at the chimney. The inner, or crimped, end of the stovepipe should always be in the direction of the stove.

In cases where you want (or are forced) to ignore the 10-foot stovepipe length regulation, use four sheet-metal screws at each junction. At intervals of 3 feet, loop wire tightly once around the stovepipe and secure it firmly to the ceiling (making sure you maintain your minimum 18-inch clearance).

The need for this type of security in long pipe runs will become obvious if you ever have a chimney fire. A fire would cause the stovepipe to whip around like something demented. If not securely fastened, the stovepipe will tear apart and bring your house down in flames. The rush of air in a chimney fire is very, very heavy.

Many older homes were heated by long lengths of stovepipe running across a 20-foot or longer room. In such cases, you basically get more heat from a wood stove. But the difficulty arises with the rapid cool down of the stovepipe which then condenses more creosote. This raises the chances of a chimney fire. If you do decide to run a long stovepipe to get more heat from your wood stove, I would recommend that you install at least one T fitting every 8 feet or so to enable you to keep a good check on the build up of creosote. In addition, you should make creosote checks every few weeks instead of twice a year.

Some years ago, I temporarily put in a wood stove, and I ran stovepipe out the window and up the side of the house (well away from any combustible surfaces). I got away with it for two winters, but I realized it was barely worth it. That 25 feet of stovepipe running up the side of the house had to be taken down about every three weeks. It became very nearly choked with creosote in that short period of time. This was during a time when I burned nothing but seasoned maple, oak, and hickory.

Late in the second heating season, the elbow leading into the house became so choked with creosote that the stove would not hold a fire at all. That was in less than four weeks of burning dried wood. After nearly two winters of use, the interior of the stovepipe was no longer smooth. What settled tended to stay in place, unless the pipe got tapped (at which time everything settled into the lower sections, or most everything did, anyway). To say the least, this is not a recommended procedure.

Lengths of stovepipe are often used to draw more of the heat produced from a wood stove. One of the more popular ideas is to run a loop of stovepipe almost to the floor next to the stove, and then bring it back up to the flue. This will increase the radiant heating surface. All such methods create problems with creosote condensation in colder flues because of the extra length. A way must always be devised to make the sections of pipe easier to clean. The pipe *must* be cleaned every three to four weeks. In most cases, inserting a T fitting, with flap damper, at the bottom of the elbow section—rather than in place of the elbow section—at each bottom corner of the loop will make the checking (if not the cleaning out) easier.

In all such cases, at least four sheet-metal screws must be used to hold the sections of stovepipe together. And the stovepipe itself must be supported in someway. Plumber's strapping or fairly heavy wire can be looped round the stovepipe at least one complete turn and then secured to a wall or ceiling framing members.

In cases where long pipe runs are in use (longer than 10 feet no matter the design), you must always keep a close eye on creosote buildup. If a pipe runs almost level over a long horizontal distance, the buildup of pyroligneous acids (creosote) will be greater than if there is a rise of a quarter inch or so per foot of pipe toward the flue. Any such horizontal section over 6 feet long needs support with looped wire or plumber's strapping. Even with the stovepipe slanting down toward the stove, you might find some odd problems if stove use is heavy. At one time, I found the creosote from a long pipe run had been dripping so heavily into a circulating wood heater that the grates were actually clogged with a mass of the stuff (twice in one winter). This occured not because I used a lot of green firewood, but because the wood heater was over-sized and ran with the damper almost all the way closed about 90 percent of the time. Plus the pipe run was about 18 feet long. Using a stove that is too large is a great producer of creosote. Being able to open the wood-heating appliance up to full blast for at least an hour a day is one way to reduce the buildup.

Several things can be done to help reduce the buildup of pyroligneous acids in the flue. First, always keep stovepipe as clean as you can. A monthly cleaning is a good idea on runs up to 10 feet; biweekly cleaning should be done on longer runs. Make certain any long stovepipe runs inside a house have the exiting ends at least a couple of inches higher than the end leaving the last bend of the pipe vertically over the wood stove. Then avoid long stovepipe runs whenever possible. Whenever possible, avoid using conifers, such as pines and cedar, for firewood. Burn as little green wood as you can. Conifers have a higher resin content than do hardwood, or deciduous, trees. Although a really hot fire will get rid of much of the resin buildup, avoiding the buildup is the simplest and cleanest way to do things.

A TYPICAL EXTERIOR WALL INSTALLATION

Let's run through a fairly typical fireplace installation of a heat-circulating unit in an exterior wall (Fig. 4-50). This might be a little easier job than building an all-masonry fireplace from the ground up, but it still requires a great deal of care, patience—and time.

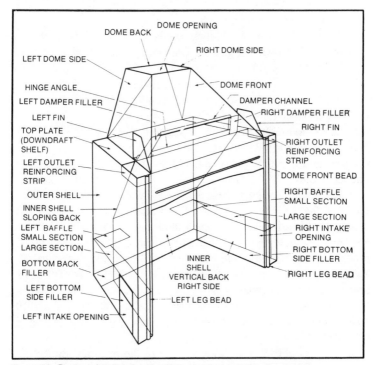

Fig. 4-50. Design details of a Heatilator heat-circulating fireplace.

First, you must select the location. You can usually ignore wall features such as windows because the wall will have to be reframed where it meets the fireplace anyway. To determine the size of the footing you need, you must know the total exterior dimensions of the circulator. Let's say you want to install a model with the following dimensions: 36 inches inner width, 20½ inches deep, 43 inches overall front width, 32 inches outside width at the rear. You must figure in the sizes of the non-combustible materials that will cover the exterior: 4 inches of brick, a couple of inches or so of glass wool insulation (which protects the masonry from excessive heat and contact with the firebox as it expands and contracts), and any decorative stone or brick that you might want.

Next up is a check of local building codes to see how large the footing must be and how deep the frost gets in your area. If the footing is not poured below frost level, problems become persistent and grow with the years. Frost heave could eventually tear the installation away from the house (possibly taking the entire end of the house with it).

If the local codes don't specify, the footing should be at least 1 foot thick and extend 6 inches beyond each side of the ready-to-be-installed fireplace. So the 36-inch fireplace will need a footing with dimensions as shown in Fig. 4-51. The footing should meet the house foundation, but should not be attached to it. This allows for differing rates of settling. If you live in an earthquake area (something else your local building codes will tell you), you'll have to install reinforcing bars to strengthen the footing.

Once the footing is poured, it's time to open up the wall of the house. You should have all your materials on hand before starting so the job can be completed as quickly as possible once the wall is opened to the weather. (Obviously this is not a job for cold winters.)

You should locate the fireplace on a wall, that does not bear some of the weight of the roof. Sidewalls under roof eaves are usually load-bearing, but most gable-end walls are not (though there are exceptions). If your house has a truss-roof framing system, you'll probably be safe even in the very center of the gable. If the wall is load-bearing, have appropriately sized 4 × 4s ready to go in place as braces the moment your cuts are made and the opening becomes large enough to accept the timbers. Make the opening about 10 inches wider than the outside of the fireplace and about 6 feet long (70 to 74 inches, depending on fireplace size).

Install double 2 × 4s on each side of the opening. Butt them where possible up against any existing framing that remains in the

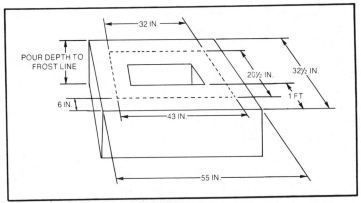

Fig. 4-51. Dimensions of a footing for a 36-inch, heat-circulating fireplace.

opening. The 2 × 4s on the inside of the opening should be 9½ inches shorter than the outside ones. These shorter supports will hold up a header (a horizontal crosspiece) of double 2 × 10s if the fireplace is under 5 feet wide, and and double if the fireplace is over 5 feet wide. Use 16-penny nails for all framing work. The header pieces should be nailed together at intervals of 16 inches or less before installation. Toenail the wall to the headers, which must, of course, meet the wall for proper support. Toenailing means driving the nails obliquely so they pass through both the headers and the wall.

You can make the chimney exterior the same size as the fireplace or you can make it smaller. The smaller chimney is lighter, cheaper, and easier to construct. Use a plumb bob to insure that vertical pieces are truly vertical. Cut back the roof framing so that it will clear the chimney by 1 inch—no more, no less. Make careful cuts because your completed work will probably be visible from the ground. If you offset the chimney to one side or the other, make sure the angle from the center of the fireplace is no more than 30° (15° is preferable). The greater the offset, the greater the soot buildup and the more your draft is affected.

Next, lay a series of block courses to bring the footing up to the proper height for the hearth. If you want an ashpit, you should set in its frame, top, and outside doors after you've laid the block courses. Fill the area to be covered with the firebox with small masonry rubble (stone, broken block, broken brick). Then lay the firebox floor. Firebrick must be used for this purpose because regular brick or stone will last almost no time at all.

Once the mortar has set around the firebrick, you can put the circulator unit in place (Fig. 4-52). Install the code air boxes at hearth level. Next, cover the unit with the insulation provided by the manufacturer. You can now begin the brickwork.

Common bricks are 8 by 4 by 2¼ inches. The mortar joints should be three-eighths of an inch. Cement mortar is stronger and more heat resistant than lime mortar. Use a level to make sure the brick courses are on target (Fig. 4-53). Do the same with cement blocks if you're using them on the exterior. Various brick course starting aids are provided by the makers of circulators.

For example, Majestic provides a set of angle seals with slotted bolt holes that fit at the sides of the fireplace opening. These must be plumbed and tightened before you start brickwork. As you continue

Fig. 4-52. Setting the fireplace unit in place (courtesy of Majestic).

Fig. 4-53. Checking masonry with a level.

up the fireplace with the masonry, you must keep leveling everything. You can make up a miss on one or two rows fairly easily, but if things get too sloppy the entire job will look shoddy. When you reach the top of the firebox, install the lintel.

First, place a layer of insulation between the lintel and the firebox lip. Then level the lintel and run the bricks across the front of the fireplace opening. Before you cover too much of the firebox, you'll need to pay attention to the circulator air passages. You must make passages through the masonry for each set of cold air and warm air boxes. The passages must be sized to the vents in the fireplace and the grills the manufacturer has supplied. The interior of these passages should receive a smooth coating of mortar to facilitate the flow of air.

Brickwork will start to taper inward as you reach the top part of the fireplace. You can keep it vertical if you want. Simply leave the upper reaches of the fireplace free of masonry and fill in with rubble or broken stone. This is a procedure that should be followed when there is any major air space between the firebox and the masonry. If the masonry is kept vertical, you might want to buy some metal ducting for use inside the rubble to carry warm air. This is much easier than trying to build mortar-lined tunnels through loose rubble.

Chapter 5

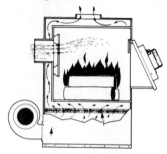

Chimneys

Because of the great importance of flue size and construction, this chapter begins with charts of recommended flue sizes for specific fireplace sizes. Remember that each fireplace or wood stove *must* have its own flue. Though a separate chimney might not be needed, an individual flue is essential to proper draft, which is essential to proper burning. Tables 5-1 and 5-2 list flue sizes.

Recommended flue sizes are the same for fireplaces with openings of 2400 to 3000 square inches. If your fireplace is larger than that, and your chimney is about 15 feet high or more (from hearth to chimney top), the flue opening, or flue area, should be about 1/10 the area of the fireplace opening; the flue area should be about the area of the fireplace opening if the chimney is under 15 feet high. Select the nearest commercially available size and use that for chimney construction. All the sizes listed in Tables 5-1 and 5-2 are commercially available.

If a single flue won't handle your fireplace, you can install two flues in a single chimney. It's more work and should only be done if there is no other way to get a flue of sufficient size. The flues, if doubled, must receive the same treatment as any separate flues. There must be at least 4 inches separating them, and one should be 4 inches higher than the other to prevent downdrafts. If one flue of a double set causes a downdraft into the other, the fireplace will smoke almost as badly as if it had a single flue receiving a downdraft.

It's also possible to build a flue too large. Too large a flue area is almost as bad as one that's too small. Do not exceed the recom-

Table 5-1. Fireplace Flue Sizes (in inches).

fireplace opening			standard rectangular flue, outside dimensions	round flue, inside diameter
width	height	depth		
28	24	16-18	8½ × 8½	10
30-32	28	18	8½ × 13	10
36	28	18	8½ × 13	12
42	28	18	8½ × 18	12
48	32	18-20	13 × 13	15
54	36	20	13 × 18	15
60	36	22	18 × 18	18

mended sizes. If the chimney height is exceptional, then a slight reduction in flue size can help to keep the draft within limits.

MASONRY CHIMNEYS

As stated earlier, all chimney tops should rise at least 2 feet above the roof ridge on peaked roofs. On flat roofs, the chimney should rise a minimum of 3 feet above the surface. This distance can be increased, but under no circumstances should it *ever* be reduced. In the case of peaked roofs, a chimney should extend at least 2 feet above the highest point within 10 feet. With proper placement the chimney need not always rise 2 feet above the *ridge peak*. If there are large trees near the house, you might have to increase the height of the chimney to prevent downdrafts. Disturbed air currents around those trees could knock smoke back down the flue and into

Table 5-2. Alternate Flue Sizes.

area of fireplace opening in square inches	standard rectangular flue, outside dimensions	round flue inside diameter
1000	8½ × 18	12
1200	8½ × 18	12
1400	13 × 13	12
1600	13 × 13	15
1800	13 × 18	15
2200	13 × 18	15
2400	18 × 18	18

the room (Fig. 5-1). In some cases, you'll almost certainly find it simpler and easier to remove obstructing trees or branches rather than run a silly looking chimney a couple of dozen feet over the roof line of your house.

You'll need a reasonably careful study to figure final chimney height. In almost all cases, whether you're putting up a masonry or a prefabricated chimney, a trip to the roof to take measurements and a careful look at surrounding buildings, hills, and trees can save a lot of later grief.

You can use a straightedge, tacked to the side of the house where the chimney will rise, as a guide. Tie the end of a 10-foot length of mason's cord to the straightedge and locate the highest point on the roof within the reach of the cord. Then measure from the highest point 2 feet upward. The distance from 2 feet above the highest point to the throat of the fireplace is the height of your chimney. The throat of the fireplace is where the flue starts.

The exterior of the masonry chimney can be built with several materials in several ways. Cement blocks still are the least expensive (and the least attractive when left unfinished). Bricks with a fireclay flue liner offer sufficient thickness (4 inches) but take time to lay. Because of their small size, common bricks are time consuming to lay, but are also quite attractive and appeal to a good many people. Cement blocks offer the greater construction ease, but they usually require some sort of covering, (brick veneer or some special painting or stucco).

As the flue liner is set in mortar and built on up (Fig. 5-2), the exterior of the chimney should be maintained just one or two tiles behind. This makes for greater working strength for the flue liner and also makes the job look a bit more orderly at the end of each working day. Flue liner by itself doesn't supply much strength. The surrounding masonry keeps you from knocking it over as quickly as it goes up. Try to bring the course of blocks, stone, or brick almost to the top of the final flue tile installed on any given day.

In most cases, you'll need scaffolding to do the masonry work on the chimney because you'll need to have quite a lot of mortar, bricks and tools on hand at working height. A chimney maker trying to work from a ladder is giving up a lot of working ease just to save a few bucks rental fee. The scaffolding will allow you to work all around the chimney and will only need to be raised after every 4 or 5 feet of chimney is laid.

Flues without flue liners will have very rough interior mortar seams. Such rough seams interfere with air flow. One worker I

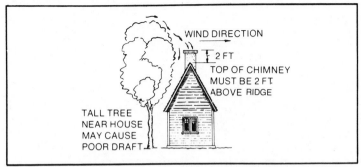

WIND DIRECTION

2 FT

TOP OF CHIMNEY
MUST BE 2 FT.
ABOVE RIDGE

TALL TREE
NEAR HOUSE
MAY CAUSE
POOR DRAFT

Fig. 5-1. Tall obstructions near a house can cause chimney draft problems.

know has a good way to cut down on seam roughness. First, he takes
a heavy cloth sack and stuffs it full of wood shavings or straw. Then
he ties the neck securely and fits the bag snugly into the flue just
above the fireplace. A heavy piece of twine leads from the bag on up
to his chimney working platform. After he finishes a course or two of
flue tile, he pulls the bag up. The snug-fitting bag slides up the flue,
smoothing down mortar joints as it goes. This technique means that
little or nothing can work its way down the flue and mess up the
smoke shelf of the fireplace. For best results, the bag should be
twisted as it is pulled up.

The simplest type of flue installation is the straight flue (Fig.
5-3). This kind of flue runs straight up from the fireplace. It leaves
little space for debris to collect and it presents the first-time builder
with the fewest problems of any masonry chimney construction.
Offsets in any direction can be built into any chimney, but they can
add to soot accumulation, resin and creosote buildup, and draft
problems. They are also more complicated to build. As stated
earlier, in no circumstances should any flue offset exceed 30 degrees (Fig. 5-4). For a chimney with a 30-degree offset, it's a good
idea to increase the flue size (cross-sectional area) by 15 or 20

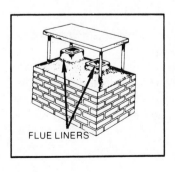

FLUE LINERS

Fig. 5-2. A pair of flues set in mortar
atop a capped chimney (courtesy of
Majestic).

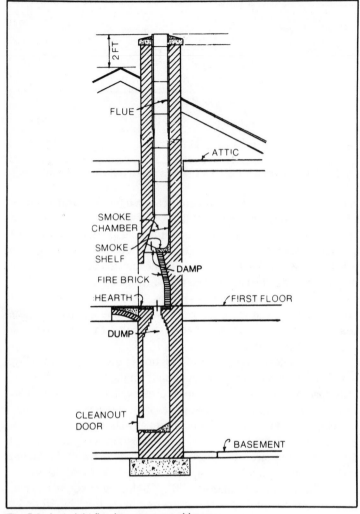

2 FT

FLUE

ATTIC

SMOKE CHAMBER

SMOKE SHELF

DAMP

FIRE BRICK

HEARTH

FIRST FLOOR

DUMP

CLEANOUT DOOR

BASEMENT

Fig. 5-3. A straight flue in a masonry chimney.

percent. A 5 or 10 percent increase in flue size is helpful with a 15-degree offset.

The final step in masonry chimney construction is to make sure that the final fire clay flue liner section is at least 4 inches from the chimney's exterior surface. A taper or bevel of concrete should be laid to within 2 inches of the liner top (as shown in Fig. 5-2). This bevel helps rain water run off and will provide some help in forming an updraft to help prevent smoking of the fireplace.

You must make a careful check to ensure that the completed chimney will not leak smoke to the inside of the building. Such smoke leaks can be dangerous. One problem with any masonry fireplace and chimney is the length of time you have to wait before using the installation. Mortar must have time to cure properly before much heat is applied.

You should make a leak test as soon as the installation is completed. A smudge fire putting out little heat, but a lot of smoke, is needed. If you have access to one, a smudge pot will do a fine job. Otherwise, use a metal stand (such as a small hibachi or barbecue). Build a fire with a few sheets of paper, a few handfuls of damp straw, and perhaps a couple of old asphalt shingles. While the fire is going, place a plate of some sort or a batch of wet newspapers over the chimney flue opening. Even small leaks will quickly become obvious as the dark smoke rises and gets forced back down the chimney (which is why you want a *small* smudge fire; otherwise, the whole house ends up smelling of smoke). If the chimney does leak anywhere, take steps immediately to solve the problem.

Masonry chimneys and fireplaces should cure from 2 to 3 weeks before being used for a *regular* fire. At the outset of use, fires should be rather small and not too hot. After a week or two, a large fire is fine.

PREFABRICATED CHIMNEYS

Most factory-built fireplaces, as well as most wood stoves, come with prefabricated low- or no-clearance insulated chimney sections with built-in flues (Fig. 5-5). These 2-foot and 3-foot chimney sections make chimney installation a breeze. All the lead-

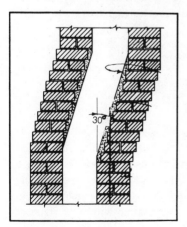

Fig. 5-4. A flue offset of 30 degrees in a masonry chimney.

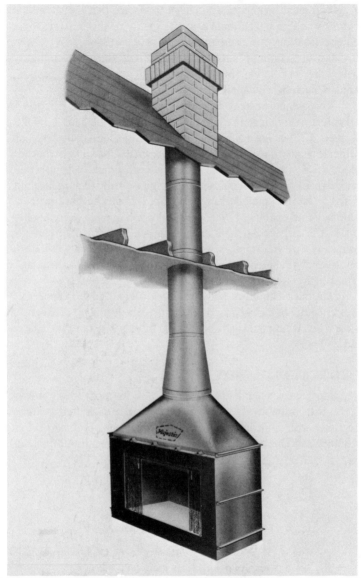

Fig. 5-5. A Majestic fireplace with a prefabricated chimney.

ing chimney systems come with twist locks or snap locks to give a
tight seal between sections. Standard straight sections are available
in 2-foot and 3-foot lengths and weigh less than 30 pounds apiece.
Chimney heights of up to 90 feet are possible with only standard

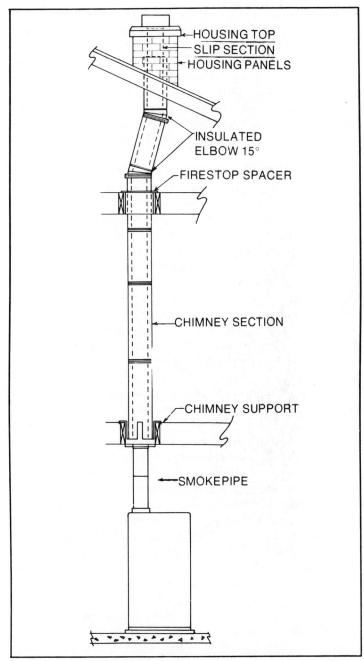

Fig. 5-6. A typical prefabricated chimney installation (courtesy of Heatilator).

111

chimney supports and no special foundations. Elbow sections, or offsets, are available in 15-degree and 30-degree pieces. Fortunately, they require no trimming or cutting. (One of the worst things about building an offset masonry chimney is the need for accurate cutting of fire clay tiles.) The larger twist-lock sections (8 and 9 inch diameter) can be adapted for use on 30-inch and 34-inch heat-circulating fireplaces by adding a masonry-to-metal base plate adapter after the fireplace surround has been nearly completed. The savings in effort and money will make this adaptation well worthwhile.

Most installed freestanding fireplaces and wood stoves have about 6 feet of standard smokepipe leading from them. Usually the smokepipe fits into a firestop spacer above and is connected there to an insulated prefabricated chimney (Fig. 5-6). Elbows can be used to bring the smokepipe through the wall at the side of the house instead of through the roof. This is true as long as there is an 18-inch clearance between the smokepipe and any combustible surface (usually the room's ceiling).

If a fireplace or stove has been designed for a top-mounted smokepipe (vent), like most freestanding fireplaces and stoves, then the first stovepipe section installed should be the piece which has the damper in it. If a stove or fireplace is designed for a side- or rear-mounted vent, then the first stovepipe section installed should be an elbow (which connects with the straight piece of smokepipe containing the damper). Side- and rear-venting wood stoves without internal baffling can be slightly more efficient than top-venting wood stoves without internal baffling. Less heat is lost straight up the chimney with the rear and side vents.

All the prefabricated chimneys I've seen require only a 2-inch clearance from combustible surfaces. They also require firestop spacers every time they pass through a wall, ceiling, or roof. If a prefabricated chimney is extra long, or has several flues, it will need chimney supports. You can buy chimney supports from the manufacturer of your particular chimney; you can also easily make them of scrap steel at home. Some building codes might require such supports more often than the manufacturer feels is essential. A quick check with the local building inspector can prevent some later headaches.

All the basics for chimney installation hold true for prefabricated chimneys. You still need the 2-foot clearance above the highest point on the roof within 10 feet of the chimney; the chimney top still must be 3 feet above a flat roof surface. The minimum chimney height (from throat to chimney top) for most prefabricated chimneys is about 15 feet. The chimney cross-sectional flue area must still be from 1 / 10 to 1 / 12 the area of the fireplace opening.

Let's go step by step through the fairly complex installation of the prefabricated Majestic Majestitherm chimney. Install the fireplace on the base framing. This will be necessary if there is a raised hearth because it changes the number of chimney sections needed. The chimney will be much easier to position if the fireplace is in its final location.

Use either a plumb bob or a straightedge taped to a level to mark the ceiling over the top of the fireplace. You should take the marks from the outside edge of the chimney installation plate on the firebox. Then mark the outline of the firestop spacer on the ceiling. After that, open up the ceiling using a drill and a keyhole or saber saw. If there is a second floor, repeat the process for the second ceiling. Each opening should be properly framed. The ceiling opening(s) should be 17½ × 7½ inches. The roof opening should be about 17½ × 18 inches (Fig. 5-7).

Once the framing is completed, install the starter section of the prefabricated chimney on the fireplace (Fig. 5-8). On the Majestitherm, the starter section is a triple-walled unit. The three sections (inner, middle, and outer) can be installed one at a time, starting with the inner one, or it might be necessary to hold the middle and outer sections up toward the ceiling opening while installing the inner section. Make sure that all three sections are firmly engaged (they use snap-lock fasteners) to the proper rims on the fireplace flue outlet.

At each ceiling level install a firestop spacer. Nail it to the joists and headers. No firestop is required at roof level with the Majestitherm. Most other brands will accept some sort of firestop if you want to install one.

Install the triple-walled intermediate sections in the same manner as the starter section and continue right on up into the attic area (Fig. 5-9). In the attic, install the air intake section. The higher

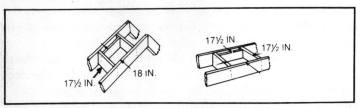

Fig. 5-7. Ceiling and roof openings for the Majestitherm.

113

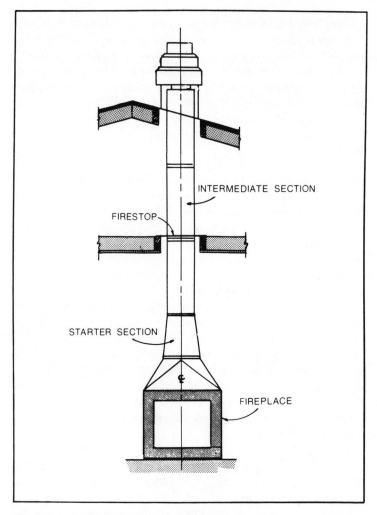

INTERMEDIATE SECTION

FIRESTOP

STARTER SECTION

FIREPLACE

Fig. 5-8. A prefabricated chimney showing the position of the starter section (courtesy of Majestic).

you locate the air intake section, the more heat you will get because heat is gained from the chimney surface. Other manufacturers do not use this sort of triple-wall chimney, nor do they use an air intake section. The installations are correspondingly simpler.

Whether or not an electric blower is added to the air intake section, the air intake section must have a minimum of 18-inch clearance (height). The chimney must remain perfectly vertical (always maintaining its 2-inch clearance from any combustible surfaces). Attic ventilation should meet minimum F.H.A. standards for proper, safe operation.

If an attic has one-fourth square inch of ventilator for each square foot of attic space, it is properly ventilated. If not, you can install extra vents in end gables or under the eaves. In drastic cases, you can also install a vent in the side or end of the chimney housing.

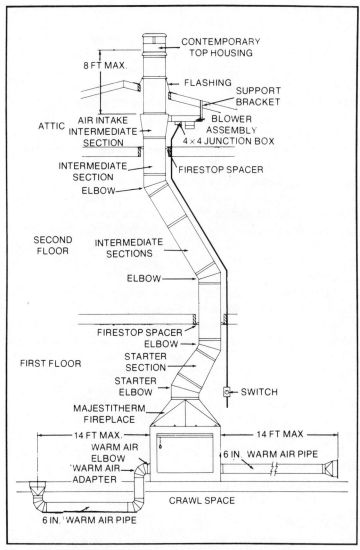

Fig. 5-9. A Majestitherm fireplace and prefabricated offset chimney.

For the Majestitherm, you must install the air intake section within 8 feet of the top of the rain cap for efficient and proper operation. The closer to the top the better. You can install the section in the housing just a couple of feet under the rain cap. The air intake section has a large bell shape on one end. The bell shape must always be at the top of the installation (Fig. 5-10).

In all installation work, make sure that the snap locks are firmly engaged. This holds true for all prefabricated chimneys (whether they use snap locks or twist locks).

Next, install the electric blower. There are predrilled holes in the air-intake section. The blower attaches directly to these (motor side down). An adjustable support bracket secures the blower to the floor or to a rafter. Check the blower wheel to make sure it is free turning. Simply give the shaft a quick spin to make sure it moves freely and causes no scraping noises.

Install the blower motor according to local electrical codes. Make sure that all wiring runs on the *outside* of the firestop spacers. A solid-state control switch and plate are supplied for installation near the fireplaces. Continue the intermediate sections of the chimney on up until they extend through the roof (at least 3 inches beyond the highest part of your already cut roof opening).

You can select top housings to fit the roof pitch or you can build your own top housing and chase. If you do build and if you are using a Majestitherm unit, you'll need to install two louvered vents to allow enough air to circulate down the chimney.

And that's about it. The fireplace and chimney, once they're checked for smoke leaks, are ready to go.

In some installations, whether masonry or prefabricated, one other thing might be necessary: a cricket. A cricket is a section that fits between the roof and the chimney to prevent debris and snow buildup (Fig. 5-11). It is a little peak made to match the pitch of the roof and the wall of the fireplace housing. It is usually, if small, made of 2 × 4 framing nailed together with 16-penny nails. It is covered with sheathing board or exterior grade plywood (three-eighths inch for spans of 2 feet or less, one-half inch for longer spans). It is then nailed to the roof, covered with roofing paper, then flashed and shingled. In general, crickets are not required if the side of the fireplace facing the roof peak is under 18 inches wide.

CHIMNEY CARE

Chimneys, if properly installed, will cause you no problems for years and years (especially if you clean them once every two or

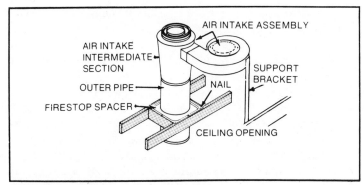

Fig. 5-10. The Majestic air intake assembly.

three years). If you use a lot of resinous firewood, you can use table salt to cut down on the amount of buildup. Get the fire roaring hot and then toss on a handful. You can also use a solution of table salt and water to wash down the chimney walls every few years (though it's seldom necessary).

A commercial chimney cleaner can clean your chimney better and faster than you can. But it's a lot less expensive if you do the job yourself. You can easily contain much of the mess.

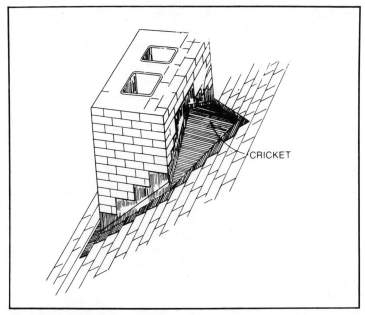

Fig. 5-11. The cricket of a chimney.

117

First, seal off the fireplace opening. If you have an asbestos board cover, simply tape it over the opening. If you use a sliding glass fire screen, use masking tape to cover the seams and any holes. First, pull the cotter pins holding the damper unit and lift it out onto a pile of spread newspapers.

Next, fill a heavy burlap bag with straw, wood shavings, or any similar substance (the rougher the bag material the better). Tie a brick to the bottom of the bag. From the top of the chimney, lower the bag slowly down the flue. Give the rope a twist every couple of feet. Repeat several times. In a pinch, the burlap bag can often be replaced by a small evergreen tree just big enough to fit snugly in the flue. Be sure to tie a brick to the bottom of the tree.

Be careful while climbing back down the ladder with the bag. The bag will be about as filthy as anything you'll ever see. Bang it around as little as possible. Don't just toss if off the roof unless you enjoy clouds of soot all over your garden. Empty the bag carefully. Then set the emptied bag aside for washing. Burlap bags, though not fantastically expensive, are getting hard to come by in many areas. This is particularly true because many feeds are now packed in plastic sacks. The whole idea of doing this somewhat nasty job yourself is to save money.

If the resin buildup in the chimney is severe, tie a heavy chain on a rope and lower it down the chimney (twirling it hard as it goes down). This procedure will knock a lot of the resin loose, but use it only when the buildup is heavy—it's bound to be hard on mortar joints and fire clay flue tiles.

By the time you store the bag and put the ladder away, most of the mess trapped inside the fireplace will have settled. Sit down and rest for a half hour or so anyway. The extra time might not be needed, but if you uncover the fireplace opening too soon you'll have a real dirty house on your hands.

Peel off the tape and remove the fireplace covering slowly. Stand it on newspaper. Set everything well to one side and immediately install and close the damper. Any sort of downdraft at this time could be a disaster.

Don't sweep the soot from the fireplace. Vacuum it. If at all possible, don't use your household vacuum cleaner. A shop vacuum cleaner that can be used wet or dry is a much better tool for this job because it allows you to use a garden hose to it to get rid of some of the internal mess. It also doesn't have an air-permeable bag inside to allow soot to blow all over the house should anything go wrong. In any case, make sure all the vacuum's filters are clean.

Although resinous buildup cannot be *totally* removed by anything other than chipping with a putty knife, the chain treatment should be a big help. Chemical removers, as far as I can discover, don't work very well. Some might combine with the soot to cause a dangerous explosion or a bad chimney fire. The creosote formed by burning wood resins is much harder to remove than soot. This is a good reason for avoiding resinous wood whenever possible.

Chipping is most difficult in masonry chimneys; they have more rough edges to catch the buildup and are more easily damaged because of mortar joints. Obviously, the interior of any chimney over a few feet high is going to be very difficult to chip free of anything. Your best bet is to hope the buildup remains minor.

In a pinch, you can take down a prefabricated chimney for cleaning. This is a distinct advantage for those areas where burning wood for fuel means burning resinous wood. You can also take down smokepipes for cleaning. Where sections are only a few feet long, cleaning is much easier.

Chapter 6

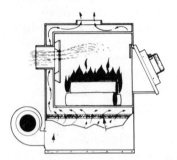

All-Masonry Fireplaces

If you're a true traditionalist, an all-masonry fireplace is the only kind of fireplace for you. Never mind that it usually costs twice as much as any other kind of fireplace. Never mind that it's more difficult to build. *This* is a fireplace!

One of the basic advantages of the masonry fireplace is that you can build it in virtually *any* shape or size. Nevertheless, you must maintain the proper relationship between flue size, fireplace opening, fireplace depth, and fireplace taper. You must also insure proper throat and smokeshelf sizes and the proper incline for the upper part of the back wall. There are more than just one or two complexities in the construction of a masonry fireplace.

THE COMPONENTS

Building an all-masonry fireplace is no cinch. Each component requires precise planning and careful work (Fig. 6-1). The masonry fireplace must have the same kind of footing as that required for masonry chimneys and exterior-wall installations. The footing prevents the masonry from settling improperly or toppling over. Pour the concrete at least 1 foot deep and 1 foot wide below the frost line.

Hearth

The fireplace hearth should project at least 24 inches in front of the fireplace opening (the floor inside the firebox itself is also called

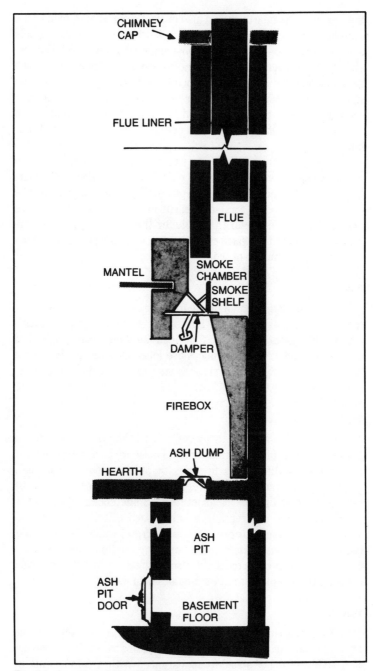

Fig. 6-1. A sectioned view of a fireplace.

the hearth). The hearth should also project from 6 to 12 inches, at a minimum, to each side of the fireplace. There are so many materials and so many methods of hearth construction that it would be impossible to cover even a majority of them here. It is suffice to say that a hearth should have at least a 4-inch thick base of poured concrete (though a brick hearth can be thinner). Terra-cotta, stone, ceramic tiles, and copper tiles can be used as a finish covering, and so can any non-combustible material that seems attractive to you and your family.

A hearth flush with the floor is easy to clean out. It also offers a quick and easy sweep-up of wood chips and such because they can just be swept directly into the fireplace. The flush hearth is usually easier to install than a raised hearth in an all-masonry fireplace because there's no need to cantilever the poured concrete. The raised hearth offers a warm seat and a convenient spot under which to store a fair amount of wood.

Ashpit

Built under the rear of the hearth, the ashpit offers an easy way to clean out the ashes (Fig. 6-1). Today's ashpits are covered with tight-fitting cast-iron doors that lead into pits made of either ceramic or metal. Cleanout doors are located either in a basement or on an outside wall of the chimney structure. The doors are handy but not essential (Fig. 6-2).

Walls

Most building codes today require that the back and sides of any masonry fireplace be made of solid masonry or concrete at least 8 inches thick (lined with firebrick or other approved material). Approved materials include steel linings; these are supplied by heat-circulating firebox manufacturers. Some codes allow you to eliminate linings of firebrick or other such materials if you use 12-inch solid masonry (or reinforced concrete) walls. Regardless of codes, I would not recommend eliminating the lining because heat from a wood fire can have a disastrous effect on any masonry wall (causing the fireplace to need almost constant repair).

Jambs

Fireplace jambs are those upright parts on the sides of the fireplace opening. You should design the jambs to provide construction stability and a pleasing appearance. With a 3-foot wide or

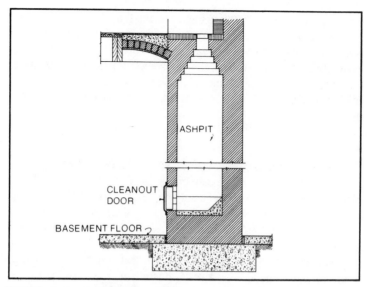

Fig. 6-2. A cross section of an ashpit.

smaller fireplace opening, I'd recommend a 12-inch width for the jambs. Proportionate increases in that width should be made according to the size of the fireplace opening. The jambs can be faced with ornamental tile or brick, but wood should be avoided at any point closer than 6 inches to the fireplace opening.

Lintel

A lintel is the support for the masonry that crosses the top of the fireplace opening. With an opening of 48 inches or less, you can use one-half inch flat steel bars for the lintel; you can also use 3½ × 3½ × one-fourth inch angle iron. Also, you could use specially designed damper frames. Heavier lintels are needed for wider openings. If a masonry arch is used, the lintel must be increased in size by a large enough amount to resist the thrust of the arch. It might be a good idea to check with an architect, architectural engineer, or civil engineer to find out what exact size you need to prevent collapse. Any fee should be minimal because it will only take a few minutes work for the professional to come up with the figures you need.

Throat

Any improperly shaped throat will ruin the draw of the fireplace. The sides of the fireplace should rise vertically to the throat (which must begin from 6 to 8 inches above the lintel bottom). The cross-sectional area of the throat must at least equal that of the flue, and the length must at least equal the width of the fireplace opening. Five inches above the throat, the sidewalls start sloping in to meet the flue. A large fireplace must have a much greater slope than a small fireplace. And the slope is absolutely determined by the throat size.

Damper

Dampers are cast-iron frames with a hinged lid that can be opened or closed to vary the size of the throat opening (Fig. 6-3). In older fireplaces, dampers were not only often installed incorrectly, but they were often not installed at all. It's usually the undampered fireplace that operates at a net heat loss for the house (unless a fire is kept roaring all the time).

The damper not only controls the draft for the fire in the fireplace, but helps to keep already heated air from flowing up the chimney when the fireplace is not in use. For that reason, a tight-fitting damper is essential. You can also adjust throat opening to reduce heat in the room while the fire is going. Though a roaring fire with resinous wood might need a full throat opening, a slow-burning hardwood log can often last all night if the throat opening is cut down to an inch or so. A good damper can keep the bugs out of the house in the summer. If you think that's a facetious remark, you've never lived in an insect-ridden area with three fireplaces in the house and not a damper between them. I have! Some of today's dampers are also designed to take the place of lintels and they can save a fair amount of worry in fireplace building.

Smoke Shelf and Smoke Chamber

The smoke shelf has one simple and important reason for existing. It is there to prevent downdrafts (Fig. 6-4). You make a smoke shelf by moving the brickwork at the top of the throat back to the line of the flue wall for the full length of the throat. It's depth, from 6 to 12 inches, depends on the depth of the fireplace. The smoke chamber is the area from the top of the throat to the bottom of the flue. Smoke shelves and smoke chambers should be plastered with at least a one-half inch covering of cement mortar.

Flue

Properly sizing the area of the fireplace opening to the flue—taking into consideration the height of the flue—is the single most

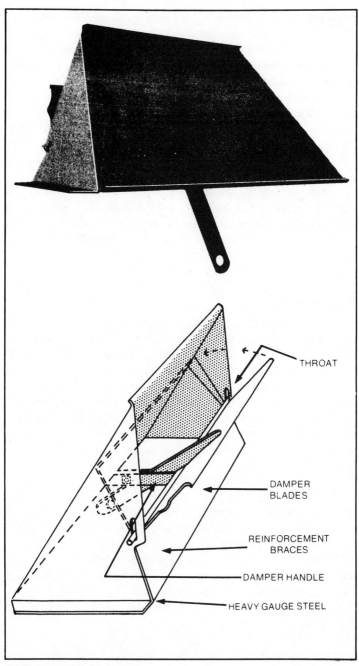

THROAT

DAMPER BLADES

REINFORCEMENT BRACES

DAMPER HANDLE

HEAVY GAUGE STEEL

Fig. 6-3. A Heatilator damper.

125

important factor in preventing smoking fireplaces. Remember, if a flue is 15 feet tall or more, its cross-sectional area should be about one-tenth the area of the fireplace opening. If a flue is unlined or if it is less than 15 feet tall, the flue must increase in size to one-eighth the area of the fireplace opening. I pretty much covered the rest of the information you need for flue selection in the chapter on chimneys. But as a reminder; stay as close to the above relative sizes as possible. Too large a flue area can cause nearly as many problems as too small a flue area. Stay with the standard size rectangular fireclay flue liner whenever possible because the rectangular flue is more efficient than the round.

And that's what a fireplace is all about. The parts involved are common, in one way or another, to all fireplaces. It's only with the all-masonry fireplace that you need to get involved with shaping and building. After you've decided on placement, poured the footings, and gathered all the other materials around you, the real work begins.

BRICKWORK

Making an accurate estimate of the number of bricks you'll need for your masonry work can save you a lot of money. Bricks are based on 3¾-inch modules. However, this sizing is not exact. You'll certainly find that it pays to check the size of bricks you buy from local suppliers to make sure they're not off an eighth of an inch or so. If you do find that your brickmaker produces bricks one-eighth inch smaller than the norm, then you'll need approximately 3 percent more bricks. If the bricks are one-eighth inch larger, you'll need, 3 percent fewer (Fig. 6-5). You should allow one-half inch for each mortar joint.

Use the mortar mix recommended by your local brickmaker and then work to get the right mix feeling. Plasticity of the mix is important for easy handling, but the dry mix must be just right to provide strength. Generally, with masonry cement, you can add 4 cubic feet of sand (in damp, loose condition) to one-third of the sack of cement. Mix it until the contents are evenly stirred together. Add water until your mixing hoe can be shaken clear of the mortar. Add the water as slowly as possible. Don't get in a rush and dump in a lot of water. The less water you use, the greater the strength of the dried mortar.

If the brick is not wet enough, it could draw off too much water from the mortar. If this happens, the mortar won't cure properly and you'll end up with weakened joints. Check wetness with a sprinkle

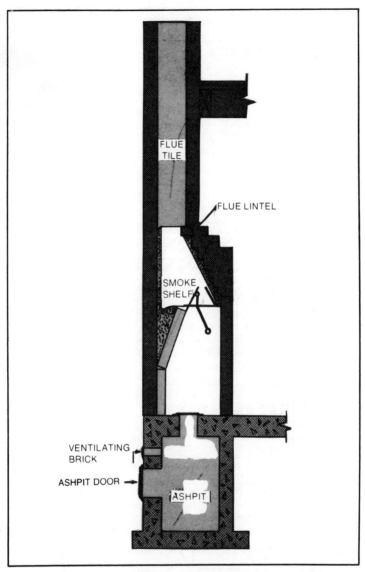

FLUE
TILE

FLUE LINTEL

SMOKE
SHELF

VENTILATING
BRICK

ASHPIT DOOR →

ASHPIT

Fig. 6-4. A cross section showing the position of the smoke shelf (courtesy of Majestic).

test. Sprinkle a few drops of water on the brick and look at your watch. If the water is absorbed in a minute or less, the brick needs to be wet down. Use a hose to wet down the entire brick pile. Keep the water flowing until you get a a good runoff from all sides of the pile.

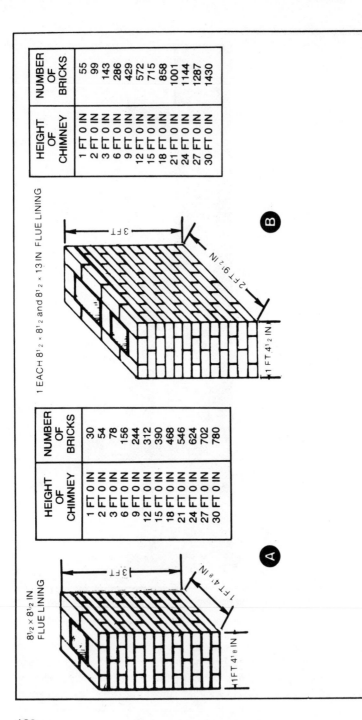

A

8¹⁄₂ × 8¹⁄₂ IN FLUE LINING

1 FT 4¹⁄₈ IN

3 FT

1 FT 4¹⁄₈ IN

HEIGHT OF CHIMNEY	NUMBER OF BRICKS
1 FT 0 IN	30
2 FT 0 IN	54
3 FT 0 IN	78
6 FT 0 IN	156
9 FT 0 IN	244
12 FT 0 IN	312
15 FT 0 IN	390
18 FT 0 IN	468
21 FT 0 IN	546
24 FT 0 IN	624
27 FT 0 IN	702
30 FT 0 IN	780

B

1 EACH 8¹⁄₂ × 8¹⁄₂ and 8¹⁄₂ × 13 IN FLUE LINING

3 FT

2 FT 9¹⁄₂ IN

1 FT 4¹⁄₂ IN

HEIGHT OF CHIMNEY	NUMBER OF BRICKS
1 FT 0 IN	55
2 FT 0 IN	99
3 FT 0 IN	143
6 FT 0 IN	286
9 FT 0 IN	429
12 FT 0 IN	572
15 FT 0 IN	715
18 FT 0 IN	858
21 FT 0 IN	1001
24 FT 0 IN	1144
27 FT 0 IN	1287
30 FT 0 IN	1430

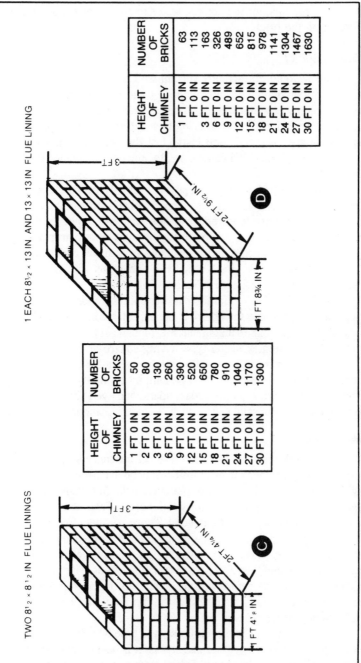

Fig. 6-5. Brick quantities for four masonry chimneys based on standard brick size: 2½ × 3¾ × 8 inches with ½-inch joints (courtesy of Heatilator).

Wait a few minutes, for the surface water to soak in or evaporate, before using the brick.

BASIC MASONRY

While I would not actually recommend that a totally novice mason consider building a lined chimney and masonry fireplace, there are plenty of spots where amateur labor can cut the cost of masonry installation on the interior and exterior of a fireplace. Some skills are essential. And instead of the normal 10 percent allowance for breakage and general waste, any novice should allow at least 15 percent.

In general, bricklaying is hard physical labor. Nevertheless, it is not extremely difficult—in its simpler forms—to carry out if proper procedures are followed. It makes no sense, however, for the true novice to try the sloping firebrick lining of any fireplace. Use a steel insert, such as those available from many companies (Heatilator being arguably the best known) or contract with a mason to finish the interior of the fireplace.

Flue liner is an essential for passing building codes in many locales (although double thickness, 8 inches, brick will often pass). Flue liner is not difficult to install, but the joints must be perfect. If a concrete block chimney of the type having square or rectangular blocks with an interior space for the flue liner is not used, I would recommend that the entire chimney be built by a competent mason. Without perfect mortar joints, smoke, spark, and even flame seepage into a home is possible. Any such leakage is dangerous.

Mortar

Proper brick masonry or concrete-block masonry starts with mortar. Mortar provides the brick-to-brick bond in masonry. It also provides the seal that keeps water out and smoke in for chimneys. Clean sand is the starting point for good mortar. From there, you must move to the type of mortar needed. There are about five or six different types. For chimneys, the best kind is the one designated for the most severe service. Begin with 6 parts of sand, add in 1 part of hydrated lime, and then add 1 part portland cement. Mix the dry ingredients thoroughly before wetting down. Mix only amounts you feel you'll use in about 1 hour. Keep the mortar in the box from setting up and being wasted.

This particular type of mortar (known as type N) is for particularly nasty conditions of weather and stress. It is best for almost all chimney applications. Type S could also be used. It is very resistant

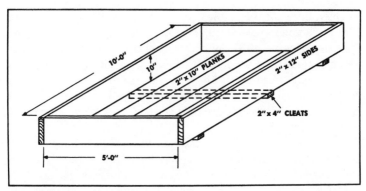

Fig. 6-6. Mortar box plans.

to stress from lateral forces (high winds). Type S mortar requires 4½ parts of sand, one-half part of hydrated lime and 1 part portland cement.

Use a large wheelbarrow or a mortar box (Fig. 6-6) to mix the mortar, and a garden hoe to mix the ingredients. Add water slowly—clean water is as essential as clean sand—and wet the mix only until it is plastic. Runny mortar is not going to give you a good bond, but neither will mortar that is dry and crumbly like cornbread batter.

Transfer the mortar to a mortar board (Fig. 6-7) for use in making joints. Mortar can be retempered if it begins to set up

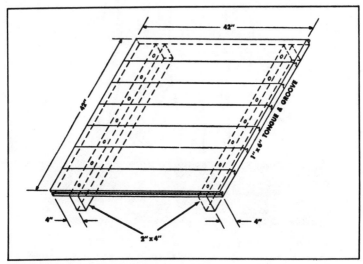

Fig. 6-7. Mortar board plans.

slightly. In most cases, if the mortar is more than a couple of hours old, you'll find it more sensible to just toss out the stiffening mix. You might "save" $10 building a chimney and fireplace if you retemper (add more water) to stiffening mortar. If you misjudge and try to retemper mortar that has really begun to take a set, you can find yourself facing severe joint leakage or weakness problems in a short while. The risks, especially considering the overall cost, is just not worthwhile.

Making a good mortar joint, once the mortar is mixed, is the next basic procedure in any form of bricklaying. The trowel must be held properly wherever space allows. The thumb is run along the top of the trowel handle, not wrapped around it, and you keep the trowel pointed down and away from your body at a slight angle (Fig. 6-8). Pick the mortar from the pile (Fig. 6-9) using the left edge of the trowel (if you're right handed, but lefties reverse).

Start with no more than enough mortar to cover three bricks. That will cover about two-thirds of a standard-sized trowel. Hold the left edge of the trowel directly over the course of bricks or over the bed where the first course is to be laid. Tilt the trowel and move it to the right while allowing the mortar to fall into place. Mortar hanging over the edge of the bricks should be scraped off and returned to the mortar board for reuse (Figs. 6-10, 6-11, and 6-12).

Fig. 6-8. The correct way to hold a trowel.

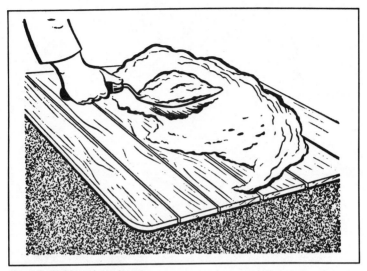

Fig. 6-9. Picking up mortar.

The bed, or base joint, is spread about 1 inch thick on the foundation. You then make a shallow furrow in the bed; taper it from the center to the outsides (Fig. 6-13). Now, you start the bricklaying, *buttering* the end of the first brick and pushing it in place in the mortar bed. Mortar for the bed joints should be run out no farther than five bricks at a time. Mortar spread too far in advance of the bricks being placed dries too quickly to provide a good bond.

Fig. 6-10. Mortar ready for placing.

Fig. 6-11. Mortar being spread.

Buttering consists of holding the brick, with one end in the air, between thumb and forefinger, and placing as much mortar on the brick's end as it will hold. If not enough mortar is buttered onto the brick ends, the head, or vertical, joints will not be full (Fig. 6-14). When bricks are placed against each other after buttering, you will

Fig. 6-12. Starting a bed joint in spread mortar.

Fig. 6-13. Note the furrow in the bed joint.

Fig. 6-14. Buttering a brick end.

need to push hard enough to force mortar from the head joint being formed.

Once joints are made, they must be tooled in one manner or another to compress the mortar and cut down on water penetration. Invariably for exterior construction, this tooling will be concave. You can use a pointing tool to do the job, or the tip of your trowel, but joint tooling is done when the mortar joint has become what is called thumbprint hard. At the time the mortar joint will barely take the print of your thumb, you need to tool it. This gives the optimum weather seal and a long lasting, tight joint (Fig. 6-15).

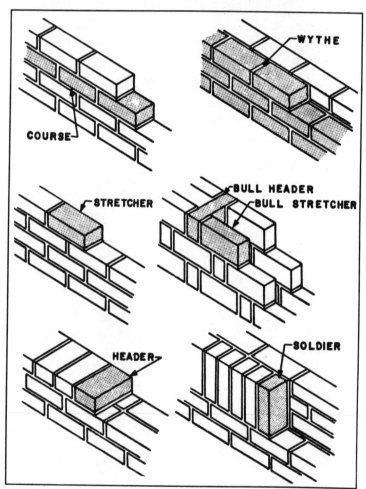

Fig. 6-15. Masonry unit and joint names.

Table 6-1. Height of Courses Using 2¼-Inch Brick and ½-Inch Joints.

Courses	Height	Courses	Height
1	0′ 2¾″	51	11′ 8¼″
2	0′ 5½″	52	11′ 11″
3	0′ 8¼″	53	12′ 1¾″
4	0′ 11″	54	12′ 4½″
5	1′ 1¾″	55	12′ 7¼″
6	1′ 4½″	56	12′ 10″
7	1′ 7¼″	57	13′ 0¾″
8	1′ 10″	58	13′ 3½″
9	2′ 0¾″	59	13′ 6¼″
10	2′ 3½″	60	13′ 9″
11	2′ 6¼″	61	13′ 11¾″
12	2′ 9″	62	14′ 2½″
13	2′ 11¾″	63	14′ 5¼″
14	3′ 2½″	64	14′ 8″
15	3′ 5¼″	65	14′ 10¾″
16	3′ 8″	66	15′ 1½″
17	3′ 10¾″	67	15′ 4¼″
18	4′ 1½″	68	15′ 7″
19	4′ 4¼″	69	15′ 9¾″
20	4′ 7″	70	16′ 0½″
21	4′ 9¾″	71	16′ 3¼″
22	5′ 0½″	72	16′ 6″
23	5′ 3¼″	73	16′ 8¾″
24	5′ 6″	74	16′ 11½″
25	5′ 8¾″	75	17′ 2¼″
26	5′ 11½″	76	17′ 5″
27	6′ 2¼″	77	17′ 7¾″
28	6′ 5″	78	17′ 10½″
29	6′ 7¾″	79	18′ 1¼″
30	6′ 10½″	80	18′ 4″
31	7′ 1¼″	81	18′ 6¾″
32	7′ 4″	82	18′ 9½″
33	7′ 6¾″	83	19′ 0¼″
34	7′ 9½″	84	19′ 3″
35	8′ 0¼″	85	19′ 5¾″
36	8′ 3″	86	19′ 8½″
37	8″ 5¾″	87	19′ 11¼″
38	8′ 8½″	88	20′ 2″
39	8′ 11¼″	89	20′ 4¾″
40	9′ 2″	90	20′ 7½″
41	9′ 4¾″	91	20′ 10¼″
42	9′ 7½″	92	21′ 1″
43	9′ 10¼″	93	21′ 3¾″
44	10′ 1″	94	21′ 6½″
45	10′ 3¾″	95	21′ 9¼″
46	10′ 6½″	96	22′ 0″
47	10′ 9¼″	97	22′ 2¾″
48	11′ 0″	98	22′ 5½″
49	11′ 2¾″	99	22′ 8¼″
50	11′ 5½″	100	22′ 11″

Bricklaying

Once you've gotten the idea of bricklaying from the mortar and joint standpoint, you've reached the time of actual practice. Get the cement sacks ready, the sand in place, and the wheelbarrow or mortar box ready to go. You'll need a garden hose, and mortar board, two trowels (one small, one regular), and a jointing, or pointing, tool. Even for a chimney, your yard will probably seem overwhelmed by pallets of bricks. Tables 6-1 and 6-2 give the needs for single wythe (single layed) walls with both three-eighth and one-half inch mortar joints. Your mortar estimates are subject to variation. But a rough guess will likely show that for every 500 bricks used, you will need two to three bags of portland cement—with proportionate amounts of sand and lime (Table 6-3).

If you were a professional bricklayer, you'd be able to pick up enough mortar in a single trowel load to place from three to five bricks. If you've never worked with brick before, your best bet is to pick up a lot less mortar. Try to start with no more than two bricks per trowel load. Toss the mortar onto the bricks, with a flick of the forearm muscles, as the trowel is turning through a half circle. End the flick with the trowel upside down. Use the trowel point to spread the mortar into a layer that's a bit thicker than one-half inch Scrape off any overhang on the sides with the trowel edge. Each brick, as it is laid, must have its end covered with mortar (called buttering) so that the vertical joints will also be filled with mortar.

Butter each brick and then lay it to the right of its final position (if you're working from left to right). Use a downward, slanting motion to slide the brick into its final position. Tap the brick with the trowel until it aligns with the previously laid bricks. As each brick is so laid, you'll have to scrape off the mortar that is pushed out by the laying operation.

To keep your lines straight, use a line for each row of brick. You can tie the line around the already laid corner bricks. Brickwork always starts at the corners; the corners are built up to from five to eight rows high before any interior bricking is done. The line should fall about one-thirty-second of an inch outside the brick wall and should be drawn as tight as possible. If the mortar in the corners has not set, be careful not to yank the corner brick out of the wall. No brick should touch the line. Masons' cord and masons' distance pieces are available at most building supply and hardware stores. They are very useful. The novice bricklayer should check the level of each course of bricks several times (possibly as often as every three bricks). Though constant checking is a time-consuming chore,

Table 6-2. Height of Courses Using 2¼-Inch and ⅜-Inch Joints.

Courses	Height	Courses	Height
1	0' 2⅝"	51	11' 1⅞"
2	0' 5¼"	52	11' 4½"
3	0' 7⅞"	53	11' 7⅛"
4	0' 10½"	54	11' 9¾"
5	1' 1⅛"	55	12' 0⅜"
6	1' 3¾"	56	12' 3"
7	1' 6⅜"	57	12' 5⅝"
8	1' 9"	58	12' 8¼"
9	1' 11⅝"	59	12' 10⅞"
10	2' 2¼"	60	13' 1½"
11	2' 4⅞"	61	13' 4⅛"
12	2' 7½"	62	13' 6¾"
13	2' 10⅛"	63	13' 9⅜"
14	3' 0¾"	64	14' 0"
15	3' 3⅜"	65	14' 2⅝"
16	3' 6"	66	14' 5¼"
17	3' 8⅝"	67	14" 7⅞"
18	3' 11¼"	68	14' 10½"
19	4' 1⅞"	69	15' 1⅛"
20	4' 4½"	70	15' 3¾"
21	4' 7⅛"	71	15' 6⅜"
22	4' 9¾"	72	15' 9"
23	5' 0⅜"	73	15" 11⅝"
24	5' 3"	74	16' 2¼"
25	5' 5⅝"	75	16' 4⅞"
26	5' 8¼"	76	16' 7½"
27	5' 10⅞"	77	16' 10⅛"
28	6' 1½"	78	17' 0¾"
29	6' 4⅛"	79	17' 3⅜"
30	6' 6¾"	80	17' 6"
31	6' 9⅜"	81	17' 8⅝"
32	7' 0"	82	17' 11¼"
33	7' 2⅝"	83	18' 1⅞"
34	7' 5¼"	84	18' 4½"
35	7' 7⅞"	85	18' 7⅛"
36	7' 10½"	86	18' 9¾"
37	8' 1⅛"	87	19' 0⅜"
38	8' 3¾"	88	19' 3"
39	8' 6⅜"	89	19' 5⅝"
40	8' 9"	90	19' 8¼"
41	8' 11⅝"	91	19' 10⅞"
42	9' 2¼"	92	20' 1½"
43	9' 4⅞"	93	20' 4⅛"
44	9' 7½"	94	20' 6¾"
45	9' 10⅛"	95	20' 9⅜"
46	10' 0¾"	96	21' 0"
47	10' 3⅜"	97	21' 2⅝"
48	10' 6"	98	21' 5¼"
49	10' 8⅝"	99	21' 7⅞"
50	10' 11¼"	100	21' 10½"

there's nothing worse than having to tear a lopsided wall down and having to start over again.

For fireplaces and chimneys, you should lay the first course of bricks on the footing or on the block wall on top of the footing if the footing is so deep the first course of bricks won't reach ground or hearth level. All such foundation work should be done with blocks or poured concrete because it is a lot less expensive than laying bricks below grade. Lay the first row of bricks dry to figure out how many bricks will be needed and where to make any cuts that might be necessary. You should allow for a one-half inch mortar joint between bricks so that any cuts will be accurate. A few chunks of folded and taped cardboard, premeasured to one-half inch, can help maintain this distance as you move along the wall.

After you get your measurements, lay that first course again (this time with mortar). Build up the corners five or six rows high and begin laying the courses between the built-up corners. When you reach the top of the corner, repeat this process until you reach your final height or the point where the brickwork must change direction or shape.

Just about anyone can lay those fine smooth joints you see on professional brickwork. A concave pointing tool is used to press squeezed out mortar back into the joint and to scrape off any excess. The tool can have a V-shape or a U-shape. The compressed mortar in the joint aids waterproofing as well as appearance.

A masonry firebox will need three-eighths inch fireclay joints. Even cement masonry won't withstand the heat of the firebox for very long. The fireclay is essential to a good, long-lasting job. Firebrick is usually $9 \times 4\frac{1}{2} \times 2\frac{1}{2}$ inches. You can lay it with either the $2\frac{1}{2}$ inch or the $4\frac{1}{2}$ inch face exposed. Local building codes should be checked first to make sure the firebox wall will be thick enough if the $4\frac{1}{2}$ inch face is exposed. At any rate, the lower back and the sides of the fireplace will present few bricklaying problems. When you reach the proper height for the fireplace back to start its forward slant, care becomes very necessary. You'll probably have to slow down to give the fireclay joints more time to set or the whole works might tumble out on you. An experienced mason can do this sort of work in one shot, and getting it right demands a bit of experience. Patience is a good replacement for novices.

If you expect too much trouble, you can build up a form from plywood; you can then lay the bricks from outside the firebox. The form is just two pieces of plywood; the top one is angled properly for the slant of the back wall. The form should be braced with $2 \times 2s$.

Table 6-3. Quantities of Materials for Brick Walls.

Wall area sq ft	Wall thickness in inches							
	4 inches		8 inches		12 inches		16 inches	
	Number of bricks	Cu ft mortar	Number of bricks	Cu ft mortar	Number of bricks	Cu ft mortar	Number of bricks	Cu ft mortar
1	6.17	.08	12.33	.2	18.49	.32	24.65	.44
10	61.7	.8	123.3	2	184.9	3.2	246.5	4.4
100	617	8	1,233	20	1,849	32	2,465	44
200	1,234	16	2,466	40	3,698	64	4,930	88
300	1,851	24	3,699	60	5,547	96	7,395	132
400	2,468	32	4,932	80	7,396	128	9,860	176
500	3,085	40	6,165	100	9,245	160	12,325	220
600	3,712	48	7,398	120	11,094	192	14,790	264
700	4,319	56	8,631	140	12,943	224	17,253	308
800	4,936	64	9,864	160	14,792	256	19,720	352
900	5,553	72	10,970	180	16,641	288	22,185	396
1,000	6,170	80	12,330	200	18,490	320	24,650	440

*Quantities are based on ½-inch-thick mortar joint. For ⅜-inch-thick joint use 80 percent of these quantities. For ⅝-inch-thick joints use 120 percent.

This causes some problems with getting smooth mortar joints on the fire side of the firebox, but this can be partly helped by using less mortar on the front side of the brick so that no extra is squeezed out.

After you build up the firebox to the proper height, imbed the damper and install the lintel (if needed) across the fireplace front. Dampers are available from many manufacturers in many sizes, but they all have one thing in common. They need to be set in a bed of rock-wool insulation to allow the metal of the damper to expand and contract. Your damper manufacturer will specify a flue size to fit the damper you purchase.

All firebox joints should be trowel finished. They should be scraped off flush with the face of the brick using the side of the trowel.

Corbeling is the method used to slant in, or slant out, the brick walls surrounding a fireplace or chimney. For slanting *toward* the fireplace, this is done by slipping the top row of bricks 1 inch off the flush line toward the fireplace. Repeat the process until you reach the point where you want to continue upward in a straight line again (Fig. 6-16). If a great deal of weight must be supported, you should consider doing the corbeling with a second row of bricks *inside* the offset.

As the fireplace grows, the spaces between the outer brick walls and the firebrick walls should be filled with masonry rubble (such as broken bricks, dried cement, small rocks, etc.).

Once the top of the chimney is reached, the flue liner should be extended about 8 inches above the top of the chimney bricks. A mortar bevel should be laid on to taper from about 2 inches below the top of the flue liner to the outside edges of the brick (for a double-wythe chimney). For a single wythe chimney, run the flue liner about 4 inches above the bricks, and taper the mortar down from about 2 inches below the top of the flue liner (Fig. 6-17).

Many forms of chimney caps are available or they can be made. I recommend quite strongly that you install a cap. It is best, whenever possible, to use or make the type of chimney cap that can be fairly easily removed. At some point in the life of any fireplace, or wood stove, the chimney will have to be cleaned. If the chimney cleaner, or you, must chip away mortar that is holding a slate chimney cap in place, the time, the materials and the cost, will go up in a rush. Slate can be drilled to accept bolts. Make sure any such bolts are aluminum or that they are galvanized. Commercial chimney caps are generally designed to be readily detached. See Tables 6-4, 6-5, and 6-6.

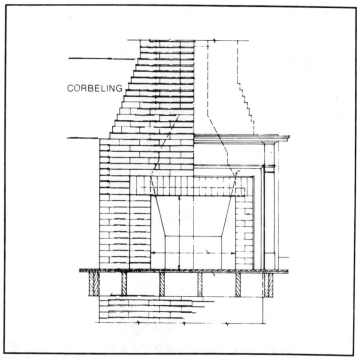

Fig. 6-16. Corbelling on a brick chimney.

After you complete the fireplace, it will require at least one week to cure. Even then the first few fires must not be roaring, leaping demons of heat. Small fires can help the curing process of the mortar and the fireclay, but roaring blazes can upset the process and create smoke leaks.

Table 6-4. Alternate Flue Sizes.

Area of fireplace opening in square inches	Standard rectangular flue, outside dimensions	Round flue inside diameter
1000	8½ × 18	12
1200	8½ × 18	12
1400	13 × 13	12
1600	13 × 13	15
1800	13 × 18	15
2200	13 × 18	15
2400	18 × 18	18

Table 6-5. Conventional Fireplace Dimensions in Inches.

Finished Fireplace Opening							Rough Brick Work			Flue Sizes[a]			Steel Angle[b]
A	B	C	D	E	F	G	H	I	J	K	L	M	N
24	24	16	11	14	18	8¾	32	18½	19	10	8	12	A-36
26	24	16	13	14	18	8¾	34	18½	21	11	8	12	A-36
28	24	16	15	14	18	8¾	36	18½	21	12	8	12	A-36
30	29	16	17	14	23	8¾	38	18½	24	13	12	12	A-42
32	29	16	19	14	23	8¾	40	18½	24	14	12	12	A-42
36	29	16	23	14	23	8¾	44	18½	27	16	12	12	A-48
40	29	16	27	14	23	8¾	48	18½	29	16	12	16	A-48
42	32	16	29	14	26	8¾	50	18½	32	17	16	16	B-54
48	32	18	33	16	26	8¾	56	20½	37	20	16	16	B-60
54	37	20	37	16	29	13	68	22½	45	26	16	16	B-72
60	37	22	42	16	29	13	72	24½	45	26	16	20	B-72
72	40	22	54	16	31	13	84	24½	56	32	20	20	C-84
84	40	24	64	20	28	13	96	26½	61	36	20	24	C-96
96	40	24	76	20	28	13	108	26½	75	42	20	24	C-108

[a] Flue sizes conform to modular dimensional system.
[b] Angle sizes: A—3 × 3 × 3/16 in.; B—3½ × 3 × ½ in.; C—5 × 3½ × 5/16 in.
[c] This dimension is listed to provide a minimum thickness of the fireback.

Fig. 6-17. A conventional fireplace.

ROCK MASONRY

From prefabricated fireplace systems to brick (or cement block) masonry to rock masonry—that's the order of difficulty in building fireplaces. For best results, you must build the rock masonry fireplace around a firebrick hearth and firebox with a

Table 6-6. Fireplace Flue Sizes (in Inches).

Fireplace opening			Standard rectangular flue, outside dimensions	Round flue, inside diameter
width	height	depth		
28	24	16-18	8½ × 8½	10
30-32	28	18	8½ × 13	10
36	28	18	8½ × 13	12
42	28	18	8½ × 18	12
48	32	18-20	13 × 13	15
54	36	20	13 × 18	15
60	36	22	18 × 18	18

fireclay flue. But it is possible to save a fair amount of money by working with native stone found on or around your own property. Brick prices vary around the country, but one thing can be said: bricks are expensive. Rocks are everywhere and they can make attractive and sturdy fireplaces and chimneys.

There are, unfortunately, a few catches that make rock masonry more difficult than brick masonry. First comes the problem of estimating the number of rocks you need. It's close to impossible using found field stones to make an accurate estimate. Brick estimates are simple; each brick is of a uniform size and the mortar joints are also uniform. Rocks close to 1 cubic foot are on the not-recommended list because a lot of rocks weigh from 150 to 180 pounds per cubic foot. That is kind of heavy to work with, even with scaffolding. Bricks might have to be trimmed for fit, but unlike rocks they don't have to be chipped to fit a mortar joint. Rocks have to be trimmed at certain fault areas and then slowly chipped to size. This sort of work requires a devilish amount of splitting and chipping. Still, it is possible. And if you've got more time than money, it can be much more economical than many other installations.

Rock masonry fireplaces require the same kind of footing as any other masonry fireplace. Two types of rocks are commonly available. Igneous rocks, granite and basalt, are more difficult by far to work with, but they are generally a lot stronger. Stratified rocks, limestones and shales, which are much easier to work with, but they are susceptible to moisture deterioration. The colder and wetter your climate, the more likely you are to have problems with this sort of deterioration. Igneous rocks are usually available in machine-cut styles, but this again runs your expenses right back up there with brick.

Ease of working depends on the weight of the rock. Granite is a very heavy stone (about 170 pounds per cubic foot) and it is matched in weight by limestone. Sandstone is also heavy but not as heavy as granite. Sandstone weighs about 150 pounds per cubic foot. Slate is heaviest of all at around 175 pounds per cubic foot.

Rock is laid pretty much the same way brick is laid. However, with rock masonry there's no need to level each course. Rocks are usually easier to lay if you trim the face sides flat. You can use a line to keep the stonework as close to vertical along its face as possible.

You should give rocks the same sprinkle test used on bricks. If a few drops of water disappear into the rock in a minute or less, soak down the entire pile.

You'll need at least twice as much mortar as you would need for a comparable brick wall (probably a great deal more). It depends in large part on how tight you plan to make the mortar joints and how closely you trim the rocks. You can use small rocks to space out the joints to cut down on the amount of mortar you use. Mortar ingredients for rock masonry are the same as those for brick masonry. Random-rubble masonry is the most difficult rock masonry to lay, but trimmed stratified-rock masonry is the easiest because it closely resembles the course-by-course laying of bricks and concrete blocks. Random-rubble masonry is done with junk rock or brick (bits and pieces of rock or brick laid in a random pattern).

The mason's, or bricklayer's chisel is an absolutely essential tool for rock masonry work. You'll probably also want a maul or small sledge. For most people, a 2-pound maul is adequate. Exceptionally strong people might prefer a 3-pounder. Look for cleavage lines (even in granite) because rock is more easily broken and trimmed along these natural lines. Use a mason's, or bricklayer's, hammer for the fine trim chipping of stone.

In the actual construction of a wall, use longer stretcher stones, about every 6 square feet, to make sure that wall strength is maintained and that all parts of the wall are tied together. You can align the wall precisely by using a stake at each end of it. Stonework doesn't allow for wrapping the line around a corner as you do with brick work. Stretch a line tautly from stake to stake at the proper height and as close to the front surface of the stone as you can get without touching the stone. Of course, you must lift and level the line as the wall moves up. If you must lift a stone out and reset it, clean the mortar from both it and any stones where it had been set. Use fresh mortar for the resetting. Wash all stones before using because dust will prevent the formation of a proper bond between mortar and rock.

Select the flattest rocks for the final course on a chimney and any final courses at other spots. Then use sufficient mortar to get a level top on the construction. Use a jointing tool to tool the mortar joints; clean away any mortar that drops on the stones. As a substitute for a jointing tool, use a stick with a smoothed end to tool mortar joints. Use a rough, wet sponge to clean off any mortar on the stone facing. Dry mortar is very hard to remove and almost always leaves a mark on stone.

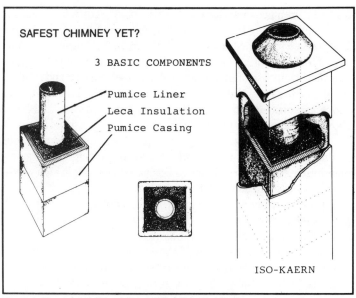

Fig. 7-1. Norweigian Wood Stove's Iso-Kaern chimney.

your flue size can stand a couple of inches reduction without ruining the draft for your wood stove or chimney (and a great many older chimneys can), such a relining job should solve all leakage problems for a long time to come (Fig. 7-2).

The company's claim is that there are over half a million of these chimneys in use in Scandinavia (which amounts to about one for every 10 families there). A test in 1980 showed that, with a flue gas temperature of 1832 degrees F., the exterior of an Iso-Kaern chimney reached only 102 degrees F (Fig. 7-3).

Certainly such a repair method beats the insertion of steel stovepipe down inside the old flue liner. This method serves, but the stovepipe doesn't aid insulation values of the chimney. And it will not last long; it will probably need to be replaced at three-year intervals.

TROUBLESHOOTING

Fireplaces pouring smoke into the room, or wood stoves doing the same thing, usually do not present the danger that chimney leaks present. But a smoke-filled house is not one of the great pleasures of the Western world. Sitting around with one's eyes dripping water from irritation does not add to any pleasure you might get from saving money with wood heat. Think of just sitting in front of a fireplace or parlor stove, with your feet up and a brandy in your hand, toasting the end of a hard week. And then to have your face greeted with great rolls of smoke from the heating unit. No fun.

Troubleshooting for smoking fireplaces and wood stoves begins on the outside of the house. Take a tape measure and a ladder and get on the roof. Make certain your chimney top is at least 2 feet above any obstruction within 10 feet on a peaked roof, and 3 feet above roof level on a flat roof (Fig. 7-4).

If actual chimney height is not a problem, you'll need to look around a bit for trees that might have been growing more rapidly than you expected. Large limbs can cause a downdraft in high winds, kicking smoke out into the house at times.

If chimney height and obstructions don't pose problems, you'll now need a very powerful flashlight and some rope. Tie the flashlight on the rope and lower it down the chimney; allow it to turn so that all sides of the chimney are illuminated. Check for any internal obstructions that might interfere with the draft (bird's nests, fallen or partially fallen stones or bricks in unlined chimneys, etc.). Look for any indication that even small branches might have blown into the chimney.

If this still doesn't solve your problems, you'll have to look possibly, a bit further afield. Look at the trees surrounding your house. Even if there are none close enough to cause obvious draft obstruction, trees can sometimes cause wind currents to vary in such a way that you'll get an occasional downdraft. Trees that were short enough and far enough away when the house was originally built might take only a dozen years to send out branches, or gain enough height, to cause difficulties (even though they are outside the ten foot limit).

A chain saw and some rope is the answer. If you do not have experience with a chain saw, this kind of work is not a good idea. The use of climbing spikes, safety belts, and the techniques for using a chain saw while in a tree require a bit more experience than cutting wood on the ground. If you don't have several years of chain saw use under your belt, I would advise hiring a professional to do this trimming for you. It will certainly cost a great deal more, but hospital time is non-productive.

If necessary, you could fell the entire tree. But a simpler solution is the installation of a chimney cap to redirect possible downdrafting air. Extending the flue lining 4 inches above the top of the chimney and then cementing a rain slant or bevel to within an inch or two of the flue's top will also help to prevent downdrafts by

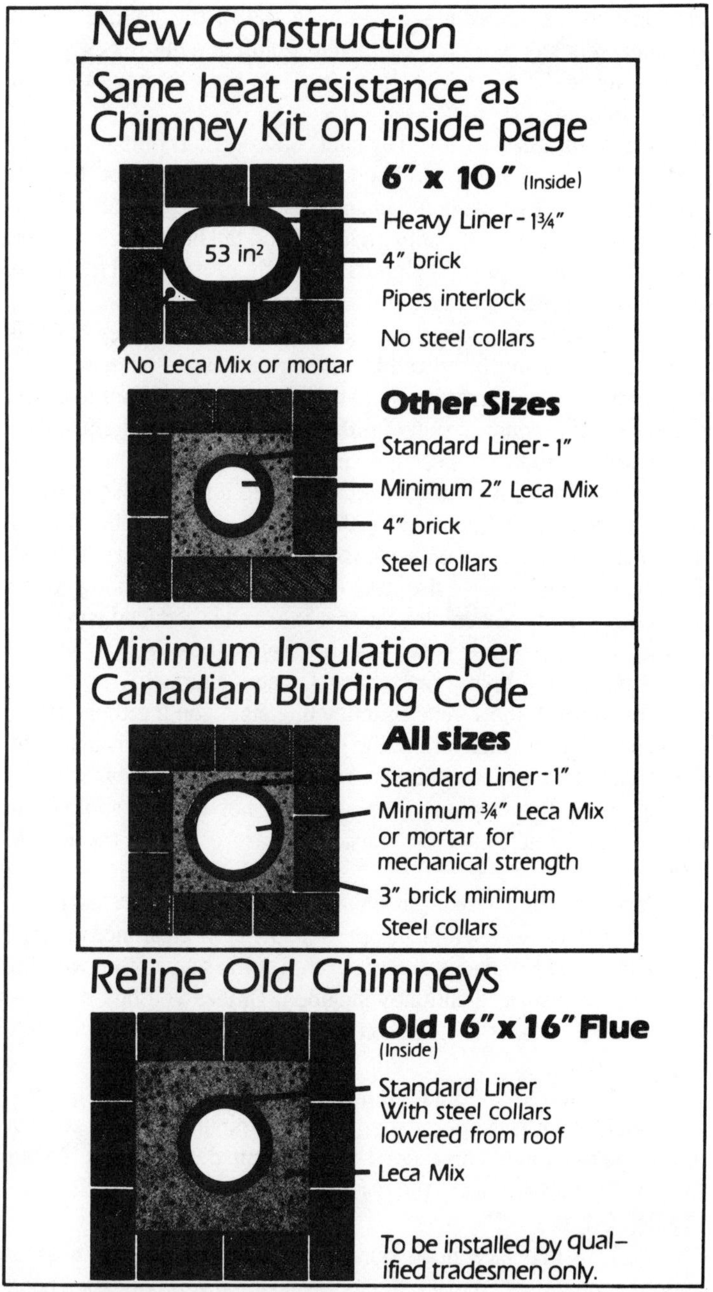

New Construction

Same heat resistance as Chimney Kit on inside page

6" x 10" (Inside)

53 in²

No Leca Mix or mortar

- Heavy Liner - 1¾"
- 4" brick
- Pipes interlock
- No steel collars

Other Sizes

- Standard Liner - 1"
- Minimum 2" Leca Mix
- 4" brick
- Steel collars

Minimum Insulation per Canadian Building Code

All sizes

- Standard Liner - 1"
- Minimum ¾" Leca Mix or mortar for mechanical strength
- 3" brick minimum
- Steel collars

Reline Old Chimneys

Old 16" x 16" Flue (Inside)

- Standard Liner With steel collars lowered from roof
- Leca Mix

To be installed by qualified tradesmen only.

Fig. 7-2. The Iso-Kaern chimney liner system (courtesy of Norwegian Wood Stoves).

cleaning up the air eddies around the top of the chimney. This technique doesn't work too well when a bluff or a hill too close to a house causes the downdraft. In such cases, the chimney cap is the better solution.

If downdrafts are caused by land conditions, a chimney several feet higher, with a cap or hood, might be the answer to your problems. Nearby high buildings can also cause downdraft difficulties. In some cases, with both high hills and tall buildings involved, your only solution will be to build the chimney on up until it is out of the turbulence that is causing downdrafting at the flue.

Improperly shaped sections of a fireplace or a chimney cause as many, probably more, downdraft difficulties as do external influences (the twisting and turning of the air currents). In some cases, some sort of reconstruction of either the chimney or the fireplace could well be the only possible cure.

For example, if a flue is sized too small for a fireplace firebox opening area, you'll find a reasonably simple cure available (though at first it sounds as if you'll have to reconstruct the entire firebox). Simply put, you'll need a fireplace hood that drops far enough down in front of the firebox opening so that the area is reduced enough to fit the flue size (otherwise, you can reline the firebox without removing the old lining, or construct a new chimney).

If you don't know your chimney flue size, you'll either have to climb a ladder and measure at the chimney top or slither inside the fireplace to take a measurement. I recommend the process with the ladder. Even the cleanest fireplaces are not exactly spotless in areas where you'll have to reach to measure (above the smoke shelf).

Incorrect flue sizes can exist on even factory-prefabricated fireplaces. This very seldom happens on the zero-clearance models. Zero-clearance fireplaces are most often sold as a package with the correct size insulated chimney included. Unless you buy the base unit and fit a reducer to its flue collar, reducing the size is virtually impossible.

Fortunately, any required hood can be made of many decorative metals such as copper (expensive!), aluminum, or sheet steel in any shape that might correspond to your home decor. Measure your fireplace opening. Locate the correct-size opening for the flue size (Tables 5-1 and 5-2).

Build a fireplace hood that shuts out the required area of over-size opening. To make things even simpler, if building a hood is more work than you care for, a narrow metal strip beneath the

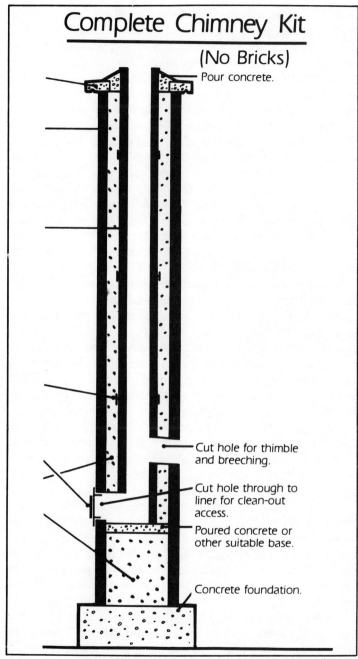

Complete Chimney Kit

(No Bricks)

Pour concrete.

Cut hole for thimble and breeching.

Cut hole through to liner for clean-out access.

Poured concrete or other suitable base.

Concrete foundation.

Fig. 7-3. The Iso-Kearn chimney system (courtesy Norwegian Wood Stoves).

breast of the fireplace (where the lintel is installed) can do as good a job. And it takes only a short time to measure, cut and fit in place.

Or you can lay a second course of firebrick, with fireclay mortar, to the hearth of the firebox to cut down on the opening area. New firebrick can also be run up the sides of the firebox, too, but the contours of most fireplace innards make such a job far more difficult than merely laying an extra layer of hearth bricks.

If you find you really need a drastic reduction in opening area, all these ideas can be combined. But it is probably far better to start with the strip beneath the breast of the fireplace, or a hood, and then lay a new hearth before considering any other measures. It's possible to run metal strips up the sides of the firebox opening, as along the top, in order to reduce size. That can be considered as a less drastic step than installing new firebrick lining over the old lining.

Modern houses are much more tightly sealed than were those of our ancestors. A house that is too tight can often cause fireplaces to gust smoke back into the rooms. If you have a series of wood-heating appliances in a tightly caulked, heavily insulated house, the added need for air for combustion when a fireplace or wood stove is used can draw air down the flue and cause smoke to billow out into the room.

This sort of tightness can cause smoking even when one or more inside doors are opened to allow more air into the room being heated. Generally, this opening of interior doors is the accepted method of improving combustion so that the smoke actually goes up the chimney where it belongs.

In a too tightly sealed house, the chimney is forced to draw down outside air to feed the wood stove, fireplace, or possibly even a hot water heater or another appliance using air for combustion. A tight-fitting damper can prevent much of any heat loss in tight houses. Remember that as outside air is drawn into the house, heated air will pass on up the chimney—causing a net heat loss for your home. The only real solution when a fireplace or wood stove smokes too much because of too little air for combustion is for you to find some way of providing more air. If opening interior doors doesn't work, you might find it necessary to crack open a basement window or even a window in the room with the wood-heating appliance.

In some cases, you might find it necessary to install a ventilating grille of the type used for hot-air heating systems. In the most extreme cases, you will need to vent to the exterior to provide cold air for combustion. If a grate is needed to provide exterior air, it is

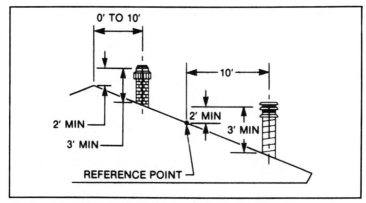

Fig. 7-4. Observe the 10 foot height rule (courtesy of Majestic).

best to vent it directly to the wood stove or fireplace (when at all possible). This helps prevent the flow of cold air into the house where it is not needed. Any such grate should be of a type that can readily be closed tightly when not in use.

Some ventilation to allow movement of air in the house is always needed. Check for proper ventilation in crawl spaces and attics. In gable roofs, there should be a good-sized screened vent at the gable end peak on each end of the house. Screened vents in the soffits will also help airflow.

When a single chimney has more than one flue installed, there can be one problem with several different causes. In a poor chimney design, one flue can suck smoke from another and right into the room served by the second flue (whether or not the wood-heating appliance on that flue is being used).

It is probably more likely that an operating flue will have its smoke forced down the flue of a non-operating appliance, but occasionally—with both flues in operation—both will smoke. Sometimes the only way you can solve such problems is to reconstruct the chimney so that the flues are at least 4 inches apart, separated by 4 inches of solid masonry.

If the flues are too close together, there is no need to tear down and rebuild the chimney. Simply make sure one flue rises at least 4 inches higher than the other, and then provide separate caps for each flue. The caps will cut out any trouble that might persist because of localized downdrafts around the flues (Fig. 7-5). Because the flue passing smoke to another can suddenly, with the correct wind currents, become the one receiving downdrafted smoke, the capping of all flues is a good idea (Fig. 7-6).

Fig. 7-5. The FLUE KAP from Jo Moco Products, Inc.

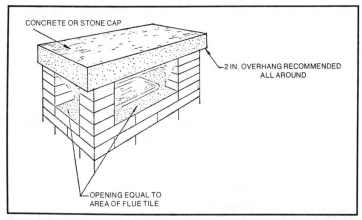

CONCRETE OR STONE CAP

2 IN. OVERHANG RECOMMENDED
ALL AROUND

OPENING EQUAL TO
AREA OF FLUE TILE

Fig. 7-6. A typical rain cap for masonry chimneys (courtesy of Vega Industries Inc.).

Construction faults might range from simple sloppy workmanship to a poor choice of building materials. If the brick used is perforated (or too porous), and the workmanship on the mortar joints is a little below standards, the possibility of flue to flue leakage is greatly increased. Without tearing out the whole works and starting over, there is really very little you can do about perforated or porous bricks. Sloppy mortar joints on the chimney exterior can and should be repaired.

Sloppy mortar joints on the interior of the flue are a bit more of a problem, but they can often be handled without major reconstruction of the chimney. A straw-filled or newspaper-filled burlap sack (or even a plastic feed sack) will be a handy tool. Make sure the bag, full of straw tightly packed, wood shavings or crumpled newspaper, is a tight fit in the flue.

Remove the damper, where possible, by pulling the cotter pins and tilting it out. Set the stuffed burlap sack on the refractory hearth and drop a moderately heavy rope down from the top of the chimney. Lift the sack almost to the flue liner inside the chimney and cover its top heavily with mortar (firebrick mortar).

You'll probably need a helper at this point or there will be a lot of scrambling on and off the roof. Draw the sack very slowly up the flue, twisting the rope as it comes up, and adding mortar as that on the top of the sack is forced into the joints. Repeat the process as needed until any flue-to-flue leakage of smoke is stopped. If more than a single pass is needed, you will find it best to run a clean, tight-fitting sack through the flue after each pass in order to keep

159

the mortar from building up too heavily on the inside of the flue liner.

A mortar-choked flue can cause smoking, but more often the choked off flue will be filled with other kinds of obstructions. You might find a bird's nest. Squirrels and other rodents sometimes build nests in unused flues. If you've built your fireplace the easy way, with a straight flue with no offset, the removal of such obstructions is no great problem. You simply pull the cotter pins holding the damper control in place, lift it out, and use a long stick to poke any obstructions down. They'll fall all the way to the hearth or lodge on the smoke shelf where they can easily be lifted out. In a chimney with one or more offsets, you could run into real difficulty. It's possible to get junk lodged in these offsets that is almost impossible to budge with a long pole of any kind. If that happens, try a bundle of logging chains on a rope. And if that doesn't work, you're in trouble. The only solution remaining is to rip out the chimney at that point, remove the obstruction, and rebuild the chimney. Screening off the top of the chimney is a good way to keep most kinds of debris out of the chimney.

Improper smoke chamber construction can also obstruct the flue. The final course of bricks that hold the flue tile should be offset just enough to fit the flue lining without cutting into the opening of the flue. Any bricks that do cut into the flue opening will have to be removed and reset.

A clogged ashpit can also cause problems. Usually this problem will only come about if the wall around the ashpit leaks water. In a correct installation, the ashpit door will be large enough to allow you to take a poker and jam around in the mess to clean it out. If clogging happens more than once, consider doing a waterproofing job on the wall surrounding the ashpit (but only after checking the flashing at the top of the chimney for possible leakage). Defective flashing can allow water to drain right down the sides of the chimney into the ashpit.

Damage from ice, snow, and rain can cause a lot of problems in older fireplaces and in some newer ones. Because there is a slightly different contraction rate for each of the various materials used in chimneys, you can expect some cracking of the mortar joints and of the beveled rain cap over a period of years. Improper mortar mixtures, poor construction techniques, and too short a curing time can cause cracks very quickly. An annual check of the cement rain bevel at the top of the chimney should be routine. This rain bevel is the most likely point for the entry of moisture, which can then freeze and expand the cracks, causing rapid disintegration. Make periodic checks of all mortar joints on the exterior of the chimney.

Use of andirons or a firebasket can help with some flue size problems, although you'll usually need to take other corrective measures. Either accessory will make fires easier to start and keep them burning more brightly. The firebasket is the better of the two at this job, as is a grate, because both provide more support than do andirons (which often allow the middle of the fire to collapse).

Fireplace depth is of great importance. Too shallow a fireplace will prevent you from building much of a fire without bringing smoke and flame into the room. Too deep a fireplace will provide its own share of smoke problems because the front of the fireplace will stay considerably cooler than the rear of the fireplace (causing eddies that throw smoke into the room).

A shallow fireplace throws more heat into a room than does a deep one with the same fireplace opening area. A good minimum depth is about 16 inches for even the smallest of fireplaces. This depth allows a reasonable-size fire to burn without the danger of burning logs rolling out onto the floor. A fair maximum depth, for fireplaces up to 6 feet wide and 40 inches high, is about 26 or 28 inches. As an example, the Majestic heat circulator, 54 inches wide and 31 inches high, offers a 19-inch depth (which the company considers more than enough).

Heatilator's 60-inch unit offers a 21¼-inch depth. These units were designed to increase fireplace efficiency by circulating more heat.

A fireplace of more than half the depth of the fireplace opening width can waste heat and money has been wasted in building materials. Masonry fireplaces that are too deep can have a row of firebrick added to their backs to take up as much as 4½ inches of the space being wasted. Make sure there is no interference with the flue.

Chapter 8

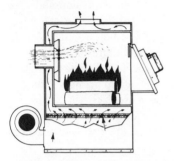

Wood for Burning

Too many people seem to feel that just flipping any old log into a wood stove or fireplace will provide a fire that has to work. Someone who does a major part of his home heating with wood needs to know a great deal more than that. Wood heat production varies as much as wood weight (and wood weight can vary from a low of about 25 pound per cubic foot on up past 70 pound per cubic foot. Because wood provides some 7000 British thermal units (Btu) of heat per pound—resinous woods provide a bit more, but cause more problems—it's easy to see that heavier, more dense woods provide more heat per cord than lighter woods. But that's not the entire story. Most dense woods are difficult to ignite, but the lighter woods, particularly those with a lot of resins (such as the pines), are handy for starting fires. For full-time use, resinous woods should be avoided if at all possible.

You should consider a combination of things then if you're to build the ideal fire. First, use resinous light wood to start the fire. Then add heavier wood for a lasting high-heat blaze.

Woods available in the United States and Canada vary a great deal. There are few spots in the country where wood of one kind or another is not available (around some cities hardwood is scarce and expensive).

The 7000 Btu of heat per pound of wood is an ideal figure. It is based on the burning of *air-dried* wood under ideal conditions. You won't get 7000 Btu under *actual* conditions in your house. By the same token, there is a fuel value of 140,000 Btu in each gallon of number 2 fuel oil for home heating. You won't get that either. Most oil furnaces in good shape will provide a 65 percent efficiency rating for the fuel burned. This means you'll get about 91,000 Btu worth of heat from each 140,000 Btu gallon you burn. With wood-burning appliances ranging so widely in efficiency, from a low of under 10 percent to over 65 percent, it's difficult to estimate just how much of the actual available Btu value in a cord of wood will actually become usable heat in your home.

Making things even harder is the difficulty in getting an accurate measurement of the amount of wood in a cord. A cord of wood is considered to be a well-stacked pile 8 feet long, 4 feet wide, and 4 feet high. While there is a wild chance that one cord in every 50 billion might actually have a full 128 cubic feet, the odds are excellent you will get much less than that. Logs when stacked leave gaps. The larger the unsplit logs, the larger the gaps and the fewer cubic feet actually in the cord. You might, with a fair number of smaller logs and split logs, find a cord which actually contains 95 cubic feet of wood. If you buy your wood, make sure the logs are well mixed between split and unsplit, with a good number of 3 inch and 4 inch logs.

How can you figure the fuel value of wood? First, locate or devise a rough efficiency figure for the wood-burning unit being used. If the unit is a heat-circulating fireplace, expect 20 to 25 percent (the 25 percent rating will come only with constant tending and perfect wood use). With modern wood stoves, such as those made by Jøtul, Ashley, and Riteway, you might be able, with proper tending, to reach an efficiency rating of 60 percent or more. But it's probably more sensible to figure on a rating of 50 percent or a bit less. No one really wants to spend more time tending the fire than is essential to keep the house warm. Older stoves will range from 30 to 50 percent efficiency. Begin overly optimistic about the efficiency of your wood-burning unit can mean running short of fuel at the wrong time.

Once you've decided on an efficiency rating for your wood-burning applicance, take 7000 Btu and multiply that by the weight of your wood for an average tightly stacked cord. This provides, at least, a starting point for figuring costs. For example, you might want to use 80 cubic feet of wood per cord. This would probably be on the low-side of average for even a purchased cord of wood. Running out of firewood in the middle of the winter is no pleasure at all if wood is your main source of heat. Low-side averages are always the safest.

Let's assume the fuel wood is sugar maple or one of the hard, heavy maples such as black maple. To get the air-dried weight, add 20 percent to the dry weight of 44 pounds. The weight will be 52.8 pounds per cubic foot. Multiply that by 80 and you have 4240 pounds per air-dried cord. At 7000 Btu per pound, you then have over 29 million Btu of heat *available* for use from a single cord of firewood.

Now multiply the 29 million Btu by the percentage of efficiency for your wood-heating applicance and you'll know just how many of those Btu will *actually* benefit you. With a fireplace heating at 25 percent efficiency (quite high for standard fireplaces), you'll receive almost 7½ million Btu of actual heat per cord in your home. That's the equivalent of about 80 gallons of fuel oil at 65 percent efficiency. At about $100 a cord, assuming fuel oil in your area costs $1.26 per gallon, you could break even. At that price, you're probably better off cutting the wood yourself unless you live in a rural area where it is still often possible to get a cord of wood for under $85.

With a more efficient fireplace, or a wood stove, the cost factor becomes an entirely different thing. At 50 percent efficiency, you'll get about 15 million Btu of heat from that same cord of firewood. At $1.26 a gallon, the wood equivalent to 160 gallons of fuel oil, would give you a break even cost of $191 (plus) per cord. If you can get your firewood for $100 a cord—a not impossible situation in many areas—and use 8 cords a year at that price, your savings will be on the order of $728.

Any savings, naturally, will be much greater if you cut your own wood. A single year cutting your own wood, if you have an accessible woodlot, will save more than enough to amortize the cost of a chain saw, a wood stove, the stove installation, and any fuel needed. Even in those areas where you have to pay a fee (known as a stumpage fee) for firewood, the savings should still be on the order of $1500 a year. Once the tool and stove costs are amortized, you have only upkeep on the chain saw, the wood stoves, and the vehicle needed to haul the wood. Such costs shouldn't work out to much over $100 a year (with any luck).

A chain saw, a splitting hammer, wedges, and a few other little gadgets should enable the average healthy person to supply his or her home with 8 cords of split and stacked wood in 10 to 15 days of moderate labor, or four to five days of good, old-fashioned hard work. Eight cords will heat most average-sized houses, or those a bit larger and well-insulated, for an entire winter anywhere but in the extreme Northern parts of the United States and Canada.

A chain saw suitable for cutting firewood will cost about $150 to $400. It depends on how much cutting you plan to do. The more cutting you need to do, the larger the chain saw needs to be. Anyone cutting more than 10 cords of firewood a year will need a farm model saw or one of the smaller professional models such as Homelite's 360 or 410. For each cord of wood you cut, you'll use about 20,000 Btu of gasoline for your chain saw. No matter how freely you lubricate your chain—the more liberal, the better—and no matter how much extra oil you slop into the two-stroke engine fuel mixture, your cost per cord of firewood should be under a buck, even today.

Most chain saw manufacturers feel that a proper example of their product will last at least a decade with no major engine repairs. From what I've seen they're probably correct for homeowners use. Over the past few years, I've used saws from almost all the major manufacturers. Most have stood up extremely well to my heavier than standard use for firewood. Some smaller parts do wear out more rapidly than the engines.

In most cases, the guide bar will have to be replaced every third year or so. For moderately heavy use, figure on a new chain and sprocket about once a year. A new bar and chain today can cost you well over $40 (depending on bar length), but in general the overall repairs for two years of heavy homeowner use (not counting depreciation and internal wear) for a 16-inch chain saw should run no more than about $55 or $60 tops (unless something drastic does go wrong).

Although locating wood, cutting it, and splitting it are essential to burning wood, knowing what sort of wood to use and how it will burn is just as important. The woods in the following list are not broken down into hardwood and softwood categories. Such a breakdown is often inaccurate because many of the softwoods are harder and more dense than some hardwoods. The distinction doesn't exist botanically anyway. I've listed the woods according to the geographical area in which they are found. Where possible, I've included the air-dried weight per cubic foot. You can use this to determine the heat value of the wood. If you want to supply your own hardwood/softwood classification, conifers are usually classified as softwoods. Deciduous trees are considered hardwoods. Conifers include such woods as pines, firs, spruces, cypresses, and cedars.

The listings include wood characteristics such as hard, close-grained, and so on. Hardwood, which has a close grain, is harder to cut than softwood (which has a coarse grain). Hardwoods will dull your saw more rapidly. These facts should be weighted against the fact that if you burn softwoods you'll spend more time feeding the fire and will need to cut a larger amount of wood to get through the winter.

I've included information on resin content because you need to know how much of a mess a particular wood can make in your flue. Many of the conifers produce a few hundred Btu more heat per pound of wood than the hardwoods. But they are resinous woods, and therefore the chimney gets clogged more quickly. In most cases, conifers burn quicker. This, again, will force you to spend more time cutting wood.

I've included wood aroma in the listings where applicable. A fire of apple or cedar can do much to lighten an otherwise gloomy winter evening. A great deal of the aroma goes up the chimney, and that might well please your neighbors too. Generally, the aromatic woods tend to be either expensive (apple, cherry), rare (cedar). They should be saved for special occasions. Almost all fruit trees are aromatic, with the burning wood exuding the fragrance of the fruit. Nut trees are the same way. Many conifers are also aromatic.

The East, particularly the Northeast, abounds in hardwoods such as oak and maple. The West has fewer of these hardwoods and many more large conifers (usually much larger than Eastern trees). Hardwoods develop in older forests, while forests in earlier stages of development have the great pines and redwoods of the world, as seen in the West. Often, when conifers are removed from a forest, hardwoods take over. When the hardwoods move out, in the next cycle, the conifers will move back in. What maples, oaks, and so on there are in the West are generally smaller and often less hardy than the same trees found in the East.

I've not listed *all* the trees in this country that can be used as fuel. There are probably more than 700 species of trees in the United States. Some are too small for fuel use. Some are too localized for a general list. Some are too rare. The rest can generally be found over a wide area, often over most of the country, and in Canada.

EASTERN TREES

American Beech. A medium hard, moderately strong, close-grained wood in the moderately heavy range at 52 to 53 pound per cubic foot. Beech is exceptionally hard to split, but makes a good fuel and is slow burning. The mature tree is 60 to 80 feet tall with a 2 to 3 foot diameter. Found from Nova Scotia south to northern Florida and west to southeastern Oklahoma.

American Linden (also known as basswood, whitewood). A very soft, weak, brittle wood weighing 30 to 31 pounds per cubic foot. A poor fuel. The mature tree is 60 to 80 feet tall with a 2 to 3 foot diameter. Found from New Brunswick west across the Great Lakes, south to Northeast Texas, east to Virginia. Not found on the Gulf Coast and the Atlantic coastal plain.

American Rowan Tree (also known as mountain ash, mountain sumac). A soft, weak wood that weighs 40 to 41 pounds per cubic foot. It is easily split and makes a fair fuel wood. Aromatic with a slightly tart or bitter smell, the mature tree is about 30 feet tall with a 12 inch diameter. Found from Quebec south to Maryland; also in northern California, Washington, Oregon, and British Columbia.

Arborvitae (also known as northern white cedar, cedar). A durable, aromatic, close-grained softwood. Extremely light at 23 pounds per cubic foot. Splits easily, burns quickly. Resinous. The mature tree will reach about 60 feet with a diameter from 1½ to 2 feet. Found from Nova Scotia to Manitoba, south to New England, Minnesota, north and east Wisconsin, northern Illinois, and Ohio.

Basket Oak (also known as swamp chestnut oak). A tough, close-grained hardwood that weighs 61 to 62 pounds per cubic foot. It is an excellent, slow-burning fuel wood. The mature tree is 60 to 80 feet tall with a 2-foot to 3-foot diameter. Found from New Jersey south to central Florida, west to Texas, and north to southern Illinois.

Big Rhododendren (also known as great laurel). A hard, strong but brittle wood weighing 47 to 48 pounds per cubic foot. A good fuel that seldom needs splitting. A mature tree is no more than 35 feet tall with a 1-foot diameter. Found from southern Vermont to Georgia and inland as far as central Ohio.

Black Ash (also known as hoop, basket, swamp, or water ash). A soft, weak, coarse-grained wood weighing 47 to 48 pounds per cubic foot. It is very easy to split. A good fuel. The mature tree is 40 to 60 feet tall with a 1-foot to 2-foot diameter. Found from western Newfoundland to north of the Great Lakes past Minnesota, southeast to the Ohio River Valley, across northern Tennessee to northern Virginia (Fig. 8-1).

Black Cherry (also known as rum or whiskey cherry). A hardwood weighing 42 pounds per cubic foot. It is easily split and it is a good fuel wood. The mature tree is 40 to 60 feet tall with a 1-foot to 3-foot diameter. Mature trees are a lot more valuable for lumber than for firewood. Found from Nova Scotia to the north shore of Lake Superior, south to central Texas, east to central Florida (Fig. 8-2).

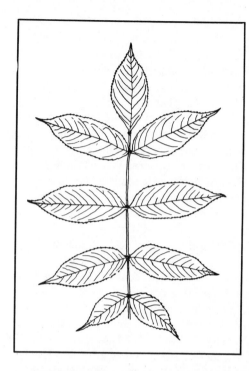

Fig. 8-1. Black ash.

Black Gum (also known as sour gum, tupelo). A medium soft, strong wood weighing 47 to 48 pounds per cubic foot. It is so cross grained that you must rip it with the chain saw; the wood simply won't split! Fair to good fuel. A mature tree is 40 to 80 feet tall with a 1-foot to 3-foot diameter. Found from western Maine across the Michigan peninsula, south to south central Texas; also on the East and Gulf Coast; found in northern Florida.

Black Haw (also known as stagbush, sweet haw). A hard, strong wood weighing 62 to 63 pounds per cubic foot. A fine fuel which seldom needs splitting because the mature tree is only 20 to 30 feet tall with a 6-inch to 1-foot diameter. Found from New York City south to Georgia; found in central Michigan, Missouri, Illinois, and Kansas.

Black Hickory. A midwestern version of the general hickory class. Lighter than other hickories at 54 pounds per cubic foot. Grows to 70 feet tall.

Blackjack Oak (also known as scrub oak). A hard, strong wood weighing 54 to 55 pounds per cubic foot. This wood is an excellent fuel and it is easy to split. The mature tree is small (20 to 30 feet tall), with a trunk 6 inches to 1 foot in diameter.

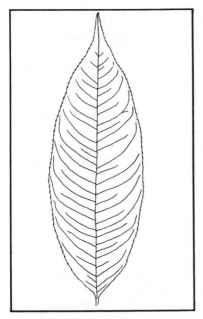

Fig. 8-2. Black cherry.

Black Locust (also known as yellow, white, red, green, or post locust, bastard acacia). A very hard, strong, stiff wood weighing about 58 to 59 pounds per cubic foot. It is easy to split and makes an exceptionally fine fuel wood. The mature tree is 40 to 60 feet tall with a 1-foot to 2-foot diameter. Found in most of the Eastern states. Sometimes into the Western states.

Black Maple. A very tough, strong hardwood weighing 52 to 53 pounds per cubic foot. The mature tree is 60 to 80 feet tall.

Fig. 8-3. Black oak.

169

Black Oak (also known as yellow or tanbark oak). A hard, strong, coarse-grained wood that weighs 51 to 52 pounds per cubic foot. It is easily split and makes an excellent fuel. The mature tree is 50 to 70 feet tall with a 2-foot to 3-foot diameter. Found through most to the Eastern and Central states with the exception of the Atlantic coastal plains and Florida (Fig. 8-3).

Black Walnut. A medium strong, hardwood, that is moderately heavy at 47 pounds per cubic foot. It is easily split and burns well, but retains such value as a lumber tree that few people use it for fuel. Single trees of good size can be worth several thousand dollars for lumber! The mature tree is 60 to 90 feet tall with a 2-foot to 3-foot diameter. Some old specimens may be as tall as 150 feet with a 6-foot diameter. Found from western Massachusetts to the North Carolina coast, through the northern Gulf states into central Texas and Oklahoma. Also found across southern Ontario to southern Minnesota and central Nebraska and Kansas (Fig. 8-4).

Blue Ash. A hard, strong but brittle wood weighing 54 pounds per cubic foot. It is easily split and makes an excellent fuel. The mature tree is 40 to 50 feet tall with a 1-foot to 2-foot diameter. Found from western Pennsylvania to central Illinois, south to Tennessee and northern Mississippi.

Box Elder (also known as sugar ash). A soft, close-grained, weak wood weighing 32 to 33 pounds per cubic foot. It is easily split and makes a fair fuel. The mature tree is about 75 feet tall with a 4-foot diameter. Found from southwest New England to eastern Oregon and Washington. Found in central Florida and Texas.

Broom Hickory (also known as brown or black hickory or pignut). A very strong, tough, heavy wood at 60 to 67 pounds per cubic foot. It makes an excellent fuel wood, it's tough to split. Slow burning. The mature tree is 60 to 80 feet tall with a 1-foot to 2-foot diameter. Found from southern and western New England to southern Michigan, Illinois, and southeastern Iowa, south to Georgia.

Bur Oak (also called the mossycup oak). A hard, tough, close-grained wood which weighs 54 to 56 pounds per cubic foot. It is moderately hard to split, but makes an excellent fuel wood. The mature tree stands from 60 to 80 feet tall with a 2-foot to 3-foot diameter. Found from New England and the Middle Atlantic States on west past Wisconsin and south from Delaware to central Florida.

Butternut (also known as white walnut). A soft, weak wood, that is coarse-grained and light at 30 pounds per cubic foot. Easily split. Burns quickly. The mature tree is 30 to 60 feet tall with a 1-foot to 2-foot diameter. Found from New Brunswick south on the

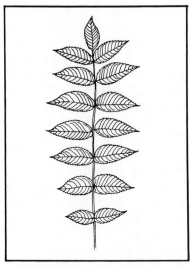

Fig. 8-4. Black walnut.

Atlantic Coast to Delaware and the Virginia mountains (Fig. 8-5).

Canada Plum (also known as horse plum.) A hard, close-grained wood that weighs 51 to 52 pounds per cubic foot. It is easy to split and makes a good to excellent fuel. The mature tree is 25 to 30

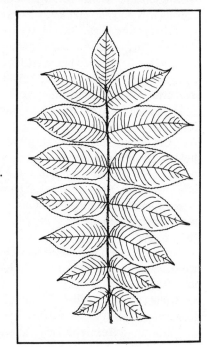

Fig. 8-5. Butternut.

171

feet tall with a diameter of 1 foot or less. Found from western New Brunswick to the north shore of Lake Superior, west to Manitoba. And in New England, central New York, and western Wisconsin.

Cherry Birch (also known as black, sweet, or mahogany birch). A medium hard and medium strong wood. Very similar to yellow birch in characteristics and range. It doesn't extend quite as far west and has a maximum mature height of 55 to 75 feet.

Chinkapin Oak (also known as rock oak, chinquapin). A very strong, close-grained hardwood that weighs 64 pounds per cubic foot. It is moderately hard to split, but it makes an excellent fuel wood. The mature tree stands from 50 to 70 feet tall with a 1-foot to 3-foot diameter. Found from western Vermont south through the District of Columbia to western Virginia, on to western Florida, west through southern Ohio to southeastern Minnesota and Nebraska, west to eastern Kansas and eastern Oklahoma.

Common Juniper (also known as gorst). A close-grained, hard, durable wood, that is medium light at 30 to 32 pounds per cubic foot. Seldom thick enough to split. Fast burning, aromatic (the berry provides gin with its characteristic flavor). Resinous. The tree is small (seldom growing over 24 feet tall). Found from Greenland and Newfoundland to Alaska. Also found in Pennsylvania, South Carolina, Nebraska, and West Texas.

Cork Elm (also known as rock, hickory, or cliff elm). A medium hard, medium strong, tough, close-grained wood that weighs 52 to 53 pounds per cubic foot. It is hard to split but makes a good fuel. The mature tree is 60 to 80 feet tall with a 2-foot to 3-foot diameter. Found from southwest Quebec into western New York and northern New Jersey. Also found in Kentucky, Nebraska, and Iowa.

Cottonwood. Large trees having soft, brittle wood, that is light at 32 to 33 pounds per cubic foot. It is easily split and it burns quickly. Not usually a good fuel, but it can be a fair substitute for other woods during shortages. The mature tree is 150 feet with a 6-foot diameter. Found in most of the Eastern and central states. it is seldom found to the north or south. Usually it is found near water (Fig. 8-6).

Cucumber Tree (also known as cucumber magnolia). A soft, weak, close-grained wood that weighs 34 to 35 pounds per cubic foot. It is easily split and it is a fair fuel wood. The mature tree is 70 to 90 feet tall with a 3-foot to 4-foot diameter. Found from New York to northern Georgia and west to eastern Oklahoma.

Eastern Hemlock (also known as the spruce or hemlock

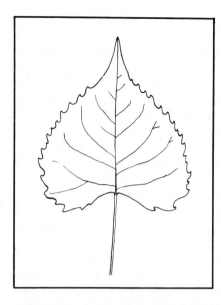

Fig. 8-6. Cottonwood.

pine). A brittle coarse-grained weak wood that is very light at 30 to 31 pounds per cubic foot. Moderately easy to split. Burns quickly and easily. Resinous. The mature tree can reach 60 to 70 feet and 2-feet to 3-feet in diameter. Found in Nova Scotia, Michigan, Pennsylvania, West Virginia, New York, New England, New Jersey, Maryland, eastern Ohio, and eastern Kentucky.

Eastern Ironwood (also known as roughbarked ironwood). An extremely hard, strong, tough wood, that weighs 60 pounds per cubic foot. An excellent, slow-burning fuel wood. Fortunately, it is seldom found in large enough sizes to require splitting. The mature tree is 40 feet tall with an 8-inch to 1-foot diameter. Found over most of the eastern states and the west central states.

Eastern Red Cedar (also known as Virginia juniper). A smooth-grained softwood, that is medium light at 36 pounds per cubic foot. Easily split. It is resinous and fast burning. The mature tree is 30 to 40 feet tall with a 1½-foot to 2-foot diameter. Found from southern Maine to the southern part of the Michigan peninsula and southern Wisconsin, south to the Badlands of South Dakota, south to East Texas.

Eastern White Oak. A very hard, very strong, durable wood that is moderately heavy at about 57 pounds per cubic foot. It splits easily. It makes an excellent slow-burning fuel. The mature tree is 80 to 100 feet tall with a 3-foot to 4-foot diameter. Found from southern Maine west to the southern Michigan peninsula and into southwest Minnesota. Also found in western Florida, the Gulf States, Texas, and eastern Oklahoma.

Flowering Dogwood (also known as Virginia dogwood). A very hard, strong wood weighing about 60 pounds per cubic foot. Usually too small to need splitting. It makes an extremely fine fuel. Dogwood is already being overcut; take only dead or dying trees. A mature tree is about 40 feet tall with a 1-foot diameter. Found from the southern tip of Maine and southern Vermont to southern Ontario, southern Michigan, and northern Illinois. Also found in southeast Missouri, eastern Oklahoma, Texas, the Gulf Coast states, and the East Coast states.

Fringe Tree (also known as flowering ash). A hard, fine-textured wood weighing about 48 pounds per cubic foot. A good fuel. It seldom needs splitting because the mature tree is no more than 40 feet tall with a 1-foot diameter.

Gray Birch (also known as small white birch). A medium soft, weak, close-grained wood of medium weight at 42 pounds per cubic foot. Moderately easy to split. No birch burns very well without being split because the bark is too good an insulator. The mature tree is 20 to 30 feet tall. Found from New England down to Pennsylvania and Delaware into the uplands of Virginia.

Hackberry (also known as sugarberry and nettle ash). A hard, tough, flexible wood that is classified as medium light though no specific weights are available. It is easy to split and should be a good fuel. The mature tree is 50 to 120 feet tall with a 1-foot to 2-foot diameter. Found from New York (it is rarely found in western New England) to Florida, west to Texas, and north to the Black Hills of South Dakota.

Honey Locust (also called sweet, thorn, or black locust and honeyshucks). A very hard, durable wood weighing 52 to 53 pounds per cubic foot weight. The wood is slow-burning and makes a good to excellent fuel. The mature tree is 50 to 75 feet tall with a 2-foot to 3-foot diameter. Found from central New York west to southern Ontario and Michigan, on to southern Wisconsin, south to east central Texas.

Hop Tree (also called wofer ash, quinine tree, swamp dogwood). A hard, close-grained wood weighing 61 to 62 pounds per cubic foot. Seldom grows large enough to need splitting. The mature tree is 20 to 25 feet tall with a 6-inch to 8-inch diameter. An excellent fuel. Found from southern Quebec to Virginia and throughout the central states. Also found in New Mexico, southeast California, Arizona, and West Texas.

Jack Pine (also known as scrub pine or black pine). A thick white sapwood. Soft and very light at about 35 pounds per cubic foot, air-dried. Splits easily, burns quickly. Resinous. Found from Nova Scotia to New Brunswick, north almost to James Bay, northwest to the Yukon, south to northern and eastern Minnesota. Also found in northeast Illinois, northwest Indiana, and throughout Maine. The mature tree stands 60 to 80 feet tall and has a 2-foot diameter.

Kentucky Coffee Tree (also known as coffeenut, stump tree). A medium soft, strong wood weighing 49 to 50 pounds per cubic foot. It is easily split and makes good fuel. The mature tree is 50 to 75 feet tall with a 2-foot to 3-foot diameter. Found scattered in central New York, eastern Pennsylvania, Maryland, Ohio, southeast Minnesota, and Alabama, and Oklahoma.

Loblolly Pine (also called the Indian pine). A weak, coarse-grained wood, weighing 45 to 46 pounds per cubic foot. Splits easily and burns quickly. Resinous. The mature tree will be from 90 to 110 feet high and 2-feet to 3-feet in diameter. Found from east Texas to central Florida, and north on the coastal plains to Cape May, New Jersey.

Mountain Maple (also known as low or water maple). A soft wood weighing 39 to 40 pounds per cubic foot. The mature tree can grow as tall as 35 feet (Fig. 8-7).

Northern Balsam (also known as blister, fir, or silver pine). A soft weak coarse-grained wood. Very light at 31 to 32 pounds per cubic foot. Easily split, and fast burning. Resinous. The mature tree is 40 to 60 feet tall and 1-foot to 1½-feet in diameter. Found from Newfoundland to the Yukon, into northeast British Columbia, south to north Minnesota and Wisconsin, northern Michigan, east to New York and northern New England, south to southern Virginia.

Northern Red Oak (also known as gray oak). A coarse-grained, medium strong wood that weighs 50 pounds per cubic foot.

Fig. 8-7. Mountain maple.

It is moderately easy to split and makes good fuel wood. The mature tree stands 60 to 80 feet tall with a 2-foot to 4-foot diameter. Found from Nova Scotia to Minnesota, south to Georgia. Not found in the coastal plains and the lowlands of Kentucky and Tennessee (Fig. 8-8).

Ohio Buckeye (also know as stinking buckeye). A weak, soft wood weighing 33 to 34 pounds per cubic foot. It is easily split and makes a fair fuel. The mature tree is 30 to 50 feet tall with a 1-foot to 2-foot diameter. Found from Pennsylvania to northern Alabama. Also found in Kansas (Fig. 8-9).

Paper Birch (also known as canoe and white or silver birch). A medium hard, medium strong wood. Tough, close-grained, and of medium weight at 47 pounds per cubic foot. A good fuel only if split. The bark provides a good fire starter. If not split, paper birch will rot before it seasons almost every time. Slow burning, and easy to split. The mature tree is 60 to 70 feet tall with a 2-foot to 3-foot diameter. Found from Newfoundland west to eastern Manitoba, south to northern New Jersey, northern Pennsylvania, and northern Minnesota.

Pecan. A hard, brittle, weak wood, that is heavy at 54 pounds per cubic foot. Difficult to split. It's a good to excellent fuel with a pleasant aroma. The mature tree is 100 feet tall with a 3-foot to 4-foot diameter. Some exceptional versions are 180 feet tall with a 6-foot diameter. Found from Texas to central Oklahoma. Also found in Ohio, southern Indiana, western Kentucky, central Tennessee, and western Alabama.

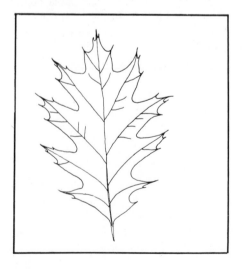

Fig. 8-8. Northern red oak.

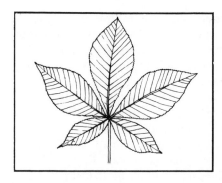

Fig. 8-9. Ohio buckeye.

Persimmon (also known as possumwood, date plum). A very strong, hard wood weighing 62 to 63 pounds per cubic foot. An excellent fuel. The trees are frequently too small to need splitting because the mature persimmon is only 25 to 50 feet tall with a 1-foot diameter. Found from southern Florida north to New Haven, Connecticut, west to central Ohio, Illinois and eastern Oklahoma.

Pin Oak. A hard, strong wood that weighs 51 to 52 pounds per cubic foot. This is an excellent slow-burning fuel wood. The mature tree is 60 to 80 feet tall with a 1-foot to 3-foot diameter. Found over most of the Middle Atlantic States into the central states.

Pin Cherry (also known as fire cherry or red cherry). A soft, close-grained, mildly aromatic wood weighing 37 to 38 pounds per cubic foot. The mature tree is 30 to 40 feet tall with a diameter up to 20 inches. It is easily split and makes a fair to good fuel. Found from Newfoundland south to Pennsylvania, from there on the high Appalachians to North Carolina, northwest to Indiana and into the Black Hills and the eastern slopes of the Rockies.

Pitch Pine (also known as the sap pine). Brittle weak wood of medium weight at 41 to 42 pounds per cubic foot. Splits easily, burns quickly and hotly. Resinous. The mature tree stands 40 to 60 feet tall and has a 1-foot to 2-foot diameter. Found across New Hampshire, Vermont, and low altitudes of New York, west to southeast Ohio, south to Georgia.

Pocosin Pine (also known as the marsh pine or pond pine). A coarse-grained softwood rated as medium heavy at 45 to 46 pounds per cubic foot. Splits easily, burns very quickly. Very resinous. The mature tree can stand as high as 100 feet, though 80 feet is more common, and will be 2 feet to 3 feet in diameter. Found from central and western Florida north to Cape May, New Jersey.

Post Oak (also known as iron or box oak). A hard, durable, close-grained wood which weighs 62 to 63 pounds per cubic foot. It makes an excellent slow-burning fuel. The mature tree is 40 to 50 feet tall with a 1-foot to 2-foot diameter. Found from Cape Cod to Florida. Also found in southern Ohio and West Texas (Fig. 8-10).

Red Ash (also known as river or bastard ash). A hard, strong wood weighing 47 to 48 pounds per cubic foot. It is easily split and makes a good fuel. The mature tree is 30 to 50 feet tall with a 1-foot to 2-foot diameter. Found from Nova Scotia west to Manitoba, south to Wyoming, south to north Georgia and Alabama.

Redbud (also known as Jonas tree). A hard, close-grained wood weighing 46 to 47 pounds per cubic foot. Easily split. A slow-burning fuel wood. The mature tree can be 40 feet tall with a 2½-foot diameter, but it is just as often only a shrub. Found from southern Connecticut and New York, west to southern Ontario, south to the Gulf States.

Red Haw (also known as thorn apple). A hard, close-grained, weak wood. Weighs 60 pound foot. It is an excellent fuel. The mature tree is 30 to 40 feet tall. The trunk is seldom thick enough to force you to split the wood. Found from northern Ohio to northern Missouri and eastern Nebraska, south to central Tennessee.

Red Maple (also known as swamp or scarlet maple). A weak, porous, close-grained, easily split wood weighing 45 to 46 pounds per cubic foot. A good fuel. The mature tree is 70 to 90 feet tall with a 2½-foot to 3½-foot diameter. Found as far south as central Florida and as far north as the Maritime Provinces. Also found in central Texas and central Oklahoma (Fig. 8-11).

Red Pine (also known as Norway or hard pine). Very close-grained, medium softwood or medium weight at 39 to 40 pounds per cubic foot, air-dried. Splits easily, and burns hotly and quickly.

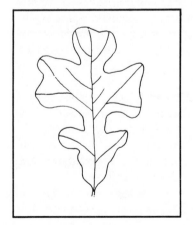

Fig. 8-10. Post oak.

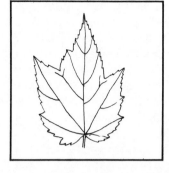

Fig. 8-11. Red maple.

Resinous. The mature tree reaches from 60 to 80 feet with a 2-foot to 3-foot diameter. Found from Newfoundland to southeast Manitoba, to south central Wisconsin, east to Central New York, south through the mountains to West Virginia.

Red Spruce (also known as yellow spruce). A soft, springy wood. Strong and light at 32 to 33 pounds per cubic foot. Splits easily and burns quickly. Resinous. The mature tree is 70 to 80 feet tall and 1½-feet to 2-feet in diameter. Found from Nova Scotia south through Maine, New Hampshire, Vermont, to Cape Ann, Massachusetts into the Berkshires, Catskills, and Adirondacks, south to New Jersey and Pennsylvania, above 3500 feet in Virginia, above 4500 feet in Tennessee and North Carolina.

River Birch (also called red or black birch). A strong, close-grained hardwood, that is moderately heavy at 48 pounds per cubic foot. The wood splits easily and makes a good fuel. Mature trees are 50 to 70 feet tall with 1½-foot to 2-foot diameters.

Sassafras (also known as aquetree). A soft, weak wood. It weighs 38 to 39 pounds per cubic foot. It is easily split and makes a fair fuel wood. The mature tree is 20 to 50 feet tall with a 1-foot to 2-foot diameter. Found from southern Maine west through southern Michigan, south to northern Florida, west to East Texas, north to southeast Iowa.

Scarlet Oak. A hard, close-grained wood that weighs 50 to 51 pounds per cubic foot. Moderately easy to split. It makes a good to excellent fuel wood. The mature tree stands from 60 to 80 feet tall with a 1-foot to 3-foot diameter. Found from southern Maine west through southern New York, west to Indiana.

Shadbush (also known as service tree, juneberry). A strong, close-grained wood that weighs 60 to 61 pounds per cubic foot. Moderately easy to split. It makes an excellent fuel. The mature tree is 25 to 40 feet tall with an 8-inch to 14-inch diameter.

Shagbark Hickory (also known as shellbark hickory). A close-grained, flexible, tough hardwood, that is very heavy at 63 pounds per cubic foot. This excellent, slow-burning fuel wood is very tough to split. The mature tree is 60 to 80 feet tall with a 1-foot to 2-foot diameter. Found from southern Maine to Delaware, on to southern Georgia, west to southeast Texas (except the Gulf Coast), north to southern Michigan and central Wisconsin. Also found in Massachusetts, northern New Hampshire, and northern Vermont (Fig. 8-12).

Silver Maple (also known as soft, white, or swamp maple). A hard, strong, brittle wood weighing 39 to 40 pounds per cubic foot. It is very easily split and makes a fair to good fuel. The mature tree is 60 to 80 feet tall (Fig. 8-13).

Slippery Elm (also known as red elm). A hard, strong, close-grained wood that weighs 51 to 53 pounds per cubic foot. It is hard to split, but it makes good fuel. The mature tree is 40 to 70 feet tall with a 1-foot to 2-foot diameter (Fig. 8-14).

Smoothbarked Ironwood (also known as American hornbeam). A very hard, strong wood, that is heavy at 58 to 59 pounds per cubic foot. The wood burns slowly and is difficult to split. The fuel value is excellent. The mature tree is 20 to 40 feet tall with an 8-inch to 1½-foot diameter. Found over most of the Eastern United States into the west central states.

Sourwood (also known as sour gum, arrowwood). A hard wood weighing 55 to 56 pounds per cubic foot. It is difficult to split, but it is an excellent fuel. A mature tree is 20 to 50 feet tall with an 8-inch to 1-foot diameter. Found from southwestern Pennsylvania

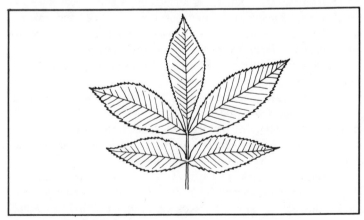

Fig. 8-12. Shagbark hickory.

Fig. 8-15. Sugar maple.

stands 40 to 60 feet high with a 2-foot to 3-foot diameter. Found from southern Missouri south to Florida, west to East Texas, north to southern Illinois.

Swamp White Oak. A medium hard, moderately strong, tough, close-grained wood that weighs about 56 to 57 pounds per cubic foot. It is moderately easy to split and makes a good to excellent slow-burning fuel. The mature tree is 50 to 70 feet tall with a 2-foot to 3-foot diameter. Found from New Hampshire west to southern Wisconsin and south to western Virginia.

Sweet Buckeye (also known as big buckeye). A very soft, weak wood weighing about 30 pounds per cubic foot. It is hard to split and makes a poor fuel. The mature tree is 60 to 90 feet tall with a 2-foot to 3-foot diameter. Found from southwest Pennsylvania, south along the Blue Ridge Mountains to northern Georgia and Alabama, west to northeast Texas and eastern Oklahoma.

Sweet Gum (also known as red gum, gum tree, alligator wood). A straight, hard, close-grained wood that weighs 43 to 45 pounds per cubic foot. It is one of the few resinous woods that doesn't come from a conifer, or softwood tree. It is easily split and is a poor to fair fuel because of the resin. The mature tree is 80 to 120 feet tall with a 2-foot to 4-foot diameter. Found from western Connecticut to central Florida, west to east Texas and north from there to southern Illinois (Fig. 8-16).

Sycamore (also known as buttonwood, planetree, water beech, Virginia maple). A hard, tough wood that weighs about 42 pounds per cubic foot. A good slow-burning fuel wood. The mature tree is 70 to 80 feet tall with a 3-foot to 8-foot diameter. Found from Maine through New York up to central Michigan; found in south central Texas and northern Florida.

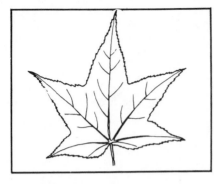

Fig. 8-16. Sweet gum.

Tamarack (also called American black, or red, larch). A close-grained, strong hardwood. Moderately heavy at 45 to 46 pounds per cubic foot. Splits easily and burns quickly. Resinous. The mature tree can reach 60 feet and 1-foot to 2-foot in diameter. Found from Labrador through Newfoundland, Quebec, Ontario, and on to the Yukon, south to Minnesota, Wisconsin, northern Illinois, Indiana, Ohio, and northwestern West Virginia north through New York.

Toothache Tree (also known as prickly ash, wait-a-bit tree, Hercules club). A very soft wood weighing about 42 pounds per cubic foot. It is easily split, but it is almost never found large enough to need splitting. A fair fuel wood. Mature trees are almost never over 20 feet tall. They usually have 6-inch diameter. Found from southern Quebec to Virginia and throughout the central states.

Tulip Tree (also known as tulip, yellow, or white poplar). A soft, tough, flexible weak wood that weighs 33 to 34 pounds per cubic foot. It is easily split and is a fair fuel. The mature tree is 80 to 100 feet tall with a 4-foot to 6-foot diameter. Found from Rhode Island to northern Florida. Also found in southern Michigan.

Water Locust. A very hard, strong wood weighing about 53 pounds per cubic foot. A good to excellent fuel. A slow-burning wood with good heat. The mature tree is 50 to 60 feet tall with a 2-foot to 3-foot diameter. Found in most of the Southern states and southern Indiana.

White Ash (also known as American or cane ash). A strong, tough, pliant wood weighing 48 to 49 pounds per cubic foot. A good fuel wood. The mature tree is 50 to 80 feet tall with a 2-foot to 3-foot diameter. Found from Nova Scotia, south to northern Florida, west to Minnesota, south to eastern Oklahoma (Fig. 8-17).

White Basswood (also known as white linden, bee tree). A soft, weak, brittle wood weighing 30 to 31 pounds per cubic foot.

The mature tree is 60 to 80 feet tall with a 2-foot to 3-foot diameter. A poor fuel. Found from West Virginia south to Florida, west to the Ohio River.

White Elm (also known as American, river, water or soft elm). A soft, weak wood that weighs about 42 pounds per cubic foot. It is coarse-grained and exceptionally hard to split. It makes a good fuel, burning fairly slowly. A mature tree is 75 to 100 feet tall with a 3-foot to 6-foot diameter. Found from northern Maine to central Florida, on west to central Texas, western Nebraska, and into the Dakotas. *Note*: Dutch elm disease continues to ravage this species. The disease causes "shotgun" holes and rust colored growth in the trees' crotches. Elm bark beetles, the carriers of Dutch elm disease, may also be present. Check with local forestry officials, though, for guidance because other diseases can cause similar symptoms. The forestry officials will also be able to tell you the best way to season and store affected white elms so the disease doesn't spread.

White Pine (also called soft pine). A soft, close-grained wood. Very light at about 30 pounds per cubic foot, air-dried. Splits easily and burns quickly. Resinous. The mature tree is from 90 to 180 feet

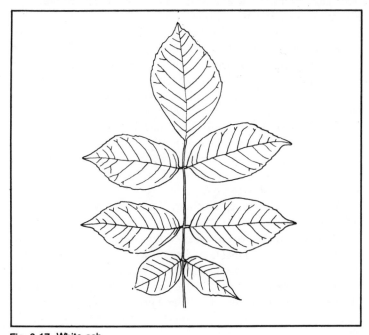

Fig. 8-17. White ash.

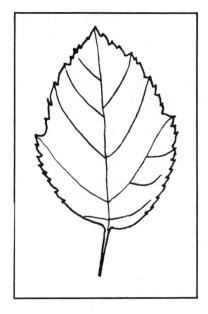

Fig. 8-18. Wild sweet crab apple.

tall and 2½ to 5 feet in diameter. Found from Newfoundland to Manitoba, south to Iowa, east through northern Illinois and Pennsylvania, south to Georgia.

White Spruce (also called cat spruce). A straight-grained softwood. Very light at 30 pounds per cubic foot. Splits easily and burns rapidly. Resinous. The mature tree is 60 to 70 feet tall and 1½ to 2 feet in diameter. Found from Newfoundland to Alaska, south to Montana. Also found in Wisconsin, northern Michigan, northern New York, Vermont, New Hampshire, and Maine.

Wild Sweet Crab Apple (also known as American or fragrant crab apple). A medium hard, weak, heavy wood that weighs 52 to 53 pounds per cubic foot. Not hard to split. This is a fine, aromatic fuel wood. Mature trees are small (from 15 to 30 feet tall and 6-inches to 1 foot in diameter. Found from western New York to Missouri. Also found in Pennsylvania and northern Delaware, and in the Appalachians to North Carolina (Fig. 8-18).

Witch Hazel (also known as winterbloom or snapping hazel). A medium heavy wood that is seldom thick enough to need splitting. A good fuel. It has very aromatic wood (many barbers still use witch hazel if you'd like a sample of the aroma). Witch hazel can make an interesting addition to your fireplace. Spreads south from Canada's Maritime Provinces down to northern Florida, then west to northern Alabama.

Yellow Birch (also known as bitter, silver, or gray birch). A medium hard, moderately strong wood, that weighs 51 to 52 pounds per cubic foot. This is a good to excellent fuel if split. It has a very tight bark, that makes splitting essential to keep the wood from rotting before it seasons. The mature tree is 60 to 80 feet tall with a 1-foot to 3-foot diameter. Found from Newfoundland to northern Maryland, south to North Carolina in the highlands, and west to the Great Lakes (Fig. 8-19).

WESTERN TREES

Alpine Fir (also known as balsam or white fir). A weak, soft wood weighing 26 to 27 pounds per cubic foot. It is easily split. Resinous. Poor fuel wood. The mature tree is 60 to 100 feet tall with a 1½-foot to 2-foot diameter. Found from coast ranges of southeastern Alaska (up to 3000 feet) along the coast ranges of British Columbia into Alberta, south through the Rockies into Idaho, Montana, Wyoming, Colorado, Utah, Nevada, Arizona, and New Mexico. Also in the mountains of Washington, Oregon, and California's Trinity range.

Arizona Cypress (also known as roughwood Arizona cypress). A soft wood weighing about 36 pounds per cubic foot. Resinous. Easily split. Slightly aromatic. A fair fuel. The mature tree is 50 to 60 feet tall with a 1-foot to 3-foot diameter. Found from southern Arizona to Brewster City, Texas.

Balsam Poplar (also known as roughbarked poplar). A soft, weak wood weighing 26 to 27 pounds per cubic foot. Easily split. A

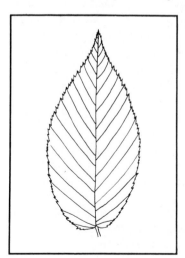

Fig. 8-19. Yellow birch.

poor fuel wood. The mature tree is 60 to 80 feet tall with a 1-foot to 3-foot diameter. Found in Alaska, Canada, Idaho, Colorado, Nebraska, Minnesota, and northern Nevada.

Bigleaf Maple (also known as Oregon or white maple). A close-grained, weak, soft wood weighing about 36 pounds per cubic foot. Easily split. A fair fuel. The mature tree is 80 to 100 feet tall with a 2-foot to 3-foot diameter. Found from British Columbia through Washington and Oregon to California.

Bitter Cherry. A soft, brittle, mildly aromatic wood weighing about 33 pounds per cubic foot. Splits easily and is a fair fuel. The mature tree is 25 to 30 feet tall with a 20-inch diameter. Found in southern British Columbia, Washington, Oregon, southern California, western Idaho, Nevada, northwestern Montana, Arizona, and New Mexico.

Black Cottonwood (also known as balm cottonwood). A soft, weak wood weighing about 29 pounds per cubic foot. Easily split. A poor fuel. The mature tree is 80 to 125 feet tall with a 3-foot to 5-foot diameter. Found from the southeast Alaskan coast south through British Columbia to Washington, western Oregon, California, northern and western Idaho, northwest Montana, and Nevada (around Tahoe).

Black Spruce (also known as bog spruce, swamp spruce, or double spruce). A soft, close-grained, weak wood weighing 39 to 40 pounds per cubic foot. Resinous. It is easily split and makes a fair fuel. The mature tree is 40 to 80 feet tall with an 8-inch to 3-foot diameter. Found from Alaska south to northern Minnesota.

Blueberry Elder (also known as blue elderberry). A soft, weak, coarse-grained wood weighing 37 to 38 pounds per cubic foot. A fair fuel. Easily split. A mature tree is 30 to 50 feet tall with a 12-inch to 18-inch diameter. Found from southern British Columbia through the Rockies of Montana, Idaho, Utah, Arizona, and southwestern New Mexico; found along the coasts of Washington, Oregon, and California.

Blue Oak (also known as western white, California rock, iron oak, jack oak, post oak, or Douglas oak). A strong, brittle wood weighing 66 to 67 pounds per cubic foot. Easily split. An excellent slow-burning fuel. It is limited to the foothills of the California Coast Ranges, the western slope of the Sierra Nevadas, and north slope of the San Gabriels.

Blue Spruce (also known as white, silver, or parry spruce). A knotty, brittle, soft, weak wood weighing 28 to 29 pounds per cubic foot. Resinous. A poor fuel. Splits with ease, but very irregularly because of the knots. The mature tree is 80 to 100 feet tall with a 1-foot to 2-foot diameter. Found from the mountains of western Montana and central Idaho through the mountains of Colorado and New Mexico (at 8000 to 11,000 feet) into some ranges of Utah and Arizona (at 7000 to 11,000 feet).

Brown Birch (also known as red birch, water birch). A soft, brittle, strong wood weighing 45 to 46 pounds per cubic foot. Easily split. A good fuel. The mature tree is 20 to 25 feet tall with a 12-inch to 14-inch diameter. Found from southern British Columbia to northeastern Washington, northern Idaho, and northwestern Montana.

Bur Oak (also known as mossycup oak). A hard, tough, close-grained wood weighing about 54 pounds per cubic foot. Excellent fuel. The mature tree is 60 to 80 feet tall with a 2-foot to 3-foot diameter. Found from Manitoba and the Black Hills of South Dakota south to central Texas.

California Buckeye (also known as horse chestnut). A very close-grained, soft wood weighing about 37 pounds per cubic foot. Easily split. A fair fuel. The mature tree is 20 to 40 feet tall with a 10-inch to 16-inch diameter. Found in the foothills and valleys of the California coast ranges (up to 5000 feet).

Canoe Cedar (also known as giant or western red cedar, shinglewood, arborvitae). A coarse-grained, soft wood weighing about 28 pounds per cubic foot. Easily split. A poor to fair fuel. Slightly resinous. The mature tree is 150 to 200 feet tall with a 4-foot to 8-foot diameter. Found from Alaska south on the sea slopes through British Columbia. Also found in Washington's Olympics (to 4000 feet), Oregon, Idaho, and Montana.

Cascara Buckthorn (also known as bearwood, bayberry, shittimwood, bitterbark, coffeeberry). A soft, weak wood weighing about 44 pounds per cubic foot. Easily split. A good fuel wood. The mature tree is 20 to 40 feet tall with a 6-inch to 20-inch diameter. Found from southern British Columbia through Washington, Oregon, and the California coast.

Chittamwood (also known as gum elastic, woolly buckthorn). A soft, weak, close-grained wood weighing about 49 pounds per cubic foot. Easily split. A good fuel. The mature tree is 30 to 40 feet tall with a 1-foot to 2-foot diameter. Found from the mountains of southeastern Arizona and southern New Mexico to West Texas.

Coast Madrano (also known as Pacific madrano, strawberry tree, madrana). A hard, strong, close-grained wood weighing about 53 pounds per cubic foot. Moderately easy to split. A good to excellent fuel. A mature tree is 20 to 100 feet tall with a 1-foot to 4-foot diameter. Found from British Columbia, on the coast, south along the coast and mountains (under 3000 feet) almost to Baja.

Coast Redwood A soft, weak, close-grained wood weighing about 30 pounds per cubic foot. It is easily split, but makes a poor fuel. Use only dead or dying trees. Coast redwoods are scarce. The mature tree is 200 to 275 feet tall and has an 8-foot to 12-foot diameter. Found along the fog belt of the California coast, 1 to 30 miles inland.

Curl Leaf Mountain Mahogany (also known as desert mountain mahogany). A very hard, close-grained, brittle wood weighing 80 to 81 pounds per cubic foot. Easily split. This slow-burning wood produces almost no ash and is an exceptionally fine fuel. The mature tree is about 40 feet tall with a 2½-foot diameter. Found from southeastern Washington and Oregon to the northern Coast Ranges of California. Also found in the Rockies from Idaho and southwestern Montana through Utah, Nevada, the Grand Canyon of Arizona, and in the Big Horns of Wyoming.

Desert Catalpa (also known as desert or bow willow). A soft, weak, close-grained wood weighing about 44 pounds per cubic foot. Good fuel. The mature tree is 20 to 30 feet tall with an 8-inch to 1-foot diameter. Found in southern California, southern Arizona, southern Nevada, southwestern Utah, and the valley of the Rio Grande in Texas.

Desert Ironwood (also known as tesota). A member of the pea family, but it has a wood that is among the hardest found anywhere in the world. Once used as arrowheads by desert Indians. It is strong and weighs 79 to 80 pounds per cubic foot. An excellent fuel. Extremely difficult to cut. A mature bush or tree is 15 to 30 feet tall with an 8-inch to 16-inch diameter. Found in southwestern Arizona and the low deserts to southeastern California. Also found in the valley of the Colorado River.

Desert Smoketree. A coarse-grained, soft wood weighing about 41 pounds per cubic foot. A fair fuel. Found in the low deserts of the West. A shrub or tree that seldom is found over 20 feet tall.

Douglas Fir (also known as Douglas, yellow, or red spruce, Oregon pine). A soft, weak wood weighing 38 to 39 pounds per cubic foot. Easily split. It is resinous and makes a fair fuel. The mature tree is 130 to 300 feet tall with widely varying trunk thicknesses. Found from the Skeena River, British Columbia (from sea level to 7200 feet) south on the Sierra Nevadas to the Santa Lucia Mountains. Also found in Wyoming, Idaho, Utah, Colorado, Arizona, New

Mexico, and the Black Hills.

Dwarf Maple (also known as Rocky Mountain, soft, or bark maple). A close-grained hard wood weighing about 45 pounds per cubic foot. Easily split. It is a good fuel. The mature tree is 20 to 30 feet tall with a 6-inch to 1-foot diameter. Found from the southeastern coast of Alaska through the British Columbia mountains and the Rockies to southwestern New Mexico and southern Arizona. Also found in the Black Hills of South Dakota.

Elephant Tree (also known as elephant bursera). A hard wood. It grows to a maximum of 20 feet in the United States. This tree is found in deserts in Arizona and the Imperial Valley of California. It has three bark layers and has a spicy aroma. Resinous. It is rare and should never be cut while alive.

Engelmann Spruce (also known as mountain spruce). A soft, straight-fibered wood weighing about 26 pounds per cubic foot. It is easily split, but it makes a poor fuel. The mature tree is 60 to 120 feet tall with a 1½-foot to 3-foot diameter. Found in the Canadian Rockies from 1500 to 5000 feet through the southern Rockies at 10,000 to 12,000 feet. Common in the Cascades.

Fire Cherry (also known as bird, pin, pigeon, or wild red cherry). A soft, close-grained, aromatic wood weighing about 37 pounds per cubic foot. A fair to good fuel that splits easily. The mature tree is 30 to 40 feet tall with an 18-inch to 20-inch diameter. Found from eastern British Columbia east to Newfoundland, south to Georgia, west to Iowa, northwestern Nebraska, and the Colorado mountains.

Gambel Oak (also known as scrub, shin, or Utah oak). A hard, close-grained wood weighing about 63 pounds per cubic foot. A really fine fuel. A mature tree is 25 to 35 feet tall with a 1-foot diameter. Very common. Found from southeastern Wyoming through Utah, western Colorado, Nevada, Texas, and Arizona.

Grand Fir (also known as lowland fir, stinking fir). A soft, fairly strong, straight-grained wood weighing 26 to 27 pounds per cubic foot. Easily split. Resinous. A poor fuel wood. The mature tree is 140 to 160 feet tall with a 2-foot to 4-foot diameter. Found from mainland British Columbia west to the Rockies of Montana and Idaho, south to Oregon and Sonoma, California.

Incense Cedar (also known as white cedar, bastard cedar, or California post cedar). A weak, soft, close-grained wood weighing about 30 pounds per cubic foot. It is easily split. Resinous. A poor but fragrant fuel. The mature tree is 80 to 120 feet tall with a 3-foot to 4-foot diameter. Found from the Cascades of Oregon south through the Sierra Nevadas and coast ranges of California into Baja California. Also found in Washoe County, Nevada.

Macnab Cypress. A soft, close-grained wood weighing 40 to 41 pounds per cubic foot. Easily split. A fair fuel. Resinous. Slightly aromatic. The mature tree is about 30 feet tall with a 12-inch to 18-inch diameter. Found in the Sierra Nevadas and north central California.

Mountain Alder (also known as thinleaf alder). Similar to the Oregon alder, but it is much smaller (ranging from shrub size to a 35 foot tree). Found from south Yukon through the Rockies of British Columbia and Alberta to Colorado, Utah, northern Arizona, and New Mexico.

Mountain Hemlock (also known as black hemlock, hemlock spruce). A weak, soft, fine-grained wood that weighs from 33 to 34 pounds per cubic foot. Easily split. Resinous. A poor fuel. The mature tree is 75 to 100 feet tall with a 2½-foot to 3½-foot diameter. Found from southeast Alaska south through the coast ranges of British Columbia into the Olympics and Cascades of Washington. Also found in Montana, Idaho, and Oregon.

Narrowleaf Cottonwood (also known as black, bitter, or yellow cottonwood, narrowleaf poplar). A soft, brittle wood weighing about 29 pounds per cubic foot. Easily split. A poor fuel. Found on stream banks (at 5000 to 10,000 feet) from southwestern Alberta south in the Rockies to western Texas and central Arizona. Also found on the high plains of western Nebraska and the mountains of eastern and central Nevada.

Netleaf Hackberry (also known as western hackberry). A soft, weak wood that is seldom thick enough to need splitting. The mature tree is about 30 feet tall with a 12-inch diameter. A good fuel. Found from northeast and south central Arizona east through New Mexico, and Texas panhandle, and the Ozarks of Oklahoma.

New Mexican Locust. A very hard, strong wood weighing about 60 pounds per cubic foot. An excellent fuel. A mature tree or bush is 15 to 25 feet tall with an 8-inch to 1-foot diameter. Found in southern Nevada, southeast Utah, Arizona, southern Colorado, New Mexico and West Texas.

Noble Fir (also known as red fir, larch). A hard, strong wood weighing about 34 pounds per cubic foot. Easily split. Resinous. A poor to fair fuel wood. The mature tree is 150 to 200 feet tall with a 4-foot to 6-foot diameter. Found from the mountains of western Washington and Oregon, south on the coast ranges, and in the Cascades to Crater Lake.

Oregon Alder (also known as red alder). A soft, weak, brittle, close-grained wood weighing 36 pounds per cubic foot. Easily split. Fair to good fuel. The mature tree is 80 to 100 feet tall with a 1-foot to 3-foot diameter. Found from Yakut Bay, Alaska south to the coast ranges of British Columbia. Also found throughout western Washington, Oregon, and the coast of northern California.

Oregon Ash (also known as water or black ash). A hard, brittle, coarse-grained wood weighing 42 to 43 pounds per cubic foot. Easily split. A good fuel. The mature tree is 60 to 80 feet tall with a 2-foot to 3-foot diameter. Found along the coasts of southern British Columbia, Washington, Oregon, and California to the Baja border.

Oregon Crab Apple A hard, close-grained, aromatic wood weighing about 61 pounds per cubic foot. Moderately hard to split. It is a fine fuel wood. The mature tree is 30 to 40 feet tall with a 1-foot to 2-foot diameter. Found from the Aleutions south to western Washington, Oregon, and the northern Coast Ranges of California.

Oregon White Oak (also known as western white, Pacific post oak). A very tough, close-grained, hard wood weighing 55 to 56 pounds per cubic foot. An excellent fuel. The mature tree is 50 to 70 feet tall with a 2-foot to 3-foot diameter. Found in Washington below 3000 feet, on the Olympic Peninsula, in Oregon, on the Colorado River and the Williamette, and on the California coast ranges.

Osage Orange (also known as bois d'Arc, bowwood, yellowwood, hedge apple). An extremely hard, tough, flexible, coarse-grained wood weighing 57 to 58 pounds per cubic foot. It makes an excellent fuel. Moderately easy to split. The mature tree or bush is 20 to 30 feet tall with a 1-foot to 2-foot diameter. Cedar-like aroma. Found in southeastern Oklahoma, southwestern Arkansas, northwestern Louisiana, Texas, and most of the East and South.

Pacific Dogwood (also known as California dogwood or flowering dogwood). A very hard, strong, close-grained wood weighing about 56 pounds per cubic foot. An excellent fuel. A mature tree is 20 to 40 feet tall with a 1-foot diameter. Found along the coasts of British Columbia, Washington, Oregon, and northern California.

Pacific Mountain Ash (also known as Sitka mountain ash). A soft, weak wood weighing about 41 pounds per cubic foot. Easily split. It's a fair to good fuel. The mature tree is about 30 feet tall with a 1-foot diameter. Found from the southwest coast of Alaska to western Montana, Idaho, Washington, Oregon, and northwest California. Also found in southeastern Oklahoma, southwestern Arkansas, northwestern Louisiana, Texas, and most of the East and South.

Pacific Plum (also known as western wild, hog, or Sierra plum). A hard, close-grained, mildly aromatic wood weighing about 48 pounds per cubic foot. A good fuel. The mature tree is 10 to 20 feet tall with a 10-inch diameter. Found from central Oregon south to northeastern California.

Port Orford Cedar (also known as Oregon cedar or ginger pine). A strong, hard wood weighing 34 to 35 pounds per cubic foot. Easily split. Resinous and highly aromatic. A fair fuel. The mature tree is 140 to 180 feet tall with a 4-foot to 6-foot diameter. Found from Coos Bay, Oregon south to the Klamath River in California.

Retama (also known as paloverde, Jerusalem thorn). A close-grained, hardwood weighing 45 pounds per cubic foot. A good fuel. The mature bush or tree is 15 to 30 feet tall with a 10-inch diameter. Found in the southwestern Arizona deserts, Rio Grande valley of Texas, and California.

Silver Fir (also known as white fir, red fir, or lovely fir). A soft, weak wood weighing 32 to 33 pounds per cubic foot. Easily split. Resinous. Poor fuel. The mature tree is 140 to 160 feet tall with a 2-foot to 4-foot diameter. Found in southeast Alaska, on the coast ranges of British Columbia, on the Olympic Peninsula, in Washington, and on the Cascades in Washington and Oregon.

Sitka Spruce (also known as tideland spruce or Menzies spruce). A weak, soft, straight-grained wood weighing 31 to 32 pounds per cubic foot. Resinous. Easily split. Poor fuel. The mature tree is 180 to 200 feet tall with a 3-foot to 4½-foot diameter. Found on the Alaskan coast ranges to the islands of British Columbia (from sea level to 4000 feet). Also found at the foot of the Washington mountains and at the mouths and bottomlands of rivers south to Mendocino, California.

Sugar Pine (also known as big sugar pine). A soft, weak wood weighing 26 to 30 pounds per cubic foot. It is easily split, but it is a relatively poor fuel. Resinous. The mature tree is 175 to 200 feet tall with a 3-foot to 5-foot diameter. Found up to 2000 feet in the central Cascade Mountains, Oregon, most California ranges, and Baja California.

Tan Oak (also known as chestnut oak, peach oak, bur oak, or tanbark oak). A hard, strong, brittle, close-grained wood weighing about 51 pounds per cubic foot. A good to excellent fuel. The mature tree is 70 to 90 feet tall with a 2-foot to 3-foot diameter. Found from the southern coast ranges of Oregon south to the Sierra Nevadas.

Trembling Aspen (also known as quaking aspen). A soft, weak, brittle wood weighing about 30 pounds per cubic foot. Easily split. It is a poor to fair fuel. The mature tree is 50 to 60 feet tall with a 1-foot to 2-foot diameter. Found over most of the West. Not found in southern California. Prefers modest elevations of 2000 to 10,000 feet.

True Mesquite (also known as western honey locust, Texas ironwood). A hard, close-grained, weak wood weighing 57 pounds per cubic foot. Aromatic. An excellent fuel (especially the underground stems). The mature tree or bush is 15 to 20 feet tall with a 6-inch to 8-inch diameter. Found over all of the southwest.

Utah Juniper (also known as desert cedar). A soft, brittle wood weighing 41 pounds per cubic foot. A fair fuel. Aromatic. Resinous. Seldom large enough to need splitting. More of a shrub than a tree. Found from southeastern Idaho mountains and southwestern Wyoming into Nevada, Utah, and northern Arizona.

Valley Oak (also known as white oak, California oak, weeping oak, or noble oak). A fine-grained, hard, brittle wood weighing about 55 pounds per cubic foot. Easily split. It is an excellent fuel. The mature tree is 60 to 80 feet tall with a 3-foot to 5-foot diameter. Found in the valleys of western and central California.

Velvet Ash (also known as Arizona, standby ash, or leather-leaf ash). A soft, weak wood weighing about 50 pounds per cubic foot. Easily split. A good fuel. The mature tree is 20 to 50 feet tall with a 1-foot diameter. Found up to 6000 feet from southwestern Utah to southern Nevada to southeastern Arizona and southern New Mexico.

Vine Maple (also known as mountain maple). A hard, tough wood weighing 49 to 51 pounds per cubic foot. Easily split. Excellent fuel. Maximum tree size is 35 feet tall with an 8-inch to 12-inch diameter. Found from the British Columbia coast south through western Washington and Oregon to northern California.

Western Chinquapin (also known as golden chinkapin, goldenleaf chestnut). A fairly hard, strong wood weighing about 41 pounds per cubic foot. Easy to split. A good fuel wood. The mature tree is 60 to 80 feet tall with a 1-foot to 2-foot diameter. Found from Washington's Olympic Peninsula south on the Cascades of Oregon. Also found from the Trinitys of northern California (up to 10,000 feet) down to the Kern River.

Western Hemlock (also known as Alaska pine). A hard, tough wood weighing 38 to 39 pounds per cubic foot. Resinous. It is easily split. A fair fuel. The mature tree is 125 to 175 feet tall with a 2-foot to 4-foot diameter. Found from the coast ranges of Alaska (up to 2700 feet) through the coast ranges of British Columbia into

Washington, western Oregon, and the California fog belt on the north coast.

Western Larch (also known as western tamarack). A hard, strong, coarse-grained wood weighing 55 pounds per cubic foot. A fair to good fuel. It is easily split, but it is also resinous. The mature tree is 140 to 180 feet tall with a 3-foot to 4-foot diameter. Found in the mountains of southeast British Columbia through the Cascades, the Blue Mountains and Wallowas of northern Oregon, and the Bitterroots of Montana and Idaho.

Western Mulberry. A hard, close-grained wood weighing 57 to 58 pounds per cubic foot. A good to excellent fuel that is hard to split. The mature tree or bush is 20 to 40 feet tall with an 8-inch to 15-inch diameter. Found from central Texas west through southern New Mexico and southeastern Arizona into the canyons of northern Arizona.

Western Soapberry (also known as wild chinatree). A hard, strong wood weighing 62 to 65 pounds per cubic foot. Easily split. An excellent fuel. The mature tree is 40 to 50 feet tall with a 1½-foot to 2-foot diameter. Found from southwestern Missouri to southern Colorado and central Arizona.

Western Sugar Maple (also known as bigtooth or hard maple). A hard, close-grained wood that weighs 55 pounds per cubic foot. An excellent fuel. Easily split. The mature tree is 30 to 40 feet tall with an 8-inch to 10-inch diameter. Found in northeastern Montana, western Utah, southeastern Idaho, southwestern Wyoming, southern Colorado, West Texas and Arizona.

Western Sycamore (also known as buttonwood, planetree). A fairly hard, cross-grained wood weighing about 36 pounds per cubic foot. A fair to good fuel. The mature tree is 40 to 50 feet tall with a 1½-foot to 2½-foot diameter. Found from the valleys of California through central Arizona to southern New Mexico.

Whitebark Pine (also known as pitch or scrub pine). A soft, brittle, weak wood weighing about 31 pounds per cubic foot. Easily split, Resinous. Poor to fair fuel. The mature tree is 25 to 50 feet tall with a 1-foot to 2-foot diameter. Found at 3000 to 11,500 ft in British Columbia, western Alberta, California, western Wyoming, northern Utah, Washington, and Oregon.

White Fir (also known as balsam, silver fir, white balsam). A soft, weak, coarse-grained wood weighing 27 to 28 pounds per cubic foot. Easily split. Resinous. A poor fuel. The mature tree is 120 to 150 feet tall with a 3-foot to 4-foot diameter. Found from the Cascade and Siskiyou Mountains of Oregon south to the high coast ranges of northern California. Also found throughout the Sierra Nevadas, eastern Oregon, Idaho, Washington, Utah, Colorado, Arizona, and New Mexico.

White Pine (also known as silver, soft, mountain, Idaho, or little sugar pine). A soft, weak wood weighing 29 to 36 pounds per cubic foot. It is easily split. Resinous. A poor to fair fuel. Found from southern British Columbia, south to northern Idaho and Montana. Also from 4500 to 8500 feet in the northern Coast Range of California, and in southern California in the San Jacintos and the San Gabriels above 8600 feet.

White Spruce (also known as skunk, cat, or single spruce). A soft, weak, straight-grained wood weighing about 30 pounds per cubic foot. It is easily split, but it is a poor to fair fuel because of its resin content. The mature tree is 60 to 70 feet tall with a 1½-foot to 2-foot diameter. Found from the Yukon Valley of Alaska and the Rockies of Alberta south to Montana, Minnesota, Michigan, New York, Vermont, and the Black Hills.

Wild Red Plum (also known as American plum). A hard, strong, easily split wood weighing 46 to 48 pounds per cubic foot. Mildly aromatic. A good fuel. The mature tree is 25 to 30 feet tall with a 12-inch diameter. Found in eastern Montana and Wyoming to New Mexico, eastern Oklahoma, Texas, and the Gulf. Also found east to the Atlantic Coast, except northern New England and southern Florida.

Willows. May be as tall as 70 feet, but they are often shrubs. When tree size is reached, the wood is soft and light (usually under 40 pounds per cubic foot). As a fuel they rate fair. They are found in most of the West.

Yellow Oak (also known as chestnut oak). A very hard, very strong, close-grained wood weighing 64 pounds per cubic foot. Easily split. An excellent fuel. The mature tree is 50 to 70 feet tall with a 1-foot to 3-foot diameter. Found from the mountains of West Texas west to the mountains of southeastern New Mexico.

Yellow Pine (also known as ponderosa pine). A hard, strong, coarse-textured wood weighing 35 to 36 pounds per cubic foot weight. It is easily split and makes a fair fuel. Resinous. The mature tree is 150 to 180 feet tall with a 3-foot to 4-foot diameter. Found in all the Western states from near sea level to about 10,000 feet.

Chapter 9

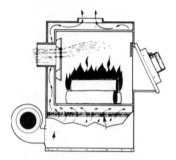

Obtaining Wood

Locating wood to burn in your fireplace can be a big problem if you've never found yourself involved in that sort of activity before. Driving around the East, you see acre after acre of unused woodlands. And acre after acre of *No Trespassing* signs. The story is the same over a major portion of the United States. Land is posted, fenced, or it is government or corporate forestland.

WHERE TO LOOK

The most fortunate among us own a few acres of woods. One quick trip onto our own property each year keeps the woodshed filled. Those of us who are less fortunate will need to search out places to cut wood. After the search is over, you must also make sure there's some sort of vehicle access to the cut wood. There's nothing quite like felling and bucking three or four cords of wood only to find that no way exists, beyond a mare and a backpack, to get the stuff back to the home fires.

In much of the country, particularly in the Northeast, woodland is in poor shape because it has received no care over the years. In many cases, no easy access is to be found. Fortunately, the terrain will often allow ample access with a four-wheel-drive vehicle. Often a regular two wheel drive pickup or van can be made to serve if you remember to take along a hoist of some sort for the bad spots.

Posted land is not all that hard to get onto if you can prove to the owner that you've got a sense of responsibility. Unless the owner is a hermit, he'll probably be glad to have you clear off dead timber each year. If he wished a more productive forest, you might also be able to get permission to thin out the trees that are over-crowding other growth.

Explain your purpose to the owner. Then invite him to watch you work the first day or two. Ask that an inspection by the owner or someone he trusts be made at the end of every two or three days of cutting. If there are changes suggested by the owner or his rep-resentative, make sure you follow up as quickly as possible.

Locating the owner of a piece of woodland is easy enough when the signs posting the land give a name or address. Just call or write explaining what you want to do. Generally, a phone call is harder to ignore. If no name or address is posted, try the nearest occupied house. You can often locate an owner right there, or find out the name of the owner if he lives elsewhere. With the name, you can then check the county clerk's office for an address. This is some-times where difficulties start to arise. Although an individual who owns land will make sure address changes reach the county clerk—for tax billing if for no other reason—corporate owners are a bit harder to deal with because of the bureaucratic structures in many businesses today. No one knows who handles what. Perserverance will often be needed to track down the person who can actually give you permission to cut wood on land owned by a corporation.

Lumber mills and sawmills offer sure sources of many types of firewood. Logs must be slabbed and trimmed before lumber is finished and ready for use in construction. Those waste slabs make fine, dry firewood. You might have to pay a few dollars per truck load now, but just as often the company will be happy to let you cart the scrap slabs and mill ends. Some mills will even provide a few hands to help; they are eager to clear out what to them is only junk wood. However, this state of affairs can't last forever because more and more people are using wood for heating. Scrap wood is getting more valuable.

In suburban and some urban areas, a check with the power company and phone company can often locate a crew that's in the process of taking down a tree or two. Usually they'll be glad to let you haul away the tree. I've never heard of one of these outfits that does other than dump this wood. Town, county, and state road repair crews often have the same type of work to do. A phone call or two might be a help. Some newspapers list street and road repairs (sometimes even detailing the type of repair). Road widening or straightening in most areas almost assures you of free wood at the end of a successful scavenger hunt.

Because not too many people are now alert to these possibilities, dumps and landfill areas are a prime source of firewood in much of the country. The wood is dumped and buried, taking up space. If you can get there before the burial, the wood will be yours. Some dump operators ask that you pay for the wood. You should avoid such payment if at all possible. You're really doing the operator a favor by keeping his dump from filling more rapidly than it would have otherwise. Unless you've got no other source of wood, refuse to part with a cent for the privilege of picking up what they've got available. According to the Department of Agriculture, as much as 30 percent of the fill in dumps is dead and discarded trees. Keep an eye open and you might be able to provide for a lot of your firewood needs without even stepping foot in the woods.

There are many state and national forests in this country. These forests need attention in the same manner as do private woodlands. Thus there is often a fair amount of fallen timber to be logged and hauled out. Permits can be had, for a nominal fee, to cut downed timber in many national forests. Most states offer once or twice yearly permission for the same type of cutting. In most cases, downed timber is all you'll be allowed to cut, but some trees might be marked for cutting by the foresters. Never take down a tree that hasn't been so marked. The fines could wipe out several year's fuel savings.

For national forest woodcutting information, contact your local forest service district ranger. For state information, you can start with your local county extension agent and move on as he advises.

BUYING WOOD

Buying firewood is a lot easier than cutting your own. But firewood is difficult to measure and difficult to qualify. So *caveat emptor* is the name of the game. Firewood is sold in one of two ways: by weight or by the cord. Neither way is truly reliable, but the worst way to buy firewood is by weight. Unless you get a chance to check the firewood for dryness, you're almost certain to be badly taken when you buy by weight.

A full cord of hard or sugar maple, air dried, will weigh no less than 4200 pounds and possibly as much as 4700 pounds. That's allowing for a reasonable 80 to 90 cubic feet of actual wood in a 128 cubic foot cord stack. But if the wood is only half dried, it may contain as much as 40 percent water instead of the 20 percent considered normal for air-dried wood. Your 4200-pound cord of hard maple will then contain only about 3360 pounds of quality wood. At

7000 Btus to the pound, that lost 840 pounds can cost you over 5½ million Btus in heat. If at all possible, avoid buying by weight.

When buying by the cord, you'll seldom be able to get all one type of wood. You'll seldom be able to get all of one kind even when you're cutting the wood yourself. The best bet is to specify hardwoods of various sizes (with no more than a certain percentage of softwoods). The percentage of softwood should help to determine the price of the cord. If a standard cord of mixed hardwood with 10 percent softwoods is going for $80, then a mixed cord with 30 percent softwoods should cost at least $5 less.

When buying by the cord, you'll also want to specify a mixture of wood sizes as well as species. This mixture makes starting a fire a bit easier. All those 1-foot thick logs burn quite nicely after the fire has gotten a good start, but a 1-foot oak log is a pain to get burning. Kindling should be included in the cord. It can cut down on any splitting you may have to do. Besides, you're more likely to get a decent number of cubic feet of wood in your cord of wood. The smaller pieces serve to fill in some of the gaps left between the larger logs.

Remember the size of a full cord of wood when buying time comes. A true cord is 8 feet long, 4 feet wide, and 4 feet high, a total of 128 cubic feet. Face cords are sold all across the country and can vary widely in cubic footage. A face cord will be 4 feet high by 8 feet long, but the logs won't be a full 4 feet long. The logs can be cut down to as short as 16 inches. A 16-inch deep face cord supplies only one-third the energy (and one-third the cubic footage) of the same types of wood in a full cord. It should be priced accordingly (not much above one-third the price of a full cord).

If you must buy by weight, dryness can be checked by knocking together two chunks of wood. A dull thump means the wood is far too wet; a sort of bowling alley ringing sound means they're as dry as you need.

Chapter 10

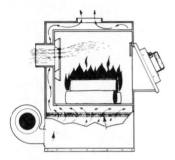

Cutting Firewood

Cutting firewood is really a simple job because of the introduction of the homeowner-size chain saw. If you know how to use a chain saw safely, you'll have very few problems. (Fig. 10-1).

CHAIN SAW USE

A chain saw is a powerful tool with an extremely sharp series of cutting edges that move very rapidly. Cutting edges are totally exposed because of the very nature of the work a chain saw is called on to do. Safety precautions must be taken by the user. Reputable chain saw manufacturers emphasize this point strongly when advertising and selling their saws (Fig. 10-2).

First, the fuel. Chain saw fuel is a premix of gas and oil. It should be poured into the saw through a funnel to help prevent spills. Much of the time, you'll be working with a hot saw; spills can be dangerous. Nearly all the time you'll be working on a forest floor. Gas can damage forest floors. Always move 20 to 25 feet away from your fueling station before starting the saw. Most of us tend to ignore this dictum, but it's much safer (especially in dry woods).

When starting the engine, make certain the saw is braced and the chain is well away from your body (Fig. 10-3). All bystanders should be instructed to stay well out of the cutting or felling area. If trees are being felled, children are especially hard to keep track of. A third party should always be on hand to take care of them. You need your concentration to keep from injuring yourself and to keep

Fig. 10-1. This sort of chain saw use isn't likely for homeowners, but note the expansion chamber to increase engine power. This cutting took place at a preliminary event for Homelite's annual Tournament of Kings contest (at Carowinds Amusement Park, Charlotte, NC). Dave Neiger, Luther, MI, is on his way to winning what is known as the hot chain saw contest to earn his third trip to the finals (courtesy of Homelite).

from knocking down power lines or dropping a tree on a building. In general, bystanders should not be allowed any nearer than twice the height of the largest trees in the felling area (Fig. 10-4).

Footing should be firm when operating the saw (with the weight of the body well balanced). Cuts should be made at chest level or below in order to maintain proper control and balance. Use a proper, firm grip to help control any kickbacks (the recoiling of the saw when the nose strikes the wood). The right hand should firmly grip the throttle handle so the saw is well balanced. The left hand should wrap around the handle bar with the thumb *around* it (Fig. 10-5). This grip provides the surest control and reduces the chances of your hand sliding into the chain.

More powerful saws pose bigger problems for the occasional user because the forces involved are greater. Kickback becomes more dangerous as power increases (as do the push/pull forces of normal cutting). *Kickback* is the normal reaction of the saw when the

Fig. 10-2. This new model 240 is indicative of the type of chain saw needed for moderate to light wood cutting (courtesy of Homelite).

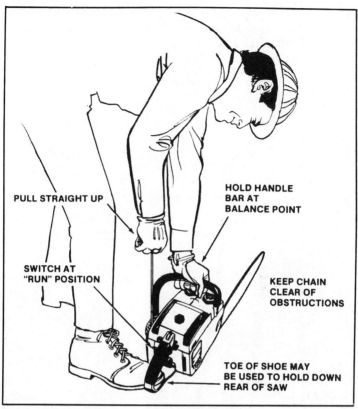

Fig. 10-3. Starting a chain saw (courtesy of Homelite).

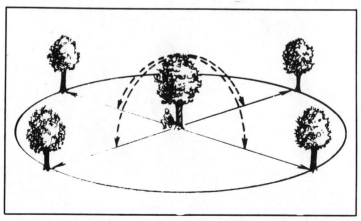

Fig. 10-4. When felling trees, bystanders shouldn't be allowed any closer than twice the height of the largest trees in the felling area (courtesy of Homelite).

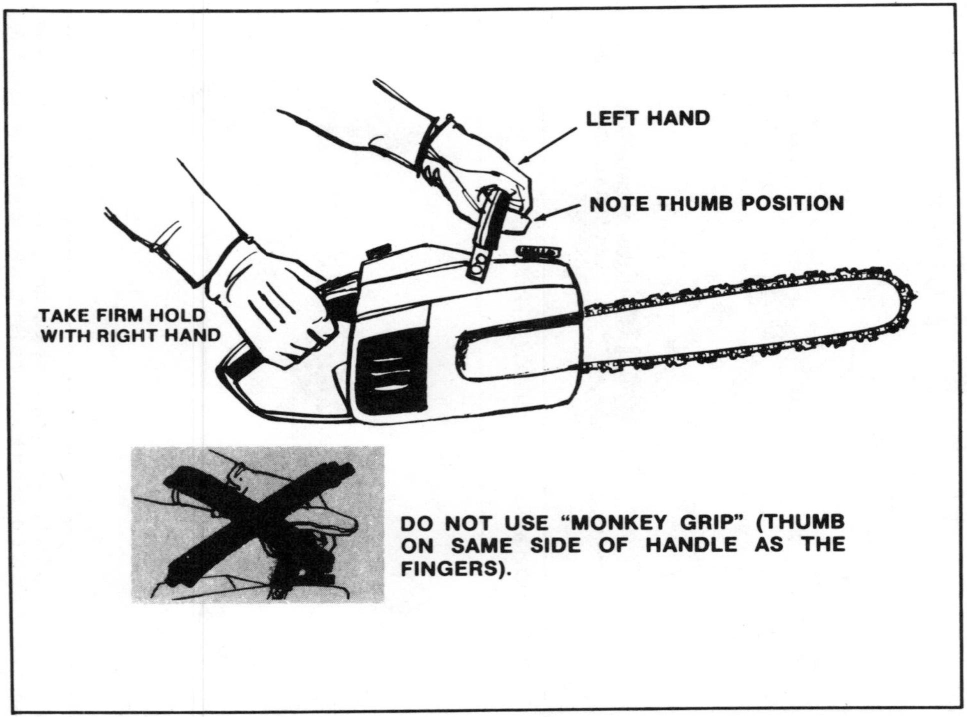

LEFT HAND

NOTE THUMB POSITION

TAKE FIRM HOLD
WITH RIGHT HAND

DO NOT USE "MONKEY GRIP" (THUMB
ON SAME SIDE OF HANDLE AS THE
FINGERS).

Fig. 10-5. Gripping the chain saw (courtesy of Homelite).

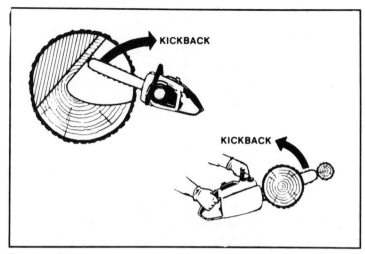

Fig. 10-6. Kickbacks occur when the chain saw nose contacts an object (courtesy of Homelite).

nose section of the guide bar and chain contacts an object (**Fig. 10-6**). The easiest way to minimize kickbacks is to consciously keep the nose of the saw from making contact with the wood (including nearby branches). **Make** cuts well back on the straight portion of the bar whenever possible. A sharp, properly adjusted chain also lessens the chances of kickback. Use care when cutting through whippy material such as brush and small trees.

Boring cuts, in which the nose of the bar is used like a drill, are almost never needed while cutting firewood. If a boring cut must be made, you should proceed slowly and carefully. Kickbacks happen frequently with boring cuts (**Fig. 10-7**).

Pull is the action you'll notice when making any top or side cut in which the bottom section of the bar is used (**Fig. 10-8**). The

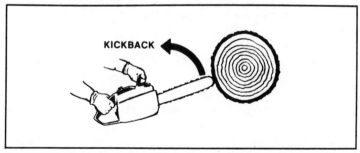

Fig. 10-7. Kickbacks occur often with boring cuts (courtesy of Homelite).

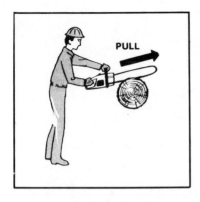

Fig. 10-8. Cutting with the bottom section of the bar produces pull (courtesy of Homelite).

operator of the saw is pulled forward, toward the saw and the log being cut. *Push* is just the reverse and occurs with bottom cuts and any other cuts in which the top part of the guide bar is used for the cutting (Fig. 10-9).

Maintaining balance is of great importance in resisting these forces. Make sure your stance is the correct one (with good weight distribution). Make sure the chain is up to cutting speed before it contacts the wood. The saw bumper or spikes can be brought into contact with the wood to reduce push or pull forces (though they'll still exist). Keep watch on the work. As soon as the push or pull force stops—at the instant the cut is completed—the throttle must be shut down so you can regain your balance as the force stops.

Clothing worn while using a chain saw can be very important. It should fit closely, but not too tightly, allowing for quick movement. No scarves or jewelery should be worn at all. Shoes should be sturdy with non-slip soles of the type make popular by Vibram. Good work gloves with non-slip palms are a help. Many people hate to work with gloves on, but chain saws require them for two reasons. While doing heavy cutting, you'll have to adjust the chain every half hour or so (and it's razor sharp when in good shape). Chain saws vibrate and can cause a fair crop of blisters if used without gloves.

Eye protection is of great importance. If you wear glasses, make sure they have safety lenses. Safety glasses are strongly recommended. If you don't wear glasses, wear safety goggles at all times while operating the saw.

A hard hat should be worn when working under large trees (whether there seems to be loose branches above or not). A widowmaker, or loose branch high up and unseen, can be shaken loose from a tree accidently. A heavy falling branch can drive several inches into the ground! You should carefully check the upper reaches of any tree you're planning to cut. Leave it be if you can't shake down *every* sizable branch that appears even a little wobbly.

For constant use of a chain saw, wear ear plugs or some sort of hearing protectors. Protectors like those used at airports are the best available, but some of the disposable waxed cotton ones do a good job too.

Physical stamina is important to safe chain sawing. For those of us who have gotten a little flabby over the years, the amount of effort needed to control a chain saw will be a surprise. Take it very easy until you work those muscles into something resembling decent shape. You need to be relaxed but alert in order to maintain safe working conditions. So getting overly tired is one of the worst things you can do. Take a break anytime you feel fatigued. Don't drink. Don't use drugs, prescription or otherwise, that might affect your balance, coordination, or judgment.

For lifting jobs, get the leg muscles into the work. Try to use your back muscles as little as possible. See Figs. 10-9 through 10-15. If you have, or think you may have, a heart ailment, or high blood pressure, or other serious condition, check with your doctor before getting involved in cutting your own firewood. The exercise might just be good for you if done intelligently. Then again it might be a little bit too much. Make sure before you start.

The chain saw requires a few accessories to be most effective and totally safe in the woods. Of course, you'll need fuel and extra chain oil while you're working. The chain oil can easily be carried in its original plastic pour jug. For any extensive wood cutting, bring along at least a quart. Fuel should be carried in a metal safety can, premixed, and ready to go. With the premix, the best bet for long engine life is to follow the oil manufacturer's directions for a proper mix.

Fig. 10-9. Cutting with the top section of the bar produces push (courtesy of Homelite).

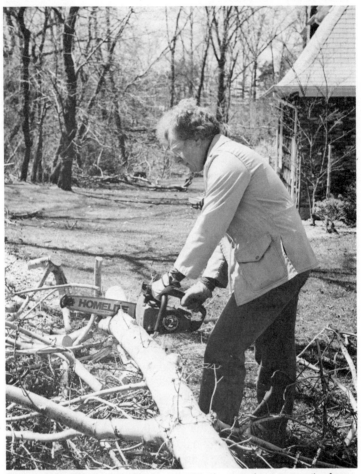

Fig. 10-10. The chain saw bumped against the log cuts down on reactive forces (courtesy of Homelite).

Most good oils require a mix of 32 parts gasoline to 1 part oil. In other words, each quart of gas needs an ounce of oil (or a gallon of gas requires half a cup). Be as accurate as possible when measuring this premix because the oil in the fuel mixture is all that stands between your chain saw engine and total failure. Those plastic baby bottles with ounce markings make ideal measurers when mixing time comes along. Bring along at least a gallon of premix. If you're using a large saw you may need much more.

The engines in most chain saws should last about a decade or more with regular homeowner use. That includes rather extensive

Fig. 10-11. An example of bumping the saw into the log (courtesy of Homelite).

Fig. 10-12. Wear no loose clothing (courtesy of Homelite).

Fig. 10-13. Gloves and eye protection are needed (courtesy of Homelite).

yearly wood cutting (possibly up to 10 or 15 cords a year). The life of the saw is really up to its owner. A lifetime of 10 years or more is not at all unreasonable with proper care and feeding.

For safety in carrying the chain saw, a chain cover can be used. A case for the entire saw can be bought with some models.

Plastic, wooden, or aluminum wedges can become essential if you misjudge a tree cut and the tree clamps down on the guide bar. Never use a hard-surface wedge to free a guide bar. And even with the soft wedges, try not to hit the bar and chain when freeing them.

If you have a roller-nose bar on the saw, you should bring along a grease gun to keep it lubricated during heavy cutting. A roller-nose bar is exactly what it sounds like. The bar has a riveted-in roller sprocket at the nose that helps increase both chain and guide bar life. Most less expensive saws use a roller-nose bar that is inexpensive at the start, but wears out quicker.

An extra spark plug and the proper sized wrench, usually supplied with any new saw, can be a help. In any case, you'll need to bring along a wrench to loosen the guide bar for adjustment (and usually a 6-by-¼-inch screwdriver to make the adjustment.

A fire extinguisher is a good idea (even in wet woods). During fall dry spells, it is essential for your own and others' safety.

Extra equipment for a day's cutting can include extra filters for the saw's air cleaner, a sharp axe or hatchet, a neon test light for the ignition circuit, and chain-filing tools. A shovel could be a help too

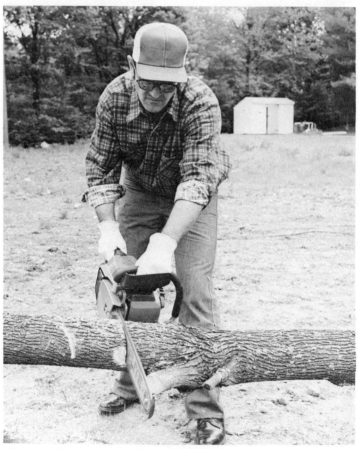

Fig. 10-14. Use proper felling procedures (courtesy of Homelite).

Fig. 10-15. Use a top quality 2-cycle oil for greatest engine life (courtesy of Homelite).

should a fire start or if you need to dig some dirt away from the bottom of a log. One or two extra chains and an extra sprocket can come in handy if you're spending a lot of time cutting hardwoods. If your saw has had a lot of use, a new starter cord might be a handy addition to your tool kit.

A first aid kit should also be carried along. It's a good idea to include one of those snakebite kits such as the one made by Cutter.

FELLING AND BUCKING

Felling and bucking in the woods are not the simple operations many people think they are. The actual process of getting a tree to fall isn't very difficult, but getting that tree to drop where you want it when you want it can be a big problem.

Assuming you've located the type and size of tree you want to cut, the next job is to look up. Make sure there are no widowmakers above. Check for fall direction. Make sure there are no power lines in the way. Make sure the tree you're felling won't end up on any other trees as it comes down. Such leaners can be very dangerous if you try to break them loose. Next, select a clear path of retreat. If necessary, clear rocks and limbs out of your way. The retreat path should be at about a 45° angle from the line of fall (Fig. 10-16). Depending on the size of the tree coming down, the butt can shoot back quite a distance. You don't really want to be there when it arrives. Clear any whippy material, such as brush and saplings, before starting to fell the tree.

Check the wind direction and the natural lean of the tree and get ready to go. Always go with natural lean direction whenever possible. Don't try to fell trees against their natural line of fall until you're well into your second or third season of felling. It can be done, but it takes an experienced eye and hand to get things just right. It often takes a block and tackle arrangement (Fig. 10-17).

Try to find out if the tree trunk is sound. This can make a lot of difference. A rotted tree can drop much quicker (sometimes even before the backcut on a large tree is more than a few inches in). You can usually tell if the trunk is rotten inside by examining the chunk that comes out with your notch cut.

The first notch cut is used to fell the tree in the correct direction. There are two types of notch cuts. One is called the *common notch* and has the first cut made parallel to the ground (Fig.

Fig. 10-16. The path of retreat should be at least at a 45-degree angle from the line of fall (courtesy of Homelite).

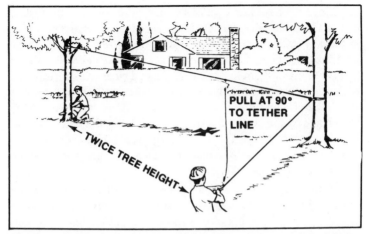

PULL AT 90°
TO TETHER
LINE

TWICE TREE HEIGHT

Fig. 10-17. Sometimes a block and tackle arrangement can be used to fell trees against their natural line of fall (courtesy of Homelite).

10-18). The other, called the *Humboldt notch*, is generally used only for logs needed for sawlog processing (**Fig. 10-19**). The Humboldt wastes a bit less wood than does the common notch. Either notch should be about one-third the depth of the tree.

Then a backcut is made 2 inches above the parallel cut (**Fig. 10-20**). For large trees, estimate 10 percent of the tree's diameter and use that as the distance above the parallel cut for the backcut. Get the backcut as level as possible or you'll end up with a stump known as a *barber's chair* and also with a split trunk (**Fig. 10-21**). Never cut all the way through to the notch! By not making a full cut, you leave a hinge of wood that serves to prevent the tree's kicking back or twisting as it comes off the stump (**Fig. 10-22**).

If the saw hangs up as the tree is going, leave it. This is a basic rule of chain saw use. If in doubt, drop the saw and beat it. Saws are cheaper then people.

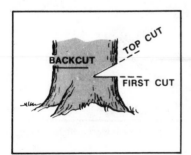

BACKCUT
TOP CUT
FIRST CUT

Fig. 10-18. The common notch cut (courtesy of Homelite).

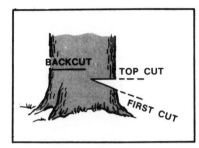

Fig. 10-19. The Humboldt notch (courtesy of Homelite).

If the tree is very large, the backcut could possibly cause the trunk to settle back onto the guidebar, pinching the saw. Wedges are used here to prevent this from happening. They should be inserted into the backcut so they don't touch the chain. The wedges can be driven in a little to jack up the tree along the backcut.

When a tree is a leaner, it presents a few special problems. This is true even if you're planning to take it down along its natural line of fall. Barber chairs and trunk splits are very common with leaners, but they can usually be prevented by using a shallower notch than normal. Try to go in only about one-quarter the diameter of the tree (instead of one-third). Shallow side notches, no deeper than the sapwood, which is the lightest colored wood in most trees, should be made (Fig. 10-23). Then bring the backcut in to leave the usual hinge. This should prevent any problems. Nevertheless, spe-

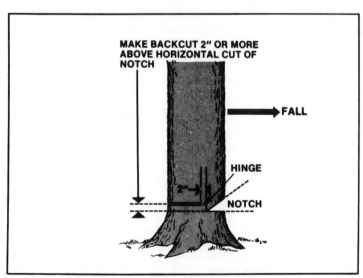

Fig. 10-20. The position of the backcut (courtesy of Homelite).

Fig. 10-21. The barber's chair stump (courtesy of Homelite).

cial care should be used in checking the footing and escape paths around any leaner.

If the tree you've selected is larger around than your guide bar is long, it can still be brought down. Usually you can bring down trees that are twice the size of your guide bar, but two or more cuts will be needed. One or two special techniques can make the job safer and easier. The notching cut is begun on one side of the tree and the saw is drawn through the cut to the other side of the tree.

This technique is used for parallel cuts and angled cuts. The backcut is a bit more complex. The saw cut is started on one side of the tree with the bottom of the guide bar. The saw is then pivoted into the cut to form the hinge on that side of the tree (**Fig. 10-24**). The saw is then removed and you reverse your position—reinserting the saw in the original cut (**Fig. 10-25**).

Be very careful as you start cutting here or the saw will kick back. Speed up the saw and draw it toward the rear of the tree. At about the two-thirds distance mark, stop. Place a wedge or two in

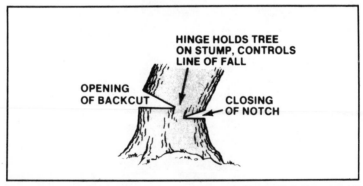

Fig. 10-22. A hinge of wood in a tree cut helps to control the tree's fall (courtesy of Homelite).

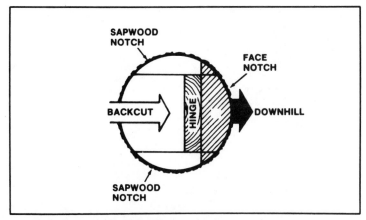

Fig. 10-23. The cross section of a tree showing the position of the side cuts, backcut, and face notch (courtesy of Homelite).

the backcut to keep the tree from clamping down on the saw's guide bar (Fig. 10-26).

With a very large tree, you might have to remove the saw and drive in the wedges to complete the felling. The tree will either fall very quickly because of its height and weight, or the strength of the wood in the hinge will force you to drive the wedges deeper. In any case, don't cut the hinge all the way through because a large trunk can kick back 20 feet or more!

After the tree is on the ground, you've got to limb and buck it in order to get it out of the woods and into your woodshed. There are a few dangers; the first of which are *spring poles*. These are saplings or branches that have been caught under the trunk and bent under tension (Fig. 10-27). Usually it's best to leave them be. Buck the tree right around them until it's possible to roll the bucked log off

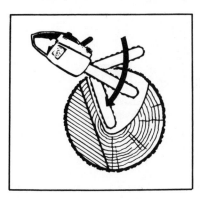

Fig. 10-24. Sawing the backcut of an oversize tree. The first cut (courtesy of Homelite).

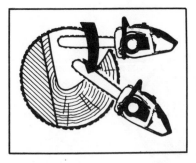

Fig. 10-25. Sawing the backcut of an oversize tree. The second cut (courtesy of Homelite).

from the side of the tree opposite the spring poles. Be careful. When that pole whips loose, it can hurt.

Limbing, the cutting off of branches, is the first job. It should be done, whenever possible, from the side opposite that on which you are standing (Fig. 10-28). Don't climb on a tree as you are limbing unless there is no other way to get at the limbs. As you limb, leave a few supporting branches along the base of the tree. These branches will help relieve stresses while you are bucking and help keep the trunk out of the dirt. Such branches can be trimmed off after the bucking is done.

Bucking is the sawing of felled trees into logs. Bucking comes in two forms: *overbucking* and *underbucking*. Overbucking is cutting from the top of the log down. Underbucking is cutting from the underside of the log up.

You'll first need to examine the log. Stresses will vary all along its length. In one area it might bend down as it's cut, pinching the guide bar in an overbuck (Fig. 10-29). A few feet away the stresses might force the piece up as it is cut, pinching the guide bar in an underbuck.

Fig. 10-26. Sawing the backcut of an over size tree. The final cut (courtesy of Homelite).

DRIVE WEDGE INTO BACKCUT TO HELP FORCE TREE OVER

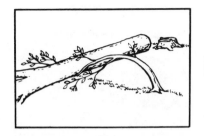

Fig. 10-27. A spring pole (courtesy of Homelite).

In such situations, two cuts must be made. In cases where the stresses will force the log down as it is cut, start with a one-third overbuck. Then remove the saw and come up from underneath the log with an underbuck to finish the job. If the log appears set so that it will rise as the cut is completed, underbuck one-third of the way through the log and finish with an overbuck. The idea is to force the cut to open up as you saw instead of allowing it to close up.

When bucking on the side of even a slight hill, *always* stand on the uphill side of the log (Fig. 10-36). Logs with no particular stresses can have a lie that will cause one part of the cut log to roll against another (which will again pinch the saw). A bucking wedge can be used to keep the cut from closing, or you can buck at an angle. To be totally sure, you can use both techniques. A guide bar pinched in a moderately large log is a real problem. It really pays to avoid pinching whenever possible.

After the bucking operation, the logs will have to be transported. The logs must be to the length needed for either easy

LEAVE SOME SUPPORTING BRANCHES UNCUT. AFTER YOU HAVE BUCKED OFF THE LOG SECTIONS, YOU CAN CUT OFF THESE LAST FEW LIMBS.

Fig. 10-28. When limbing, stand on the opposite side of the trunk from the limbs you are cutting (courtesy of Homelite).

221

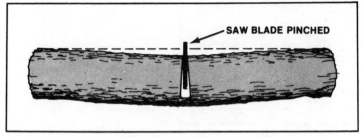

Fig. 10-29. A guide bar pinched in an overbuck (courtesy of Homelite).

transporting or for use in the wood-burning appliances you have at home.

SPLITTING AND STORING WOOD

Splitting and storing wood is not very complex, but it is often done wrong—which results in a poor fire. You'll need a splitting hammer, two or three splitting wedges, and a good pair of work gloves. It would also be wise to use your safety goggles. There's always the chance that a metal chip will fly as you smack the wedges with your hammer. An axe can also be used to split wood; it requires more work for most types of wood. Certain types of pine and cedar are so easy to split that there's little reason to prefer one tool over

Fig. 10-30. When bucking on a hill, always stand on the uphill side of the log (courtesy of Homelite).

Fig. 10-31. A typical lumber sawhorse.

another. If you do prefer an axe, select one with a thick heel so that, as the blade moves through the wood, the heel will force the split wide. A splitting hammer, that can be found in most hardware stores, is really just a 6-pound hammer with one side formed into a wedge. Usually, with woods such as green maple (hard or soft), pine, and green oak, the wedges won't be needed—unless the pieces to be split are very long. The hammer will drop right on through.

Fig. 10-32. A seasoning stack.

If the logs were cut only to transport lengths, they should be placed on the sawhorse and cut to burning length. A sawhorse is simply made; most are just a couple of wooden X's joined together with crosspieces (Fig. 10-31). A longer-lasting sawhorse can be made using 2×6s or 2×8s and lag bolts and carriage bolts to hold it together. The height of the wooden X's should be adjusted to the height of the user. The crosspieces should be about twice the length of desired firewood length. That allows you to lop off the two ends of a long piece, then move to the center and cut right through that final piece without having to move the wood around. You might need a bucking wedge for the center cut if the wood is more than a foot or so in diameter (but you most likely won't).

Once the bucking is finished, the splitting starts. Any piece of wood that is more than 10 or 12 inches in diameter should be split. Paper birch is a special problem because the bark seals so tightly the wood is likely to rot long before it's dry enough to burn. Split wood dries much more rapidly than does unsplit wood. If you're using a fireplace, you will surely want a few big logs so the fire will last. But you won't need nearly as many of the big logs as you will the spit logs. Split logs, by the way, start burning more easily than unsplit logs.

To split a log, first stand it on a soft, rock-free patch of ground or on a stump. The stump is to be preferred because it keeps the hammer or axe from hitting stones and other debris. Select, when possible, a natural crack in the wood. Raise the hammer above your head, aim, and let it drop. The weight of the hammer head will carry

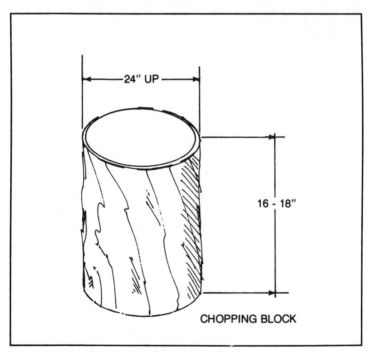

24" UP

16 - 18"

CHOPPING BLOCK

Fig. 10-33. Near ideal chopping block dimensions.

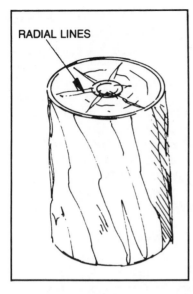

RADIAL LINES

Fig. 10-34. Radial lines. Splitting along these lines is always easier.

it right on through all but the toughest wood (where your wedges come in very handy). There is usually no need whatsoever to swing the splitting hammer with any power. It does the work if you'll let it.

If the wood you've cut is good hardwood and has had some time to season before you get around to splitting it, you're going to have to work harder. If you do your splitting in the depths of a cold winter, let the wood freeze. It splits more easily when frozen. Some woods, such as elm, are best left until frozen. Elm and some of the hickories are exceptionally hard to split. If possible, let the wood freeze first.

The size of the split wood is up to the splitter and the fire tender. Many people prefer to halve 10-inch logs and to quarter any log over 16 inches. This can vary a great deal if you've got an extra large or extra small fireplace. In a huge fireplace, the small logs will drive you crazy. But many wood stoves will burn best with even the 10 inch logs quartered.

After the logs are split, they should be stacked for seasoning. The basic seasoning stack is *not* what you see as a cordwood stack around most homes. It is to be hoped that the people who use such a cordwood stack have already seasoned their wood. If they haven't, there's a fine chance much of it will rot before it dries enough for use.

Seasoning stacks are chimney stacks (Fig. 10-32). Two waste logs, or some flat rocks, are placed on the ground. Two split logs are placed across them. Then two more logs are placed across those.

This continues on up to maximum safe height (which depends on the length of the logs). The longer the logs being stacked, the higher the stack can be before there's any danger of its toppling over. The hole up the center of the chimney stack, and the spaces on the sides, allow plenty of air to flow around the split wood—drying it rapidly and thoroughly. If possible, a tarp should be draped over the tops of the stacks. The tarp can be plastic, canvas, or anything water resistant. Use rocks or extra logs to hold down the tarp.

Wood is best cut the winter or spring before it is needed for use. This allows plenty of time for seasoning—6 to 8 months, and sometimes more. It also exposes the wood to drying spring breezes and the hot summer sun, all of which are a help. If you're cutting dead timber, the need for seasoning is correspondingly less—but it still exists.

Keep at least two day's wood stored indoors. More if possible. Less humid indoor air helps dry the wood even more. A few weeks indoors can reduce water weight by 10 percent or so. Indoor storage also means you don't have to constantly be hopping out to the woodshed or garage to grab an armload of wood to feed your fires.

The splitting of wood is a job that is seldom given a lot of consideration when things are first thought out. It is just plain hard work by hand, most people think, and so they start considering any

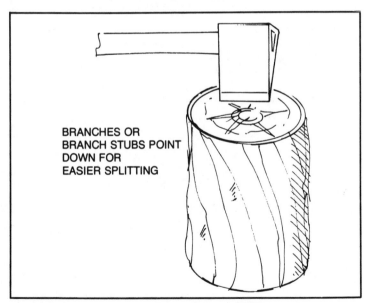

BRANCHES OR
BRANCH STUBS POINT
DOWN FOR
EASIER SPLITTING

Fig. 10-35. Branch stubs pointing down for easier splitting.

of a variety of powered wood splitters ranging in price from about $175 on up well past $500. I've used most of the versions of wood splitters on the market. I can see no reason for a healthy person who will be splitting under a dozen cords of wood a year to go with any power splitter.

It is possible for a fairly well-conditioned male to split a cord of wood by hand in about 1 or 1½ hours (barring a lot of difficult wood types). Most non-commercial wood splitters are rated at 1 cord per hour. The advantage of the powered wood splitters is that they can keep going for 10 or 12 hours and get the job done in a single day. Most of us, no matter how good our condition, will need a week or so to split a dozen cords of wood by hand. If a one-day job is essential, rent a power splitter.

Hand splitting will do any size log you have. Most under-$650 power splitters won't work on wood over 2 feet in diameter. Sooner or later, you will hit some 3-foot diameter logs. At one time, I had to split a sugar maple well over 4 feet in diameter. I did that by hand and I split it in two before I bucked it to lengths other than 8 feet.

If a power splitter *is* used, I prefer the screw type. In general, they are safer than hydraulic ram splitters and the types that mount on your car or truck wheel or a tractor power takeoff. I tested a

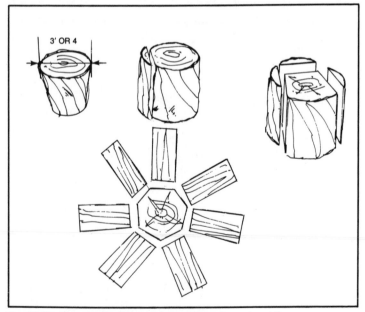

Fig. 10-36. Cloverleafing to ease the splitting of very large logs.

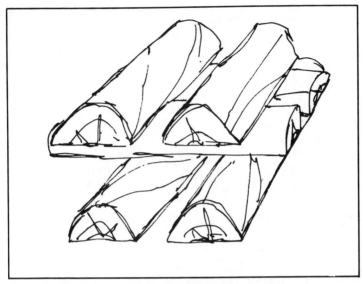

Fig. 10-37. The start of a chimney stack for rapid seasoning.

screw-type splitter bolted to a van rear wheel by splitting a seasoned hickory log (12 feet long and over a foot in diameter) with only two easy movements of the log. This is the least expensive form of power splitter to be found these days. Hydraulic ram splitters don't save any lifting at all. Where you might have to lift a chunk of wood to your 18-inch high chopping block, you'll find only a 2-inch savings in lift with hydraulic splitters.

Simply put, unless you're cutting a tremendous amount of firewood there is little point in going with power splitters. They are not safe and not really much faster than splitting wood by hand. They do save you some physical energy. Proper techniques will allow you to split logs more easily. See Figs. 10-33 through 10-37.

Chapter 11

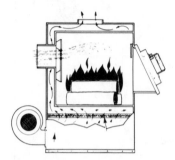

Woodcutting Tools

Chain saw and axe selection and care are important parts of heating with wood. You'll find that without proper selection and care of your tools, burning wood can be more expensive than it needs to be.

HAND TOOLS

Because the axe and the woodsplitter's hammer are the least expensive, I will start with them. I prefer the woodsplitter's hammer, or *go-devil*, over the axe. Heads are available in 6-pound or 8-pound weights, with 32-inch or 34-inch hickory handles. The hammers are specifically designed for splitting wood and should never be used for other jobs. They are also used to drive wedges when the hammer alone isn't enough. A woodsplitter's hammer should never be used to strike and break concrete or rock. One hammer should never be used to strike another. The usual sensible precautions against using tools with loose or split handles apply.

Any striking tool should be used with safety goggles. The goggles become especially important if you're using the hammer to slug a wedge down through a hard chunk of wood.

Proper use involves simply raising the hammer and letting its own weight carry it as far into the wood as it will go. This will normally be all the way through. When used in conjunction with a splitting wedge, the striking face of the hammer should always be larger than the face of the wedge. The hammer or an axe should be used to provide a starting notch for the wedge. The wedge is then placed and struck.

Any hammer or wedge with a chipped head or face, with a badly battered or slightly split head or a mushroomed head or face, should be tossed in the trash. Such tools become weapons, they continue to spray off bits of metal every time they are used.

If the bit of a woodsplitter's hammer or wedge becomes dulled or slightly chipped, it can be resharpened. The basic rules for sharpening also apply to axes. First, the tool must be returned to its original shape. All cracks must be removed while the grinding temperature is kept low. Only a medium- or fine-grit grinding wheel should be used. The wheel must be kept wet to keep temperatures low enough so the temper of the metal remains undisturbed.

The grinding wheel direction of rotation should always be *away* from the cutting edge of the tool being sharpened. This helps direct heat away from the tool's edge. Always wear safety goggles when you are sharpening tools.

If a file is used for sharpening, remove all scratches with a whetstone or hone. When doing a total regrind, move back 2 to 3 inches from the cutting edge and grind to within one-half inch or so of the edge. That remaining one-half inch or so will be sharpened with a hone or whetstone. Work for a fan shape so the cutting edge can have extra metal behind it for support (Fig. 11-1).

Axes come in so many styles and sizes it's almost impossible to list them all. Axes for woodsplitting should have a single blade with

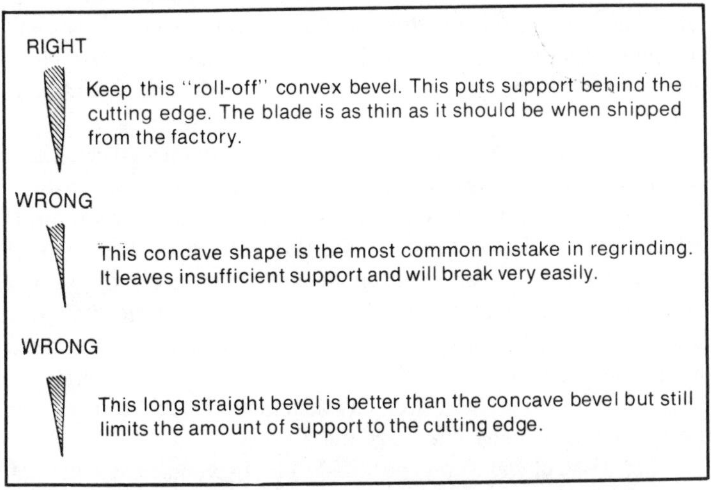

RIGHT

Keep this "roll-off" convex bevel. This puts support behind the cutting edge. The blade is as thin as it should be when shipped from the factory.

WRONG

This concave shape is the most common mistake in regrinding. It leaves insufficient support and will break very easily.

WRONG

This long straight bevel is better than the concave bevel but still limits the amount of support to the cutting edge.

Fig. 11-1. Getting the proper shape on a blade involves careful grinding.

231

a thick heel or poll and, with a 4-pound or 5-pound head. The handle should be no less then 30 inches long (on up to 36 inches). The head should be of forged carbon tool steel (as should that of the woodsplitter's hammer). The axe is used directly for splitting wood or for setting the wedge.

It does not in any other way substitute for the wedge or woodsplitter's hammer. No axe should be driven through a log with a sledge or maul. The axe should not be used to drive a wedge (Fig. 11-2). The poll is not hardened to withstand this sort of treatment and will quickly mushroom and chip when so used.

Keep an eye on the handle and tighten when needed. If it splits, or gets heavily damaged anywhere along the handle length, replacement is needed. If the head of the axe shows a crack or break around the eye section (where the handle fits into the head), discard the axe. If the striking face or cutting edges show large chips or dents, or if the face is mushroomed, the axe is good for scrap metal and nothing else.

Properly cared for and used, a woodsplitter's hammer, an axe, and several wedges should last the major part of a lifetime—even with fairly heavy use. If poorly cared for or abused, none of them will last a single wood-cutting season.

THE CHAIN SAW

The most complex of the woodcutter's tools is the chain saw. Fortunately, the most complex part of the modern chain saw, the engine, is the part not likely to need much care beyond an occasional tuneup and proper feeding. Just get the right oil, use fresh gas, and get the mixture correct. The engine should last and last. Most chain saw maintenance has to do with the condition of the chain, guide bar, and sprockets.

Selection of a chain saw can drive you crazy these days. Chain saw manufacturers usually produce more than one saw model. There are now over a dozen manufacturers to choose from. First, examine the work you'll need to do. Will you cut only a couple of cords of wood each year? If so, almost any of the smaller saws will do. Prices can range from about $120 to over $160. Basically, you'll need a saw that handles easily for you, a saw that has automatic oiling, and a saw that is as quiet as possible. Smaller saws are well built, but they lack the power and adaptability needed to chomp their way through seasoned oak and hickory.

For those of you who expect to do a lot of woodcutting, but not enough to justify buying one of the $200, 16-inch models, look for a

Fig. 11-2. Never use an axe as a wedge or a maul.

smaller saw with a roller-nose guide bar. The roller-nose increases the life of both bar and chain and allows the saw to cut a bit more coolly and rapidly. The roller-nose can be punched out and replaced when it wears out (saving having to buy a new guide bar).

For the homeowner who plans to cut more than a half dozen cords of wood a year, the larger saws will certainly prove worthwhile. Unfortunately, the move up in size and power requires a move up in price. To get more, you've got to pay more. Sometimes a lot more. It's at this point the chain saw field really begins to widen out. Prices running from about $165 on up past $400. Virtually every chain saw manufacturer in the world makes at least one 16-inch model with all the features and power anyone could want. Some manufacturers go so far as to make several 16-inch models. Others provide 16-inch guide bars on heavy duty saws. The longer the guide bar and chain, the more expensive the saw. Always buy the shortest guide bar that will be useful. A quick look at just two manufacturers and their homeowner lines will show just what I mean. Homelite produces several models that can take a 16-inch guide bar: 150 Auto, EZ, Super EZ, XL-12, Super XL Auto, XL-123 and 350 Auto. Pioneer's P25, P1200A, P40, 3270SC, and 650 can take 16-inch guide bars too.

For the homeowner's purposes, the top-of-the-line models with prices around $300 are not really necessary. These are as close to professional saws as you can get and the price reflects that. For really heavy use on farms they would be ideal. But the $200 saws can handle most cutting jobs, and they last a long time.

One of the fortunate things about chain saws is the lack of yearly model changes. The manufacturers are in strong competition and discovered years ago that their customers preferred features such as more power and less noise to new paint and sheet-metal designs that don't aid performance.

When making a chain saw selection then, determine the size of the saw you need. Make sure the model you select has automatic oiling. This feature can save a lot of wear and tear on the thumb which would have to be used to pump a manual oiler every few seconds. Another handy feature is an all-position carburetor. Now go out and test as many of the various brands as you can. You may have to rent some to use, but your friends may also let you check out their chain saw. The tryout is a good idea for several reasons. I could recommend a saw for you and be pretty sure you'd be able to use it. But the shape of your body and your skeletal and muscle structure is sure to differ from mine. A saw that handles beautifully for me might be unwieldy for you. Your hand shape will also differ. Where one model might not work very well in your hands, another might just fit right into your style of cutting wood.

When your chain saw is first started after the original uncrating, it probably will run reasonably well. Usually a brand new saw won't settle into a good idle with a clear power surge when the throttle is opened quickly. A minor carburetor adjustment is usually what is needed.

Start the saw and let it idle. Run it in short bursts every so often. Then make a few cuts in a log to completely warm the engine. Fine tuning can then follow. Locate the idle speed screw with the engine still at idle. The chain should not be turning. Turn the idle speed screw in the proper direction (most saws will have the screw turning *in* to increase idle speed) to move the speed up until the chain barely starts to move.

Now back off until the engine starts to falter a bit. Halfway between the speed at which the chain barely moves and the speed where the engine wants to stall is the proper engine idle speed at this stage. Move over and locate the low speed range needle adjustment. Adjust it until the idle speed has increased as much as possible. Now adjust the idle speed one more time. This series of adjustments might have to be carried out several times to get the carburetion right on the nose. Once you get it right, it should stay that way for a good while.

For adjusting engine pickup from idle to wide open throttle, I suggest a fast trip to the dealer's shop. Though the adjustment itself isn't difficult, an inexperienced hand at the throttle can scatter chain saw engine all over the place.

Chain tensioning is important for keeping the chain as sharp as possible for as long as possible. Proper chain tension also helps prevent premature chain wear and guide bar wear. Chain adjustment is pretty much the same on every chain saw. Minor details of screw turning will vary slightly from saw to saw.

Make sure you're doing the adjustment to the degree needed for the bar you're using. Sprocket-nose bars run with a much tighter

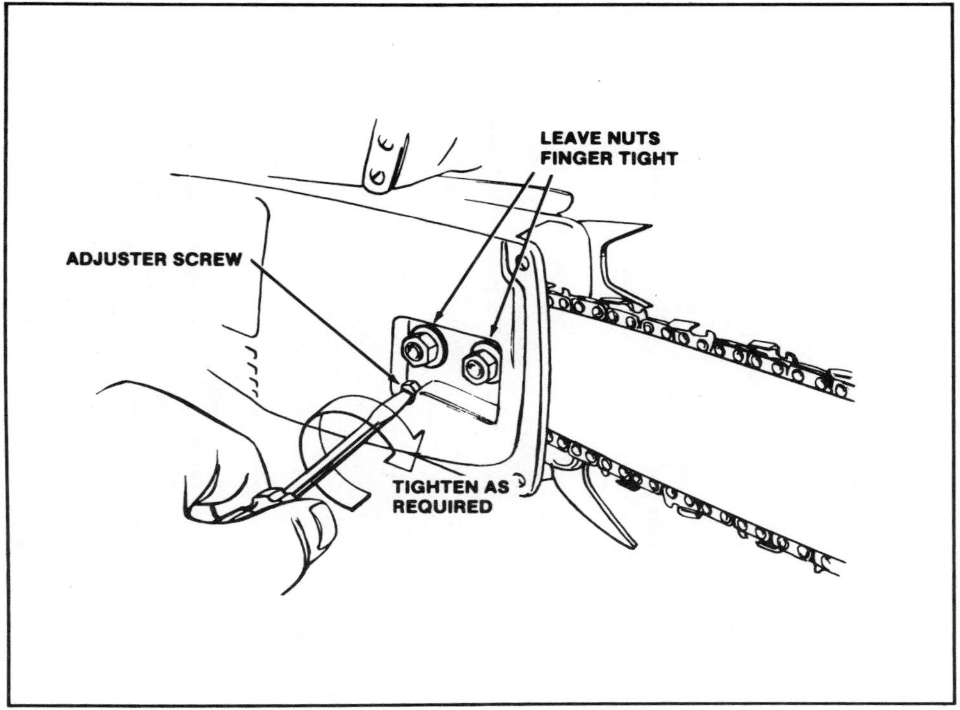

Fig. 11-3. Loosening the guide bar mounting nuts (courtesy of Homelite).

LEAVE NUTS
FINGER TIGHT

TIGHTEN AS
REQUIRED

ADJUSTER SCREW

chain tension than do hard-nose bars. Put on your gloves; the chain will be extremely sharp. Loosen the guide bar mounting nuts at the base of the bar, and then run them back up finger tight (**Fig. 11-3**). Lift up the nose of the bar. Move the chain along the bar until it reaches its tightest position. Snap the chain to remove any possible kinking: Just pull it away from the bar and let it drop back several times.

Locate the chain tensioning screw (usually at the base of the bar on the side closest to the engine). On a sprocket- or roller-nose bar, the chain should be adjusted until it is taut—without any evident dropaway from the guide bar groove (**Fig. 11-4**).

The chain should not be so tight that it binds as you pull it along the bar by hand. If the bar and chain are warm, allow more slack. On hard-nose bars, the cold tension is set to where the chain tie-straps (the connecting links between the chain sections) don't quite touch the bar rails at the center of the bar. They must not hang out more than the thickness of a dime though (**Fig. 11-5**).

When making a warm adjustment on a hard-nose bar, allow up to one-eighth inch of clearance at the bar rails. Don't adjust a warm bar unless the tangs are hanging all the way out of the bar groove.

On all types of bars, when you start with a cold chain, always recheck as soon as it warms up so that you're sure the tension is correct. A new chain will have to be adjusted fairly frequently for the first couple of hours of cutting.

When in use, sprocket-nose bars require at least daily lubrication. Use a special sprocket-nose gun and lubricate while the bar is still warm. This should be done at the end of the cutting day. The grease should be pumped in until no more dirty grease is forced out. This lubrication cleans all the sawdust and grit out of the sprocket nose and provides lubricant for the next day's cutting. Sprocket noses, by the way, are good as long as they turn freely with no roughness or binding. If a new nose sprocket is needed, the drive sprocket should be replaced at the same time (**Fig. 11-6**).

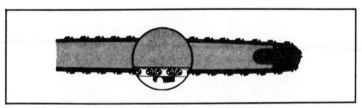

Fig. 11-4. On a sprocket- or roller-nose bar, the chain should have no slack (courtesy of Homelite).

Fig. 11-5. On hard-nose bars, the cold tension should be set to allow a little slack in the chain (courtesy of Homelite).

Guide bars last varying times, but the heavy woodcutter can expect to go through one every two years or so. Replace chain, drive sprocket, and guide bar at the same time.

Saw chains will require fairly frequent sharpening to maintain cutting ease. Using a dull chain for too long causes everything to heat up to the point where both the chain and guide bar could be

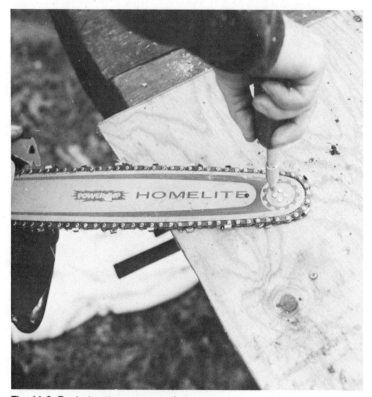

Fig. 11-6. Replacing the nose sprocket.

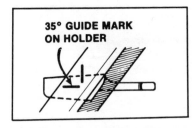

35° GUIDE MARK ON HOLDER

Fig. 11-7. The guide lines on a file holder (courtesy of Homelite).

ruined. To sharpen the chain, a proper size file and file holder are necessary. It's nice to have a depth gauge too, but generally the homeowner can get around this by having the chain professionally sharpened and the depth set every third time.

Although a chain filing vise is also a good addition to your tool kit, carrying all that gear into the woods is not essential. The chain can be sharpened on the bar by tightening up the tensioning screw so the chain can't wobble. Wear gloves to protect your hands. Do all your filing at the midpoint of the guide bar.

The file holder will have two lines on top (Fig. 11-7). These are the angle markers you must use to get the correct 35-degree filing angle for sharpening your chain (Fig. 11-8).

Hold the file against the cutter at the proper angle. Make sure the file stays level as you stroke, with no dips or rocking (Fig. 11-9). File toward the front corner of the tooth and lift the file on the backstroke. Use a firm but light stroke and avoid heavy downward pressure. Your file holder will automatically keep 10 degrees of the file above the top plate to provide the proper beveled underedge.

Use only a few strokes to each tooth and rotate the file in the holder after filing three or four teeth. Use the same number of strokes on each tooth. File all the cutters on one side of the chain; turn the saw and do all the cutters on the opposite side. Check the edge. A sharp edge does not reflect light, but a worn, dull edge does (Fig. 11-10).

Corrective filing is sometimes needed when one cutter has to be filed down more than any other. All cutters must then be filed

Fig. 11-8. The 35-degree top-plate angle (courtesy of Homelite).

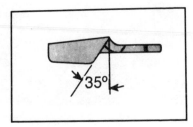

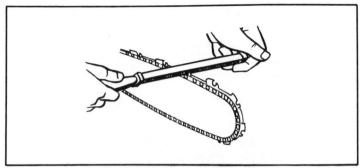

Fig. 11-9. Keep the file level as you sharpen the chain cutters (courtesy of Homelite).

back to match the length of the shortened cutter (**Fig. 11-11**). The same holds true when a tooth is damaged by hitting a rock or other hard object. The damaged tooth must be filed back past the damaged area. It is then filed to the correct shape. Then all the other teeth have to be filed to match the new size. This gives each tooth an equal chance to do its proper cutting job.

The chain drive tangs have sharp points when they are new or in good condition. In order for the bar groove to stay clear of debris (sawdust), these tangs must stay sharp. An oval or round file can be used to sharpen every fourth or fifth tang to help maintain this cleaning action (**Fig. 11-12**).

The guide bar will last much longer if it receives care and attention. Primarily, a simple cleaning is all that's needed for most bars until the saw has a number of hours on it. Using a piece of wire or other stiff object, clean any packed sawdust out of the chain groove (Fig. 11-13). Make certain the chain-oil holes in the bar are also clear because obstructions here prevent oil from reaching the chain (which results in hard cutting and premature wear on the chain).

Fig. 11-10. A sharp edge doesn't reflect light; a dull edge shines (courtesy of Homelite).

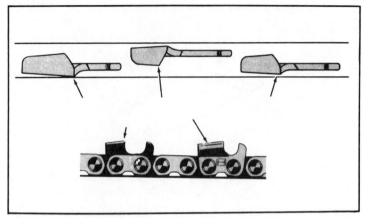

Fig. 11-11. All cutters must be filed back to match the length of the shortest one (courtesy of Homelite).

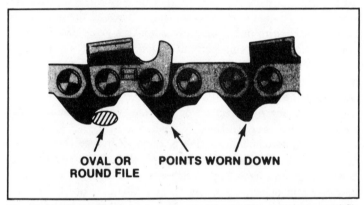

OVAL OR ROUND FILE   **POINTS WORN DOWN**

Fig. 11-12. Chain drive tangs can be sharpened with an oval or round file (courtesy of Homelite).

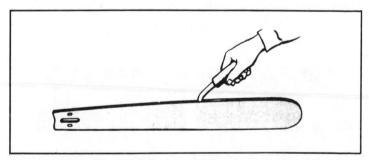

Fig. 11-13. Use a thin, stiff object to scrape sawdust out of the chain groove (courtesy of Homelite).

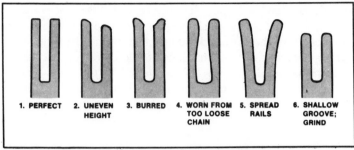

Fig. 11-14. Wear patterns of a chain groove (courtesy of Homelite).

When wear starts to show on the bar groove, it will be in the form of the patterns shown in Fig. 11-14. Most burrs can be removed with a flat file. File carefully and remove only as much material as is needed to get rid of the burrs. Check the bar for cracks and sight along it to check for straightness. Place a few chain drive tangs in the groove and check to see that they don't bottom out in the groove. If they do, the groove will have to be ground deeper. A dealer usually must handle this kind of grinding.

A blue discoloration on the bar can indicate several things. The bar and chain might not be getting enough oil. Make sure the oil holes are open and the oiler is full and operating. The discoloration could mean that you've been bearing down too hard with a dull chain. Sharpen the chain. Discoloration could also mean the guide rails have been pinched together at the discolored point. Use a screwdriver to gently pry the rails apart. Most guide bars can be turned over to help equalize wear. Turn yours after every third or fourth chain sharpening.

Sprocket noses on guide bars are very easy to replace. There will usually be four rivets holding the old nose in place. The center of these rivets should be drilled out and then the remainder punched

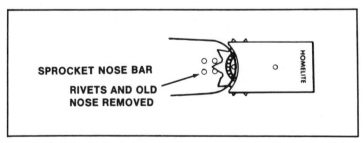

Fig. 11-15. The Homelite replacement sprocket can be slid into place right from the package.

out. The old sprocket nose will drop free. Install the new assembly directly from the package—slipping it right into place (Fig. 11-15). New rivets are then inserted and the heads peened smoothly with light taps of a hammer. Several moderate blows with the flat surface of the hammer will then spread the rivets to fill the holes. Grease and go. Proper maintenance and repairs will keep your woodcutting tools in good shape for many years.

Chapter 12

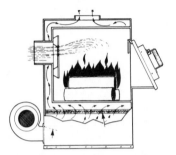

Accessories

The numbers and types of fireplace and wood-stove accessories have increased greatly in the past five or six years. Few accessories were available except for fireplace screens, pokers, bellows, and the Thermogate insert for extracting more heat. Since that time, more and more fireplace inserts have been developed. These inserts are often of a quality to increase fireplace efficiency to near that of a good wood stove. New forms of chimney-cleaning gear, new types of dampers, and other items have been developed.

FIRE SCREENS

Fire screens are not complex items. Most of the standard models are little more than wire mesh fitted into a frame that will attach to, slide across, or stand against the firebox opening of the fireplace. The finer the wire mesh, the smaller the flying sparks the screen is able to stop. The tighter the fire screen fits at the top, sides, and bottom of the fireplace opening, the less chance there is of burning brands popping out of an unattended fireplace (to either scorch floors or start fires).

More complex fire screens are available. They are most often made of Pyrex or some other brand of heat-resistant glass. Glass fire screens are useful in several ways, but they can also present you with a problem or two at times. Closing a glass fire screen, even the ventilated type, on a burning or smoldering fire helps cut down on heat loss up the flue. Closing a glass fire screen during the evening also cuts way down on the heat that is able to flow into the room from the fire.

Most of the glass fire screens now available come with a series of small holes drilled somewhere on their faces, or with louvered slots cut, so that a little more air is allowed to reach the fire and keep it burning. Most of these now have cutoffs of sliding metal to seal the holes when shut-down time arrives.

A great many of the glass fire screens are designed to fit tightly to almost any firebox opening. Usually, a mineral-wool insulation provides the seal. Extremely careful measurements must be taken or things just are not going to work out when you make the installation.

For best general use, select a glass fire screen that is combined with a mesh screen for daytime and early evening use. The inner wire mesh screen is usually of the type you can slide across the opening when no one is in the room to keep an eye on the fire. At night, the glass screen is closed, sealing the firebox fairly well, to cut down the fire. Depending on the type of screen, shutting down the glass doors will either keep the fire in a smoldering state through much of the night, or it will shut it down completely. The damper must still be left open so that air loss can occur through any vent holes in the fire screen.

For those who prefer the least heat loss, a check of glass fire screens with no ventilation holes, or ventilation holes with a tightly sealing door, needs to be considered. From this point, it is a matter of careful measurement and making sure the seal is properly done.

Asbestos millboard, or Kaowool millboard, can be used in place of a glass fire screen if all you want to do is shut down the fire at night and prevent heat loss up the chimney. Glass fire screens tend to be more than moderately expensive. This is especially true if you have a large fireplace. The board can seal things at less cost. Cut one piece of asbestos board about 2 inches higher and wider on each side than the fireplace opening. Cut a second piece of millboard to a size that will just squeeze in the opening. Place small spacers inside (two or three washers at each point is a good idea) and epoxy the thing together. Line the edges behind the larger board with one-inch thick strips of mineral fiber insulation.

Now all you need to do is set the unit in the fireplace opening when you want to shut down the fire, or prevent heat loss up the flue. The millboard, whether asbestos or Kaowool, should be reinforced with wood 2 × 2s if it is to receive extensive use. Just make sure the wood is placed on the portion of the unit that is to face into the room—not into the firebox.

Always leave the damper at least part of the way open when there is any fire in the fireplace (even if you want the fire to go out in a hurry). If the damper isn't open, you are virtually certain to fill the house with smoke even when a glass or asbestos screen is in place.

GRATES, STANDS, AND ANDIRONS

Grates, log stands, and andirons are next in importance to fire screens because they provide better bases for fires, more even burning, and greater starting ease. Of the group, grates and stands are more desirable because they don't allow a fire to collapse in the middle as andirons do. Any of the three will do a reasonably suitable job.

Grates and firestands need to be selected to fit the width and depth of the fireplace as closely as possible. This assures you of the greatest amount of heat being reflected back into the room. If the fire takes up only the very center of the fireplace, the unit cannot be very efficient in radiating heat to the room. If the entire fireplace firebox area is in use, the heating efficiency increases a great deal.

Size is not your only consideration when selecting a grate for use in a fireplace. Construction must be looked at quite carefully. Even the heaviest cast-iron grate is going to burn through, sooner or later, because the hottest portion of your fire is resting right on it. To keep things going longer, select a grate made of the heaviest metal you can find in the largest size your fireplace will hold.

Andirons are more decorative than firegrates, and they are often used in combination with grates. If looks mean more to you than does efficiency, you can go with andirons alone. Otherwise, use a grate, or andirons and a grate.

General fireplace tool sets are handy to have. The most useful tools in the sets are the poker and tongs. They provide a safe method of prodding the fire and moving logs to allow better air circulation.

Bellows are not often seen around today's fireplaces as other than decorative options. They shouldn't be needed in a properly built fireplace and tend to be messy to use anyway. They can be useful for bringing the previous night's fire back to life a bit so that the new kindling catches more easily. If a bellows is used too vigorously, ashes will fly all over the room.

Mechanical and chemical fire starters are available for those who don't want to use kindling, paper, and matches, or for people in urban areas where kindling is expensive.

Built-in gas-fired log starters seem to me to be a waste of time and money. Electric starters that are prodded into logs don't seem any better. Both will use much more power than most people will really want to spend to just light a fire.

Cape Cod style lighters are the best I've ever seen. They provide rapid fire starting and are more than reasonably safe if used properly. The Cape Cod style lighter consists of a small pot, which is used to hold kerosene, and a porous fireclay knob with a wire handle. The knob is kept in the kerosene (which should always be capped with the lid). The knob of fireclay is removed from the pot, lighted, and placed under logs. It serves as a sort of wick and provides a fairly hot, intense flame that will start a small log to burning rather quickly. If the log does not ignite on the first try, however, the starter knob should *never* be placed back in the pot without allowing plenty of time to cool down. Just pull the lighter from the fireplace onto the hearth and let it cool. Reinsert it in the pot only after the knob is totally cool to the touch.

No other chemical or mechanical starters have proved to be of much value in my experience, and some are downright dangerous. No one should ever pour kerosene or gasoline directly on logs for a quick starting fire. If you use charcoal lighter, your nerves are better than mine.

Various types of grills and pot hangers with pots are now being made for fireplace decoration. The grills often allow a fireplace to be used as an indoor barbecue during the cold months. When using a fireplace as a barbecue, expect grease to spatter. Cover the hearth with metal foil to prevent soiling. Charcoal can be used in the fireplace on many of these grills, but as a precaution you should always open a window no matter how good the fireplace draft.

Coal can also be used as a fuel in many fireplaces and wood stoves. Burning coal can cause, in wood stoves not designed for coal, premature firebox burnout. Firebrick lining shows that a stove was intended for use with coal. In a fireplace, generally all that's needed is a coal grate (which differs from a wood grate only in that the slots in the grate are smaller so the coal won't drop through).

Log holders, in the form of two loops with a spread bottom, are found just about everywhere now. Large ones stand by fireplaces in many homes. They can store as much as one-eighth of a cord of wood. They're very handy.

Wood totes can be bought or made. Garden Way Research in Vermont sells a fine one. It is fairly easy to make your own. Cut a piece of canvas about 4 feet long and about 6 inches less in width than the length of the logs you expect to carry. Using a sailmaker's needle, sew a loop of half-inch rope in each end. Those loops form the handle. You place the logs in the tote, pull the handles together, and go on about your business. To get really fancy, you can hem the sides. The tote will also last longer if that's done.

A bell-shaped item known as a *curfew* might soon be available again. It is used to cover the fire at night and has a few holes in its top to allow the fire to keep burning. Morning fire starting is thus less of a chore. To find a curfew at this time, you'll probably have to haunt antique auctions. As fireplaces continue to grow in popularity, we can expect this accessory from the Middle Ages to make a comeback.

Chapter 13

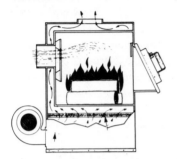

Fire Starting and Fire Tending

Some people seem to start right out knowing how to tend a fireplace or wood stove. They have what amounts to an instinct for firebuilding. The rest of us have to learn as we go along.

STARTING FIRES

The tightness of the modern home is a problem. Some sort of exhaust fan in operation in the kitchen or bathroom can draw air out and the home is too tightly sealed to allow any air in to replace what goes out. The chimney must provide a downdraft. Result: a smokey room.

Therefore, the first check to make when you are getting set to start a fire requires an open damper, a few minutes wait, and a wet finger. Hold your wet finger under the chimney throat and see if the end of your finger begins to feel cold. If it does, open a door to another room or open a window a couple of inches. Check the draft again. If this hasn't corrected the downdraft condition, you'll need to move back to the chapter on fireplace problems and their cures. If it has, you're just about ready to lay the fire.

Of course, this downdraft check won't be needed every time you build a fire. But for any fireplace or wood stove not having been used for some time it's a good idea. It's also a good idea if you've just recaulked and reinsulated the house, or if you've just had storm windows installed. It's nice to locate and cure such a problem before filling the house with smoke.

If the fireplace has been in use, you should have left an inch or two of ash on the refractory hearth. Now select your fuel. First, several crumpled sheets of newspaper are placed on the grate. Next the kindling goes on. Use sticks of 1-inch or less in diameter (if split wood) and three-fourths of an inch or less if small branches, twigs, and unsplit wood are used. If you're using pine branches, make certain the dried needles have been shaken loose first because they tend to flare badly when ignited.

Two logs should now be laid parallel to the back wall of the fireplace (with the kindling crisscrossed between them). These logs should be split if they are over 4 inches in diameter. A third log, slightly smaller in size, is then laid on top of the two logs already down (again parallel to the back of the fireplace).

Now, an optional step. A crumpled sheet or two of newspaper can be held under the chimney throat and lit. This is thought to warm the air in the flue and provide a better starting draft for the fire. It seems to work for me. Others say it does nothing much. Try it and see what you think.

Now light the newspaper under the kindling in three or four places. Long fireplace matches are available for this job and they make reaching around logs somewhat easier.

As the fire starts, it should spread through the kindling and quickly set off the smaller logs you've used as fire starters. If you're using a Cape Cod fire starter, the paper and kindling can be eliminated. But at least one of the bottom logs should be split to provide more surface for the flames to reach. Even with the Cape Cod lighter, the fire will start more easily with kindling.

Always remember that although bark stripped from a tree and dried makes good kindling in most cases, bark still on a log serves as a natural insulator for the wood (making fire starting a little bit harder). Place the split sides of the logs down so the flames can reach them easily and quickly.

As the starting firewood is consumed, you can add larger logs (with the largest going to the back of the fireplace to serve as a back log). This back log will lie directly against the back of the fireplace where it will burn best and radiate more heat into the room. The back log serves to hold the body of the fire out where it will provide more radiated heat.

FIRE TENDING

Fire tending is the simplest of all fireplace jobs. Make sure there's always more than one log on the fire. Three or four are ideal, though large fireplaces might operate best with five or six logs on the fire at one time. A single log just doesn't provide enough fuel surface for the flame to grow and provide heat.

Fireplace setup before the fire is laid might need a little attention. First, if you're using andirons, make sure they are separated by one-half or two-thirds the length of the logs. In other words, if your fireplace will hold 3-foot long logs, the andirons should be from 18 to 24 inches apart for best results. For 2-foot logs, place the andirons 12 to 16 inches apart. Paper is crumpled and very small kindling is laid on it between the andirons. The kindling should be continued on up onto the andirons. This is not essential if the wood is good and dry and you've left a 2-inch base of ash in the fireplace.

Using a fire grate is even simpler. The grate should occupy as much of the firebox as possible (with the greatest importance being attached to width). The crumpled paper and kindling can be laid on the grate, or the paper can be laid underneath. My preference is for doing the whole job right on the grate, but other people get as good results laying the paper underneath. The kindling should, as always, be crisscrossed for best burning.

Charcoal indoors is not safe when charcoal lighter is used as a starter. A small wood fire is needed to get things going. Coal fires need a wood fire to get them going. The best coal is the hardest coal. Selecting a coal size for use these days pretty much depends on luck. You take what you can find.

In any fireplace, the ashes should remain from the day before (at least until the depth reaches more than 4 inches). Then the fireplace should be cleaned to the point where there's about 1 or 2 inches of ash remaining. Logs should always have an inch or two of space between them when laid for a fire.

Trash should not be burned in a fireplace or wood stove. Paper trash generates floating ash and other debris, and extra high flames that might cause chimney fires. Trash such as plastics should *never* be burned in a fireplace or wood stove. Most plastics give off fumes that are at best very unpleasant and sometimes poisonous. There is hardly a single plastic that burns without giving off some foul odor. They might also leave deposits on flue walls. Some have enough acid in the smoke to rot out a wood stove in short order. Most also leave a sticky deposit in place of real ash.

Poison ivy and other noxious weeds also are to be avoided when burning time comes. If you do burn them, stay out of the smoke because the poison is carried in the smoke (which may not make your neighbors too happy either).

A poker can be used to move logs apart as they burn so that air spaces will remain. The poker can be used to move unburned wood ends into the main body of the fire. Fire tongs are useful, at the end of the burning day, for standing unburned logs or partially burned logs on end in the back corners of the fireplace. Such partially burned wood makes fire starting a bit easier the next day.

As time passes, you'll be able to experiment with damper openings to get the best control over your fire. A roaring fire, and a fire being started, both need a wide open damper. As the evening progresses though, and the hardwood takes on its characteristic lower flame, you can start cutting back on the damper. There is little need for the damper to be wide open unless you want to have a roaring fire. A good oak fire will radiate just as much heat from a modest blaze with a half to two-thirds closed damper. At the same time, the fire will consume less fuel and lose less warm air up the chimney.

In the late evening, as the fire dies down to a bed of glowing embers, the damper can be brought nearly to the closed position (cutting down even further on the level of heat and the amount of heat lost up the chimney). Constant fiddling with the damper isn't necessary once you learn what the various positions will do, but a few adjustments over the course of an evening can provide much more efficient, enjoyable heating.

The damper should never be totally closed when any fire, with or without flame, remains in the firebox. This holds true for wood stoves as well as for fireplaces. A glass or asbestos fire screen should be used to cut down warm air loss when the damper must be left open overnight.

Wood stoves are as easy to operate as fireplaces. Dampers will be placed differently and there might be other air control devices located on the stove. A wide-open damper at the start, and a slowly closed down air supply as the fire gains strength, will provide the best combination of heat and fuel economy. Wood for stoves should usually be split into smaller pieces than that burned in a fireplace, but otherwise the starting rules are the same.

The grate in the firebox should be clear of ashes. Sift them down into the ashbox, but don't dump the ashes until you're sure all the coals are out.

Many of the newer stoves are of the airtight variety. This means that with proper feeding and damper control you can keep a fire burning all night. Some owners claim to have used older airtight stoves without having to light more than one fire during a single heating season! Simply light the first time, feed at proper intervals (sometimes as seldom as three times a day with the draft cut back), adjust to supply the needed heat, day or night, and restart with a few small bits of wood on the hot coals when morning comes.

Most American cast-iron stoves, new or old, are not airtight. They will have to be fed more often, and will have to be relit each morning. It's a simple chore.

In both wood stoves and fireplaces, pines, firs, and other resinous woods can be used to start a roaring fire quickly, but unless no other wood is available, resinous woods should not be used as the primary fuel. As a secondary fuel, there's nothing better than a dry piece of pine or fir to really get a cheerful blaze off and flaming the first thing in the morning.

Chapter 14

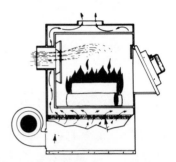

Increasing Heating Efficiency

The most obvious of the long-standing efficiency increasers for fireplaces are the heat circulating devices. Different brands use different methods of venting heat into a room to cut down on heat loss up a chimney. If you use a heat-circulating liner or zero-clearance model fireplace, you can obtain a fireplace that approaches 15 to 20 percent efficiency. This is instead of the 10 percent or so efficiency with a well-designed standard fireplace.

THERMOGRATE

Fireplace accessories and additions are available in various forms. Each is designed to gather and throw more heat into the room while allowing less of the warmth to flow up the chimney. Thermograte was one of the first companies to supply a tube-type grille or grate. There are many competitors now. These units do an exceptionally good job of supplying more heat to a room (Fig. 14-1). The Thermograte just about doubles the available useful heat. The benefits of using a Thermograte unit are demonstrated in Fig. 14-2. By adding a blower to the lower (cool air) openings of the Thermograte tubes, you will get even more rapid heat rises

Converting the findings in Fig. 14-2 to fireplace efficiency percentages is extremely difficult. This is especially true if you try figuring in the advantages of a heat-circulating fireplace at the same time. Thermograte's studies have shown that a 36-inch by 26-inch

Fig. 14-1. A Thermograte unit in operation.

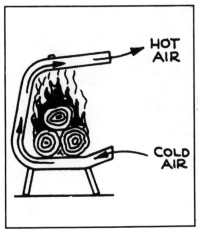

Fig. 14-2. A graph showing the superiority of the Thermograte unit over a standard grate.

firebrick fireplace produces from 7000 to 10,000 Btus per hour (all radiant heat). The same fireplace with the correct model Thermograte and a comparable fire was able to produce 25,000 Btu per hour.

Thermograte claims that adding a blower unit to the system produces a rise to 40,000 Btus per hour. That would be, for sure, a worthwhile addition even if the manufacturer's figures are somewhat on the optimistic side. Even a 50 percent increase in heat output can make a strong difference in your comfort on bitter cold days.

Fig. 14-3. The operation of the Thermograte unit.

The Thermograte is a fairly simple unit. A series of tubes, much like automobile exhaust tubing, is bent to fit the fireplace interior as closely as possible. Legs are then welded on. Cool, room air flows into the bottom tube openings. Warmed air flows out of the top tube openings and into the room (Figs. 14-3 and 14-4). Thermograte suggests that you fit the top tubes as close as possible to the top of the firebox, and as close to the top facing of the fireplace as possible (Fig. 14-5). If a wire mesh screen is used on the fireplace, the top Thermograte tubes must come below the top bracing on the screen in order or warm air to be expelled into the room. Glass fire screens cannot be used in a closed position with the Thermograte if you want any extra heat.

Though Thermograte models and the growing family of competitors seem to be made of exceptionally light materials for fire grates, wear tests have been made that are a bit surprising. Life expectancy for Thermogrates in use all day (24 hours) is over two years. With seasonal or intermittent use, that life expectancy should go way, way up. Some standard cast-iron grates wear out in less than a single heating system under heavy use. Part of the

Fig. 14-4. A Thermograte unit.

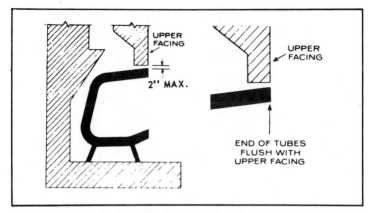

Fig. 14-5. The top tubes of a Thermograte unit should fit as close to the top of the fireplace as possible. They should not protrude past the upper facing.

reason, possibly all of the reason, according to Thermograte is that their style of fire grate does not get as hot as a conventional fire grate. The air circulating continuously through the open tubes serves to keep things cooled down very well. Heat is passed more usefully into the room instead of turning the grate cherry red.

None of the heat circulating grates should affect the fireplace draft because there's no interference with the air currents in and

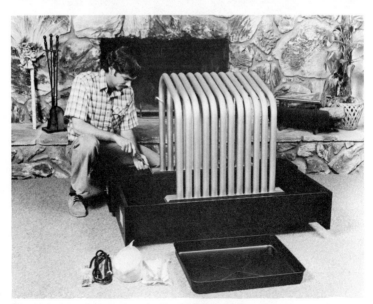

Fig. 14-6. A smokepipe ringed with aluminum garden edging.

Fig. 14-7. Near the start of assembling the Free Heat Machine (courtesy of Unique Functional Products).

around the fireplace and flue. Some, however, might offer other problems. Certain brands consist of loops running from one side of the fireplace to the other (instead of from front to back). Although such grates are effective at catching heat, they do cut several inches off the size logs you can use once the grate is installed.

A TUBE FIRE GRATE

A more sophisticated version of the tube-style fire grate comes from Aquappliances, Inc. (135 Sunshine Lane, San Marcos, CA

92069), and is called the Free Heat Machine. While calling the unit a **Free Heat Machine** is a bit extreme (after all, it costs a good bit itself, depending on the size you require), the increase in efficiency provided by the FHM should give you amortization in a relatively short time. Free Heat Machines are available in sizes that will fit masonry fireplace openings as great as 34¾ inches by 55⅝ inches. According to Aquappliances, larger sizes can be adapted by almost any experienced sheet-metal mechanic (Figs. 14-6 and 14-7).

Essentially, the Free Heat Machine consists of a tube fire grate. The tubes are set quite closely together to keep hot coals in place instead of having them drop to the bottom of the firebox. The unit has adjustable log retainers to keep the fire well back in the firebox. It is sealed with a glass front with several unusual features (Fig. 14-8).

The blower unit (a 160-cubic-feet-per-minute fan) are filtered at the front so that only clean air enters the room being heated. There is a draft panel at the bottom to allow draft control. This appears to me to be a more positive unit than many of the sliding louver type.

Fig. 14-8. Nearing final assembly (courtesy of Unique Functional Products).

There is an ash pan. The heat exchanger unit has leveling legs. Glass doors are used to provide a near airtight seal. The company says that the fireplace damper can be left totally open when the Free Heat Machine is installed. That's a good thing for those really older fireplaces where no damper was ever installed (Figs. 14-9 and 14-10).

The Free Heat Machine is claimed to fit about 90 percent of existing masonry fireplaces. The weight is about 150 pounds. Most

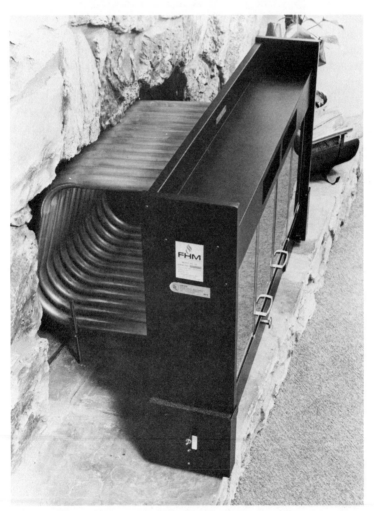

Fig. 14-9. The assembled Free Heat Machine (courtesy of Unique Functional Products).

Fig. 14-10. Slipping the unit home (courtesy of Unique Functional Products).

stove inserts weigh 450 or more pounds. Therefore, installation is a great deal easier (Fig. 14-11).

INSERTS

Fireplace wood stove inserts are quite popular these days. Better'n Ben more or less started the trend, but many manufacturers are getting in the act and doing quite a good job. Suburban Manufacturing Company offers two models (Figs. 14-12 and 14-13). The materials used are quite heavy and the construction appears to

Fig. 14-11. The Free Heat Machine in use (courtesy of Unique Functional Products).

Fig. 14-12. Suburban Manufacturing's Woodmaster/Coalmaster fireplace stove insert.

Fig. 14-13. The Woodmaster fireplace stove (courtesy of Suburban Manufacturing Co.).

be of top quality. The price range is $671.95 to $999.95 for the two models (depending on firebox size). Fuel costs savings should be possible by the second year of installation.

American Stovolator (Rt. 7, Arlington, VT 05250) also offers a glass-doored fireplace stove insert that covers the entire front of your fireplace. It gives better draft control, much higher heating efficiency, and a large reduction in wood consumption. Greenbriar Products, Inc. (Box 473, Spring Green, WI 53588) offers a fireplace stove that does the same job.

Radiated heat from a fireplace can also be increased by making sure everything is working properly and the flue is clean. Today, you have more and better chimney cleaning kits to choose from than ever before. I've been using a Black Magic chimney sweep kit for couple of years now. The unit consists of two wire brushes: square for my vertical flue liner, and round for the connecting flue liner at the stovepipe. In addition, there is 21 feet of flexible fiberglass rod. The basic 6-inch diameter round kit costs about $50 (while the extra brush cost about $20). My flue now gets cleaned three or four times a season because the job is so much easier.

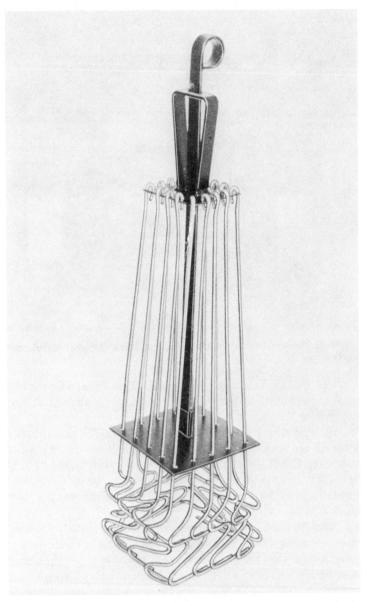

Fig. 14-14. A chimney flue cleaner (courtesy of Johnson Energy Systems Inc.).

Johnson Energy Systems, Inc. (7350 N. 76th St., Milwaukee, WI 53223) offers two brushes with fingers of what appears to be spring steel that should fit most size flue pipes. (Figs. 14-14 and

14-15). These are made to be drawn up or down a chimney with rope. Anything that makes chimney cleaning easier for the homeowner makes burning wood safer.

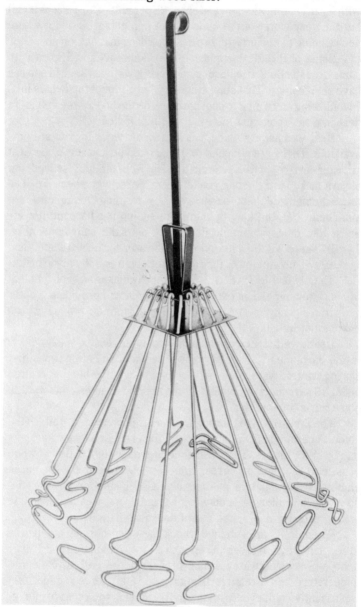

Fig. 14-15. A chimney flue cleaner (courtesy of Johnson Energy Systems Inc.).

Wood stoves offer some different challenges and more possibilities. The type and quality of the wood stove is going to directly affect the output of heat. But with a wood stove, you'll be starting with basic heating efficiency of about 25 percent to 30 percent for all but the very worst of the bunch. That percentage is about where you're going to end up with the best fireplace installation possible.

Some of the ideas applicable to wood stoves will work with some freestanding fireplace models. Both stoves and fireplaces have smokepipes. That smokepipe is where a lot of the heat is lost. But allowing more pipe to cool down inside the house will shift more heat into the room and increase heating efficiency.

Heat exchangers made specifically for wood stoves are now available. These are attached to the smokepipe and serve as a heat transfer surface increase. Some do very well, others less well, but always make sure the one you buy is made for wood heat. You can make homemade heat exchangers by forming "doughnuts" of aluminum. Use the kind of aluminum edging used around flowerbeds. Slip these aluminum doughnuts onto the smokepipe (Fig. 14-16). There will be a lot more surface area for heat transfer, and the cost will be a lot lower than any of the commercially made units.

The Louisville Tin and Stove Company makes an oven unit that fits in a stovepipe. The exterior of this oven will provide a greater heat transfer surface to the surrounding room air whenever the oven is not in use.

Heating efficiency can be added to by increasing the humidity inside the home. Cold air has very little water retention capability. During winter, warmed air is very low in relative humidity, often under 15 percent. For comfort, some method of adding moisture to home air is a good idea.

The first step is to thoroughly seal off all unneeded drafts in the home. A certain amount of air circulation is needed in any house so that fresh air enters. The fresh air aids proper combustion of wood fires, oil fires, and gas fires. Unnecessary cold drafts should be eliminated by standard tactics: increased insulation, storm windows, fresh caulking around windows and doors, weather stripping around exterior doors, and storm door installation.

When drafts are subdued, check the wood-burning appliances to see that they are receiving enough air for combustion and proper draft. Now comes water adding time. A house with a 68-degree temperature and a relative humidity of 15-20 percent might feel unpleasantly cool, even without drafts. Raising the relative humidity 35 percent might make the same temperature feel just fine.

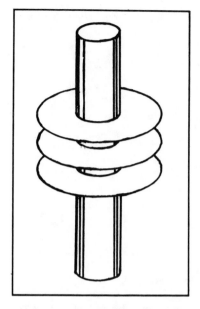

Fig. 14-16. A smokepipe ringed with aluminum garden edging.

There's a lot of variation in the amount of cold or heat that an individual can tolerate. But supplying the correct humidity to the house air will go a long way to making sure that everyone stays comfortable.

The most efficient way to humidify a wood-heat home is with the small electric powered humidifiers. These units usually hold from 3 to 8 gallons of water that is picked up on a rotating belt. The belt then passes in front of a small fan. The humidified air passes through a small grill and into the house.

The basic units, with about a 4-gallon or 5-gallon tank, should sell for no more than $70. They will have no fancy refill lights and no fancy refill gadgets. The unit will shut itself off when empty. The two small motors on the humidifiers don't use a lot of electricity, but they do use some.

Humidifying is a simple job for those who have wood stoves with flat tops. Place one or two saucepans two-thirds full of water on top of the stove. Boil the water slowly and fill as often as needed. This takes the place of the old saucepan-on-the-radiator trick.

Fireplaces present a few more difficulties. It's hard to find a spot to put a pan of water where the heat can get to it. Often it's a simple matter to install a pivoting crane that can hold a kettle.

Chapter 15

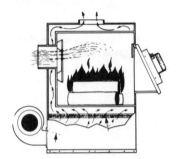

Cooking with Wood

Using wood as a fuel for cooking requires a bit of trial and error work. You can expect to ruin a few meals before everything comes together. The primary reason is that it is much simpler to standardize the heat source in an electric or gas range than when using wood as a fuel. Some woods burn hotter and faster than others, for example, and some chimneys provide more draft than others. It always takes time to become used to any particular wood range even if you've used wood as a cooking fuel for some time. See Figs. 15-1 through 15-5.

In addition, you have no opportunity of shoving a thermostat into a roast in the oven, setting a switch, and going to the opera. Wood stoves must be attended to all the time your food is on or in them. With the wood burning, you can't just turn off the heat and forget it. You must move the utensils containing the food from cooler to hotter areas as needed or things will cook unevenly (or be overdone or underdone). Because you'll have to add fuel rather often for longer cooking jobs, you'll find yourself moving things around with fair frequency.

The continual attention required to cook on a wood range is only one aspect of the work that goes into cooking with wood. There are the other jobs required of all appliances using wood as a fuel source (such as cutting, carrying and feeding the wood into the fire, and removing ashes). The firebox will need occasional cleaning and /so will the flues.

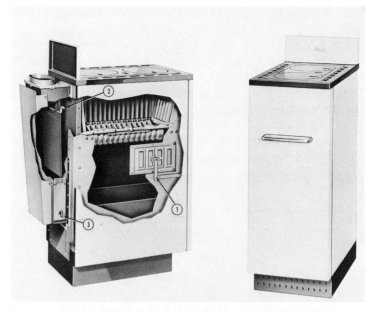

Fig. 15-1. A typical small kitchen stove (courtesy of Monarch).

In addition, using a wood range in the summer is definitely no pleasure. When it is already past 90 degrees F. outdoors and you have to cook a meal over a wood range, you begin to appreciate at least one of the troubles our ancestors had to put up with. Summer kitchens were sometimes used, but not everyone had the space and money for a separate structure to hold the wood range and protect it from the elements. My grandmother had a second chimney off a long, screened back porch and her range was moved out there during the hot months. I promise you that even then that was no place to be when the central Virginia temperatures hit 100 degrees F. The temperature on that porch would rapidly send the old alcohol-mix thermometer over its 120 degree limit. When I got stuck helping to churn butter on days canning was in progress, I rapidly moved the churn and stool out into the back yard.

COOKWARE

In my personal and not very humble opinion, the only cookware worthwhile is made of heavy cast iron. The stuff looks especially right on a wood range. It spreads heat more evenly than even the most expensive metals (and we've got copper-bottomed and triple-

269

layer stainless steel pots and pans that cost from three to five times what the cast iron did).

You can buy several kinds of cast-iron cookware; some is imported and some is made from old molds in this country. It seems to me that the cookware made in the United States is of heavier and better quality cast iron than that made elsewhere. The best frying pan I have, or have ever had, was given to me by a Wisconsin farmer. It had been in his family for nearly 50 years.

Cast-iron cookware comes with wooden handles, Pyrex lids, or with cast iron handles and cast iron lids. I would go for the all-cast-

Fig. 15-2. Combining the old and the new, a wood stove and electric stove in a single unit (courtesy of Monarch).

Fig. 15-3. Using gas with wood (courtesy of Monarch).

iron cookware. Pyrex lids on such heavy utensils don't seem to last very long. It only takes a 1-inch drop to shatter them.

Seasoning cast-iron cookware is a necessity too often done incorrectly or overlooked. If the cookware is new, coat it liberally with a salt-free vegetable oil or (preferably) animal fat and place it in an oven set at about 250 degrees for two hours. When the utensil has cooled down, coat it once more with fat and place it in a hot oven. Do this last step twice. Once this is carried out, you should have little problem with things sticking for a long time to come. If the utensil has been seasoned before, and just needs reseasoning, clean it thoroughly and coat it with salt-free fat. Place it in a hot oven for an hour. Let it cool and the pot or pan is ready for use.

Fig. 15-4. Fuel oil may also be used in combination with wood (courtesy of Monarch).

Cast-iron cookware starts out a middling gray in color. It will quickly turn black with use. This is a natural process and not a reason to scour the cookware. Some people say never to scour cast-iron cookware, but occasionally you'll find it necessary to do so to get something out of the pot or pan. Go ahead and do it, and then just season the utensil over again. It is virtually impossible to ruin cast-iron cooking utensils with any sort of normal cooking treatment. The overly concentrated heat from modern gas and electric ranges tends to remove the seasoning fairly quickly if you cook many water-based dishes in them. It is a simple matter of reseasoning them, and not tossing them in the trash as must be done with some more modern types of cookware.

Fig. 15-5. Adding wood to an electric range as a supplementary fuel doesn't cut out any modern conveniences (courtesy of Monarch).

Just imagine, for an instant, leaving a copper-bottomed or steel or aluminum-bottomed pot on medium heat or high heat for several hours after any liquid has boiled away.

Wood kitchen ranges with their less concentrated heat—it spreads over the entire top surface instead of being situated only in tiny rings—are far less likely to cause such problems. In most, the fire would go out before sticking became much of a problem. Still, biannual reseasoning of the most heavily used cookware is probably a good idea. The choice of pots, pans, dutch ovens, skillets and so forth depends on your cooking needs. Virtually everything available (except large stockpots) in other metals comes in cast iron.

Added to the durability of cast-iron cookware is its relatively low cost. In general, you can expect to save about two-thirds of the price of multi-layered steel cookware, nearly half the price of good, copper bottomed steel cookware, and possibly as much as three-quarters of the cost of so-called gourmet copper cookware. The savings can range to over $150 on a complete set. Cast iron is worth considering even if you don't care to use a wood range.

COOKING

There is a basic of wood stove cookery that can be used for most kinds of cooking. Build the hottest fire you can get with the fuel available, and then move the pots and pans around the top of the stove until you reach a spot that cooks as you want it to. Further movement will be needed as the fire dies down a bit, is re-fueled, and so on. In general, go with the hottest fire possible. The hottest spot on virtually all wood ranges will be directly over the firebox. But in some non-range stoves that can also be used for cooking. The heat is pretty intense over the entire top. In such cases, adjustments will have to be made to the fire. And not only for cooking purposes. If the day is only cool, and not cold, a roaring fire in that stove will just about run you out of the house. At least it will make you open a number of windows.

The eyes, or lids, are placed on the tops of wood ranges and cookstoves—not to indicate where the fire is the hottest—to allow you to expose a pot or pan directly to the flame. This is handy for getting things to a quick boil, but tends to leave a rather messy soot deposit on the outside of the utensils' bottoms. If you plan to do this open flame boiling, first coat the bottom of the pot or pan with a bit of liquid soap (not detergent) and the resulting mess is a great deal easier to remove.

Wood-stove cookery is very similar to any other type of cookery except that with the fuel variations you must pay more attention to maintaining the right heat levels for the various items being cooked or baked. The fuels can vary widely, too. I know of several people who swear by dried corn cobs for hot, fast fires for quick meals. In general, the people using corn cobs as a cooking fuel seem to be those who harvest a fair amount of feed corn and strip the kernels. Sometimes the cobs can be picked up at feed mills. Feed corn is normally harvested in the late summer or early fall when the amount of moisture in the corn has dropped off drastically.

Different kinds of woods, cut and split in different manners, will provide heat characteristics for almost any form of cooking. Splitting well-dried pine or fir into 1-inch sticks provides a good, hot and fast morning fire for those early cups of coffee. Use hardwoods such as oak for longer lasting, hot fires when baking or oven roasting. Oak, maple, beech, and hickory are usually split a bit larger (with most pieces 2 inches or more thick). Length of the wood must be determined by the length of the firebox on your particular wood range.

When the various draft units feeding warm air around an oven have been totally mastered and are in perfect operating condition, most wood-stove cooking experts feel there is no need to turn the contents of an oven to make sure each side is evenly browned. In my experience with wood ranges, only one was in perfect operating condition continually. And at least one turn of the loaves of bread produced a more evenly browned loaf. Biscuits probably won't need turning if the drafts are even near correct because the cooking time is short. Roasts almost always will need to be turned.

RECIPES

Wood-stove cookery starts with trial and error. Your stove will have its own little habits, and you can count on wasting at least a bit of flour and yeast in discovering just what they are. Carefully watched cookery is seldom a total waste, but I recommend that you begin your wood-stove cookery with experiments among the cheaper food elements such as breads and biscuits. Once you've mastered those, you have reached the time to slap in that $25 - or $30-standing rib roast (with far less chance of ruining things).

Start by pretty much disregarding the door thermometer on any older wood range. These things are normally inaccurate after a few years, and a good quality oven thermometer must be used as at least a monthly check against problems.

Biscuits. Most biscuit recipes call for white flour, but I tend to prefer stone-ground whole wheat. Start with 2¼ cups of sifted flour and add in a half teaspoon of salt and four teaspoons of baking powder. Sugar is called for in many recipes, but for a kick, replace that, or half of the sugar, with sifted white cornmeal. That would mean cutting the sugar to 1 tablespoon and using an equal amount of cornmeal. Ready a one-third cup of lard, 1 egg and about two-thirds of a cup of milk.

Slip the dry ingredients back into the sifter and sift once more. Cut the lard into your mixture until you get a coarse crumb-like texture. Add the milk and the egg and use a regular table fork to mix until the dough will sort of follow the fork around the bowl. Sprinkle flour on a kneading board and flop the blob of dough down and thoroughly knead the mix at least a half dozen times. (Good exercise for the wrists and forearms, too.)

Roll out to about a half inch thick and use a water glass to cut into biscuits (vary the size of the water glass to get larger or smaller biscuits, but 2 inches or so is about average). Place an inch or a bit less apart on an ungreased cookie sheet and bake in a hot oven—450 degrees F—for from 12 to 15 minutes, or until golden brown and fluffy. The result should be about 16 2-inch biscuits.

Golden corn bread is considered a northern dish. Southern corn bread supposedly uses only white corn meal.

Corn Bread. This might be considered the northern version, but it is very similar to what I've eaten in most areas of the southern states over the years. Start with a cup of sifted stone ground flour, and a quarter cup of sugar, four teaspoons of baking powder, and about a half teaspoon of salt. Now, you need 1 cup of yellow cornmeal. Sift all these dry ingredients together. Now beat 2 eggs well, and add a cup of milk and a quarter cup of softened shortening.

Dump the concoction into the dry mix and stir with a fork until the flour mix is just moist. Even if the batter has lumps, do not overstir (this was a constant fault of mine and ruined quite a lot of flour, eggs and such). Grease heavily a 9-inch or 10-inch cast-iron skillet and pop it into a hot oven for about 20 minutes, or until the top is a bit past a golden brown. Serve with fresh, sweet butter and maple syrup while hot from the oven and you'll forget about *any* diet.

Sour Dough. There seems to be some sort of cult built up around sourdough breads and biscuits, but once you've lit off your starter, the procedures are quite simple. Start with a crock or a glass bowl, never metal, and combine half a package of active yeast (dry) with 2 cups of sifted flour, two tablespoons of sugar and 2½ cups of water. Cover with cheesecloth to keep flies away and stick it in a warm spot for a couple of days. Your starter will be ready. To replenish sour dough starter, simply stir in 2 cups of warm water to 2 cups of sifted flour before the original runs out.

For sour dough biscuits, begin with 1½ cups of sifted unbleached flour or stone ground flour, 2 teaspoons of baking powder, and a quarter teaspoon of baking soda. Now add in half a teaspoon of salt and sift these dry ingredients together.

Use a knife or pastry blender to cut in a quarter cup of butter (that's half a pound and let it get good and soft or you'll go crazy).

Now add the sour dough starter and mix well. Again, roll the dough after, this time, just enough kneading to make the dough light (about half an inch thick) and cut as with regular biscuits.

To get authenticity, place the biscuits in a well greased 10-inch, cast-iron skillet. If you want, you can brush melted butter over the tops, or place a pat of butter on top of each. Give the biscuits an hour or so to rise in a warm spot and then stick them into a hot (425 to 450 degree F) oven for 20 minutes or until golden brown. You'll get about a dozen 2-inch biscuits you won't readily forget.

You can avoid using yeast in sour dough starter in at least two ways. For one, boil four unpeeled medium sized potatoes (with just enough water to cover). Pull out a couple of the potatoes and peel them, and then mash all four in the water used for boiling. Mix the mashed potatoes with four cups of any sort of flour you choose. Virtually all sour dough starters can exchange white, brown and rye flours for different flavor effects. Stir in half to three-fourths of a cup of honey. Now mix in two teaspoons of salt, and place the mix in a large crock or glass bowl, cover with cheesecloth, and stand in a warm place for three to four days. It will bubble and give off a fairly strong, sour odor when ready.

The simplest of all sourdough starters requires nothing more than a cup of milk and a cup of flour. Let the milk stand at room temperature for at least a full day and night. Mix with a cup of flour and place the cheesecloth covered mix in a warm nook for four days. Check to see if it is bubbling and if it has a sour odor.

Yeast Breads. The variations possible on a loaf of bread are probably endless. About 10 years ago, I began to test a few recipes, and found that I never wanted to even so much as see another loaf of store bought sponge again.

My favorite recipe is a rolled bread with a great richness. I can remember returning from Wisconsin to stay with my in-laws for a time and baking something like six loaves of this one afternoon. Not a slice made it to the cooling racks. And there were only four of us in the house! Start by dissolving a package of dry yeast in water (use two tablespoons of lukewarm water). Scald two-third of a cup of milk while the yeast works. Pour the milk, in a large bowl, over a quarter cup of sugar, a teaspoon of salt and some four tablespoons of butter. Set this to one side to let it cool. Add two eggs, the yeast, and the milk/sugar/salt/butter mixture to a cup and a half of sifted stone-ground flour. Beat the mix until it is very smooth. Now beat in another cup and a half of flour using a large, wooden spoon.

Cover this with a piece of clean, white muslin and stick it in a warm place to rise until it doubles in size. Once size has doubled, lift the dough out and knead it only lightly. Next, roll it out onto a lightly floured board and spread with two tablespoons of butter (melted), and sprinkle with a mix of a quarter of a cup of sugar and two teaspoons of cinnamon.

Brush the top with melted butter after rolling the dough tightly and placing it in a greased bread pan. Let the loaf stand for about an hour in a warm place when it will have doubled in size. Slip into a medium (350 degree F) oven for about three-quarters of an hour. Slice, eat and gain weight!

For a basic white bread, start with one package of active dry yeast, a quarter cup of warm water, two cups of scalded milk and a couple of teaspoons of sugar. Add two teaspoons of salt, a quarter cup of butter and half a dozen cups of stone-ground white flour.

Dissolve the yeast in the warm water. Set the yeast aside and mix the scalded milk, sugar, salt and butter in a large bowl. This must stand until it is lukewarm; Then add the yeast and half the flour. Beat until the flour disappears and then add the rest of the four during constant stirring. Turn the dough out onto a floured mixing board and knead until it is extremely smooth. This is work, but without it the bread is not good.

Place the kneaded dough into a greased bowl and let it stand until it doubles in size. In a warm spot, it will take about 90 minutes. Now punch the dough down and let it stand for another half hour. Use a sharp knife to cut off loaf-shaped chunks. Place these, after shaping, into greased bread pans. Cover again with a clean cloth. Allow to rise until size once more doubles. The result goes into a moderately hot (400 degree F) oven for half an hour. You'll be delighted with the quality of bread you've turned out.

Stew. Select a dutch oven of the appropriate size for your family (and for the number of meals you want to provide). Dutch ovens with flat bottoms (legged Dutch ovens are for campfire or fireplace use) are readily available in sizes including 5 quarts, 7 quarts, 9 quarts and 12 quarts.

I like to begin with at least 1½ pounds of stew beef in 1-inch cubes (plus left overs). I like a fairly hot fire. Melt enough butter to cover the bottom of the Dutch oven about one-sixteenth of an inch. Once the butter starts to turn brown, I drop in the meat cubes to brown. These must be turned. In between turning, cut celery, carrots, potatoes, and onions. Once the stew beef is browned, drop in the meat scraps for further browning, if needed. After that's done, add water (a good touch here is to save the juices from cooked vegetables and use that whenever possible) to cover the meat, plus half an inch or so.

Drop in four or five beef boullion cubes and two or three vegetable cubes. By this time, the potatoes—I prefer not to peel them, but do cut them into about 2-inch chunks, after a thorough washing—can go in. Next the carrots, a couple of bay leaves (to your taste), crumbled, and seven or eight black peppercorns.

Once this starts to simmer, add the onions and let the whole works come back to a good boil. Add beef short ribs if you have them. Enough water must be kept in the Dutch oven to cover the ingredients, barely, during cooking.

If you like, a tablespoon of lemon juice and about the same of Worcestershire sauce can be added. Adding the Worcestershire sauce to the butter during browning seems to impart the flavor more solidly.

Slip the Dutch oven to a part of the stove where the stew will be reduced to little more than a bare simmer. Allow that to continue until the bones pull away from any short ribs and the marrow drips from the bones. By this time, the meat will be at the stage where it can easily be forked apart and your stew is ready.

More Hints. I'm sure you've seen those double-sided grilles meant for use over fireplaces or campfires. Consider using one of those, or an old cake cooling rack, as a "charcoal" broiler for indoor cookery. Hamburgers and steaks and fish can be grilled over an open flame simply by fitting the meat or fish in the grille or on the cookie rack or cake rack and placing that over an opening where the lid has been removed from the firebox portion of the stove. Keep a box of baking soda on hand for flare-ups with steak or hamburgers.

In such cooking, I would consider the use of something other than pine. Hickory imparts a fine, woodsy flavor (and is used to make much charcoal), while apple or cherry could add interesting highlights to a wood stove, open-broiled trout. A wood stove, to me, allows for a greater imaginative range when doing many sorts of cooking.

Other benefits accrue. As the lunchtime fire burns down to coals, select a couple of large baking potatoes—or a number suitable for your family needs—and wash them well. Coat the potatoes thickly with butter or margarine, and encase in heavy duty tinfoil. Coat this foil with lard, Crisco or some soft fat product, and wrap one more time with heavy foil. Shake down the ashes until only glowing coals remain. Place the potatoes evenly across the firebox.

Cover the potatoes and coals with a slow burning, dense wood such as hickory, apple, or oak. For even very large potatoes, a poke with a fork inside an hour and a half will almost surely show them as done. They can be removed, still in the foil, and placed in the warming oven to be opened when the rest of supper is ready. The mildly scorched skins, butter soaked already, add marvelously to the enjoyment you'll experience from this often mundane vegetable.

The same, or nearly the same, procedure can be used with roasting ears of corn. Corn needs only about 15 minutes of roasting.

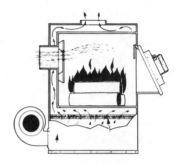

Glossary

WOODCUTTING TERMS

backcut—The felling cut made in the back side of the tree toward the undercut felling notch.

barber's chair—The stump of a tree having long wood fibers attached at the hinge section. Usually results from poor cutting practice.

boring cut—A blind cut made into the wood—principally with the nose of the bar.

bucking cut—Any cut made to section a felled tree or log.

felling cut—The final backcut that causes the tree to fall.

felling notch—A horizontal cutout, often wedge-shaped, made on the side the tree is to fall. The inside edge of the notch usually is 90 degrees to the line of fall.

hinge wood—Wood left uncut between the notch and backcut. The hinge holds the tree on the stump and guides it over.

kickback—The rapid and dangerous movement of the saw toward the operator after the chain along the top or nose of the bar has contacted the wood or some other object.

leaner—A tree with an extreme lean. Such trees require special notching and hinging techniques to avoid "barber's chair" or splitting during felling.

lodged tree—A tree partially or wholly separated from its stump, or uprooted, but that has not fallen to the ground.

"no load" speed—The rpm developed by running the engine or saw at wide open throttle without applying any work load. CAUTION: Letting the engine run at full throttle without a load should be avoided as much as possible to prevent saw damage.

overbucking—Using the bottom edge of the bar to cut downward through a log.

root wad—The roots and base of tree extending above ground level after a tree has been pushed over by wind or other means.

saw kerf—The width of the saw blade or cutting chain including the set of the teeth. Also the cut made by a saw blade or chain.

snag—Any dead standing tree or portion thereof remaining standing.

spring pole—A sapling bent and held down under tension by another fallen tree.

underbucking—Using the top edge of the bar to cut upward through a log.

widowmaker—Any overhanging limb or section of a tree that could become dislodged and drop to the ground.

BRICKLAYING TERMS

abutment—A masonry mass supporting the pressure of an arch, vault, beam or strut.

adhesive strength—The quality of the bond that mortar has for holding two masonry units together.

agglomerated mass—A mixture of aggregate with plaster, mortar, and concrete.

aggregate—Various hard, inert material such as sand, gravel, or pebbles in various size fragments mixed with cementing material to form concrete, mortar, or plaster.

alignment—A parallel or converging line of upright masonry units.

amalgamation—A mixed blend or combination of materials such as lime, cement, sand, and water.

American bond—A masonry bond with a course of headers between five or six courses of stretchers. Also called common bond.

anchor—A metal tie or strap that binds one part of a structure to another.

angle iron—Iron or steel bar in the form of an angle used to hold lintel units.

anta—A rectangular pier or pilaster formed by thickening the end of a masonry wall.

arcade—A series of arches supported on piers or columns.

arch—A curved structural support spanning an opening and resolving vertical load pressure into horizontal thrust.

arch buttress—See flying buttress.

arris—The sharp edge or salient angle formed by the meeting of two plane or curved surfaces.

ashlar masonry—Cut, sawed, tooled, or dressed stone used for facing a wall or rubble or brick.

ashlar line—The outer line of an exterior wall above any projecting base.

axis—In masonry arch work, the center or point from which a circle or arc is formed and drawn on a template.

backfill—To replace earth around a foundation wall.

backing—Unsquared stone, rubble, brick, hollow tile or concrete block used as masonry wall to support a structure.

balanced—A proportionate distribution of the load.

basement—The substructure of a building that is wholly or partially below ground level.

bat—A portion of a brick that is whole at one end and with the other end broken off.

batter—A receding slope to a wall.

batter boards—One of a pair of boards positioned outside the corner of an excavation to indicate the proper level of the structure.

batter stick—A tapered instrument used with a level to build a battered wall.

bearing stone—Stone that withstands weight, thrust, or strain.

bearing wall—A partition that supports the weight of a structure.

bed—The surface on which brick is laid.

bed joint—A horizontal masonry joint.

bed stone—A large foundation stone.

belt course—A horizontal band around pillars or columns.

bench mark—A fixed elevation mark or point of reference on a concrete post set in the ground from which measurements can be made.

binder course—A course of aggregate between the foundation and the pavement.

binders—A substance such as cement that promotes cohesion of materials.

blind bond—A masonry bond in which headers extend only half of the way through the tier of the face brick. The face bricks are all stretchers and some are split lengthwise to accommodate the headers.

block—A solid unit of masonry material formed in a uniform size.

block and bond—Laying a block bond on one side and a different unit and bond on the other side.

blocking course—The finished course of a wall laid on top of a cornice to give weight and to bind the cornice.

boasting—Cutting masonry with a broad-edged chisel.

bond—The systematic lapping of brick or other masonry units to enhance strength and appearance.

bond course—A course of masonry bondstone laid crossways partially or entirely through a wall.

boning rods—Rods to sight across masonry to keep the units level as they are laid on a horizontal surface.

breadth—The width of a masonry wall.

breaking load. The stress or tension sufficient to break or rupture.

breast (fireplace)—The front of a fireplace.

brick—Building or paving material made by baking or burning molded clay into blocks.

brick beam—A lintel of bricks with iron straps.

brick chisel—A broad-edged chisel used to trim or cut brick.

brick set—Another name for a brick chisel.

brick trowel—A flat triangular instrument used in bricklaying to spread mortar or concrete.

brick veneer—Brick facing bonded to a wall built of another material.

bricklayer—A person who constructs buildings, chimneys or other structures made of brick or block and mortar.

bricklayer's hammer—A hammer with a flat face and sharp peen used to dress or break brick.

brickwork—A structure built by laying brick with or without mortar.

bridge stone—Masonry that spans a gutter.

bridge wall—A low, separating wall of firebrick.

broken range—Random laying of masonry units.

brooming—Applying a finish to concrete with a broom.

buck—A rough doorframe placed in a wall or partition during construction.

buckstay—Either of two connected girders, one on each side of a masonry structure to take the thrust of an arch.

bulging—The spreading of a wall usually caused by excessive load pressure.

bull header—A header brick laid on edge with the end exposed.

bull stretcher—Brick laid on edge with the face exposed.

bull's-eye—A circular or oval opening in a wall.

bush hammer—A hammer with a serated face for dressing masonry units and concrete.

burning—Processing brick in a kiln at 100 to 400 degrees.

buttered joint—A thin layer of mortar applied to one end of a brick before it is laid.

buttress—A projecting structure of masonry that resists lateral pressure at a specific point.

clacine—To heat materials for manufacturing cement or lime.

camber—A slight convex arch or curve.

carve—To cut or dress brick or stone.

casting—Molded or shaped masonry.

cavity wall—A masonry wall built in two thicknesses separated by an air space designed to provide thermal insulation.

cell—An air space in a hollow tile or a cement block.

cement—A powdered mixture of alumina, silica, lime, iron oxide and magnesia burned together in a kiln and finely pulverized. When it is mixed with water it forms a plastic mass that hardens by chemical combination.

chain bond—A bond formed by building in a tie or strap.

chain course—A course of continuously fastened headers held by cramps.

chase—A groove or shallow channel in masonry for a pipe or conduit.

chimney—A vertical masonry structure for carrying off smoke.

chimney breast—The portion of a chimney or fireplace that projects from a wall into a room.

chimney cap—A device used to improve the draft from a chimney.

chimney hood—A protective covering over the indoor portion of a chimney.

clastic—Conglomerate stone.

cleavage plane—The natural division of masonry units that results in a sharp division or splitting in specific directions.

clinker brick—The result when brick is over-burned in a kiln.

clip bond—A masonry wall bond formed by clipping off the inner corners of the block or face brick to obtain a diagonal bond with stretchers.

closer—The last masonry unit in a course.

cohesive strength—The resistance to separation of masonry.

common bond—See American bond.

concrete—A solid, durable building material formed by mixing cement, aggregate, and water.

concrete finishing—Applying a smooth surface to concrete.

concrete masonry—Brick, block or tile construction.

conglomerate—Rounded fragments of sedimentary rock cemented into a mass.

coping—The highest course or the covering course of a masonry wall. It is usually sloped to carry off water.

cored brick—Brick with three holes in a single row near the center or two rows of five holes.

corbel—A masonry unit that projects from a wall upward and outward.

cornice—The top course of a wall that projects horizontally.

course—One layer or row of masonry units.

course bed—The top of the last masonry course laid.

cramp—A dovetailed form used to bond concrete block.

crown—The finishing element of a masonry surface.

curing—Chemical change in concrete obtained by maintaining proper moisture and temperature conditions.

curtain wall—A non-bearing wall between piers. Also called an enclosure wall.

diagonal bond—A masonry bond in which headers are bonded to the wall by concealed paralled bricks.

dipping—Putting masonry units into mortar rather than spreading the mortar on them.

dowels—A piece of wood driven into a hole that has been drilled into masonry.

draft—A device for regulating air currents through a chimney or fireplace.

dressing—Working the face of a brick or stone.

dry stone—Stone laid without mortar.

Dutch bond—Alternate courses of headers and stretchers. Joints between the stretchers are over the centers of the stretchers.

efflorescence—The formation of a powder or incrustation on a masonry surface due to capillary transfer of soluble ground salt.

English bond—Masonry bond where header courses are alternated with stretcher courses.

face brick—Brick commonly used for exposed surfaces. Manufactured in various colors.

fire brick—Brick made from fireclay that can withstand higher temperatures than regular brick.

fireclay—A refractory clay used in making firebrick.

fire wall—Masonry placed between joists to prevent the spread of fire.

Flemish bond—A masonry bond in which each course alternates headers and stretchers so that each course is centered above and below a stretcher.

flue—A passage or duct for chimney smoke.

flush—To bring a masonry unit even with the surface of the structure.

flying buttress—An arch spanning a passageway to a solid pier or buttress.

footing—Foundation or bottom unit of a wall.

form—A temporary frame that retains concrete until the concrete hardens.

forming—Tempering clay to produce a homogeneous mass for making brick.

foundation—The portion of a structure, usually below ground level, that supports a wall or other structure.

galleting—Filling a masonry joint with rock chips to increase the strength of the joint.

garden wall bond—Alternating two or more stretchers in each course.

graded aggregate—Aggregate with various types of sand and gravel.

grout—Mortar that has been thinned with water so that it can be poured.

header—Masonry unit laid with the shorter ends exposed.

header bond—Masonry bond in which all courses are overlapping headers.

header course—A row of headers.

hearth—The floor of a fireplace, usually made of stone or brick.

herringbone bond—Masonry bond in which the exposed bricks are laid diagonally to the wall.

interlocking—Bonding masonry units by lapping them.

joggle—To fit or fasten with dowels.

joint—The space between two adjacent masonry units bonded by mortar.

jointer—A tool used for making joints.

keystone—Masonry unit at the summit of an arch.

kneeler—A brick or stone supporting inclined masonry.

lateral thrust—Movement caused by load pressure.

lean mortar—Mortar that is deficient in bonding material.

lime—When combined with water, lime forms calcium carbonate. Used in mortar and cement.

lintel—Horizontal architectural member supporting the weight above a door or window.

mortar—Mixture of lime, cement, and water used to bond masonry.

mortar board—A small, lightweight board on which masons temporarily place mortar.

muriatic acid—Hydrochloric acid diluted with water and used to clean masonry.

neat cement—Cement and water without aggregate.

niche—A recess in a wall.

nogging—To fill open spaces of a wood frame with bricks or other masonry.

offset—To build a wall with a reduction in thickness.

parapet—An elevation raised above the main wall, generally at the edge for decoration.

pargeting—A lining of mortar or plaster for a chimney.

parging—A thin, smooth coat of mortar applied to masonry.

pier—A portion of a wall between windows or doors.

pilaster—A shallow rectangular projection from a wall, usually in the shape of a column.

pitch—To square a masonry surface by cutting with a chisel.

plumb—Having a perpendicular or vertical line that is true.

pointing—Filling masonry joints with mortar. Dress the surface of masonry with a tool.

portland cement—Hydraulic cement made by burning a mixture of limestone and clay in a kiln.

precast—To cast a concrete block or slab before placing it in a structure.

pugging—To knead clay with water to make it plastic. Fill with clay to deaden sound.

putlog—A short horizontal support.

racking bond—Stepping back the ends of a course from bottom to top on an unfinished wall.

rich mix—Mortar with an excess of bonding material.

riprap—Broken stone for foundations. A masonry wall with an irregular pattern.

rowlock—A brick laid on edge as a header.

rubble—Broken stone of irregular size and shape.

sand—Small, loose grains (usually quartz) used as aggregate.

sand cushion—A layer of sand separating paving and subsoil.

sandblasting—A blast of air or steam with sand used to clean masonry.

scaffold—A temporary structure for holding workers and material during construction.

screed—A wooden strip for smoothing the surface of concrete.

shoved joint—A joint made by shoving a masonry unit into position.

slump test—The method for determining the consistency of concrete.

soldier course—A masonry course in which the units are laid vertically with the narrow face exposed.

split—A brick half the normal thickness and used to support a course of bricks over another course that is not level.

stack bond—Masonry units positioned one on top of the other and having the same vertical joints.

story pole—A rod cut equal to the height of one story of a building with markings indicating specific heights.

straightedge—A strip of wood or metal used to test for straight lines.

stretcher—A masonry unit with its length parallel to the face of the wall.

stretcher bond—See running bond.

string course—A course of stretcher masonry units.

tempering—To bring to a proper consistency by mixing or blending.

template—A pattern, usually of wood or metal, used to make a copy of an object.

tensile strength—The resistance of a material to stress.

texture—The visual and tactile quality of a masonry surface.

tooled—Worked or shaped masonry.

tucking—Filling mortar joints after masonry units are laid.

tuck-pointing—Pointing which has an ornamental line projecting from the structure.

winning—Mining procedure where several days production are held in storage.

wythe—A continuous vertical tier of masonry. The partition dividing flues of a chimney.

Index